MATLAB Optimization Techniques

César Pérez López

Apress®

MATLAB Optimization Techniques

ISBN-13 (pbk): 978-1-4842-0293-7

ISBN-13 (electronic): 978-1-4842-0292-0

Managing Director: Welmoed Spahr
Lead Editor: Dominic Shakeshaft
Editorial Board: Steve Anglin, Mark Beckner, Ewan Buckingham, Gary Cornell, Louise Corrigan, Jim DeWolf, Jonathan Gennick, Jonathan Hassell, Robert Hutchinson, Michelle Lowman, James Markham, Matthew Moodie, Jeff Olson, Jeffrey Pepper, Douglas Pundick, Ben Renow-Clarke, Dominic Shakeshaft, Gwenan Spearing, Matt Wade, Steve Weiss
Coordinating Editor: Melissa Maldonado
Copy Editor: Barnaby Sheppard
Compositor: SPi Global
Indexer: SPi Global
Artist: SPi Global
Cover Designer: Anna Ishchenko

Distributed to the book trade worldwide by Springer Science+Business Media New York, 233 Spring Street, 6th Floor, New York, NY 10013. Phone 1-800-SPRINGER, fax (201) 348-4505, e-mail orders-ny@springer-sbm.com, or visit www.springeronline.com. Apress Media, LLC is a California LLC and the sole member (owner) is Springer Science + Business Media Finance Inc (SSBM Finance Inc). SSBM Finance Inc is a Delaware corporation.

For information on translations, please e-mail rights@apress.com, or visit www.apress.com.

Apress and friends of ED books may be purchased in bulk for academic, corporate, or promotional use. eBook versions and licenses are also available for most titles. For more information, reference our Special Bulk Sales–eBook Licensing web page at www.apress.com/bulk-sales.

Any source code or other supplementary material referenced by the author in this text is available to readers at www.apress.com. For detailed information about how to locate your book's source code, go to www.apress.com/source-code/.

Contents at a Glance

Contents at a Glance

Contents

About the Author

César Pérez López is a Professor at the Department of Statistics and Operations Research at the University of Madrid. César is also a Mathematician and Economist at the National Statistics Institute (INE) in Madrid, a body which belongs to the Superior Systems and Information Technology Department of the Spanish Government. César also currently works at the Institute for Fiscal Studies in Madrid.

Also Available

- *MATLAB Programming for Numerical Analysis,* 978-1-4842-0296-8
- *MATLAB Control Systems Engineering,* 978-1-4842-0290-6
- *MATLAB Differential Equations,* 978-1-4842-0311-8
- *MATLAB Linear Algebra,* 978-1-4842-0323-1
- *MATLAB Differential and Integral Calculus,* 978-1-4842-0305-7

CHAPTER 1

■■■

Introducing MATLAB and the MATLAB Working Environment

1.1 Introduction

MATLAB is a platform for scientific calculation and high-level programming which uses an interactive environment that allows you to conduct complex calculation tasks more efficiently than with traditional languages, such as C, C++ and FORTRAN. It is the one of the most popular platforms currently used in the sciences and engineering.

MATLAB is an interactive high-level technical computing environment for algorithm development, data visualization, data analysis and numerical analysis. MATLAB is suitable for solving problems involving technical calculations using optimized algorithms that are incorporated into easy to use commands.

It is possible to use MATLAB for a wide range of applications, including calculus, algebra, statistics, econometrics, quality control, time series, signal and image processing, communications, control system design, testing and measuring systems, financial modeling, computational biology, etc. The complementary toolsets, called *toolboxes* (collections of MATLAB functions for special purposes, which are available separately), extend the MATLAB environment, allowing you to solve special problems in different areas of application.

In addition, MATLAB contains a number of functions which allow you to document and share your work. It is possible to integrate MATLAB code with other languages and applications, and to distribute algorithms and applications that are developed using MATLAB.

The following are the most important features of MATLAB:

- It is a high-level language for technical calculation

- It offers a development environment for managing code, files and data

- It features interactive tools for exploration, design and iterative solving

- It supports mathematical functions for linear algebra, statistics, Fourier analysis, filtering, optimization, and numerical integration

- It can produce high quality two-dimensional and three-dimensional graphics to aid data visualization

- It includes tools to create custom graphical user interfaces

- It can be integrated with external languages, such as C/C++, FORTRAN, Java, COM, and Microsoft Excel

The MATLAB development environment allows you to develop algorithms, analyze data, display data files and manage projects in interactive mode (see Figure 1-1).

1

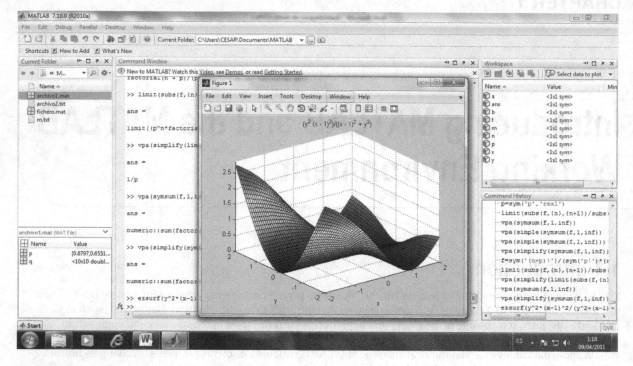

Figure 1-1.

1.1.1 Developing Algorithms and Applications

MATLAB provides a high-level programming language and development tools which enable you to quickly develop and analyze algorithms and applications.

The MATLAB language includes vector and matrix operations that are fundamental to solving scientific and engineering problems. This streamlines both development and execution.

With the MATLAB language, it is possible to program and develop algorithms faster than with traditional languages because it is no longer necessary to perform low-level administrative tasks, such as declaring variables, specifying data types and allocating memory. In many cases, MATLAB eliminates the need for 'for' loops. As a result, a line of MATLAB code usually replaces several lines of C or C++ code.

At the same time, MATLAB offers all the features of traditional programming languages, including arithmetic operators, control flow, data structures, data types, object-oriented programming (OOP) and debugging.

Figure 1-2 shows a communication modulation algorithm that generates 1024 random bits, performs the modulation, adds complex Gaussian noise and graphically represents the result, all in just nine lines of MATLAB code.

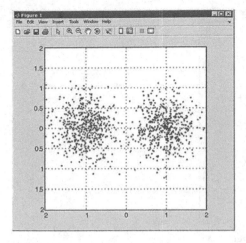

```
% Generate a
vector of N bits
N = 1024;
Bits = rand(N,1)>0.5;

% Convert to symbols
Tx = 1-2*Bits;

% Add white Gaussian noise
P = 0.4;
Nz = P*(randn(N,1)+i*randn(N,1));
Rx = Tx + Nz;

% Display constellation
plot(Rx,'.');
axis([-2 2 -2 2]);
axis square, grid;
```

Figure 1-2.

MATLAB enables you to execute commands or groups of commands one at a time, without compiling or linking, and to repeat the execution to achieve the optimal solution.

To quickly execute complex vector and matrix calculations, MATLAB uses libraries optimized for the processor. For general scalar calculations, MATLAB generates instructions in machine code using JIT (*Just-In-Time*) technology. Thanks to this technology, which is available for most platforms, the execution speeds are much faster than for traditional programming languages.

MATLAB includes *development tools*, which help to efficiently implement algorithms. Some of these tools are listed below:

- **MATLAB Editor** – used for editing functions and standard debugging, for example setting breakpoints and running step-by-step simulations

- **M-Lint Code Checker** - analyzes the code and recommends changes to improve performance and maintenance (see Figure 1-3)

- **MATLAB Profiler** - records the time taken to execute each line of code

- **Directory Reports** - scans all files in a directory and creates reports about the efficiency of the code, differences between files, dependencies of files and code coverage

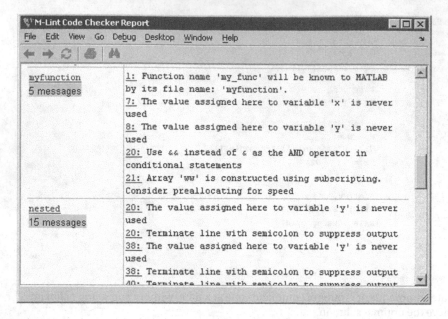

Figure 1-3.

You can also use the interactive tool GUIDE (*Graphical User Interface Development Environment*) to design and edit user interfaces. This tool allows you to include pick lists, drop-down menus, push buttons, radio buttons and sliders, as well as MATLAB diagrams and ActiveX controls. You can also create graphical user interfaces by means of programming using MATLAB functions.

Figure 1-4 shows a completed wavelet analysis tool (bottom) which has been created using the user interface GUIDE (top).

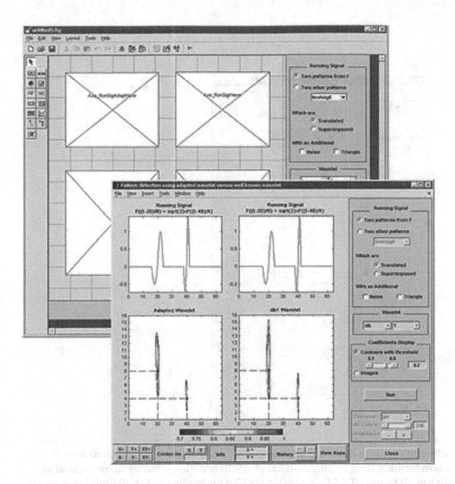

Figure 1-4.

1.1.2 Data Access and Analysis

MATLAB supports the entire process of data analysis, from the acquisition of data from external devices and databases, pre-processing, visualization and numerical analysis, up to the production of results in presentation quality.

MATLAB provides interactive tools and command line operations for data analysis, which include: sections of data, scaling and averaging, interpolation, thresholding and smoothing, correlation, Fourier analysis and filtering, searching for one-dimensional peaks and zeros, basic statistics and curve fitting, matrix analysis, etc.

The diagram in Figure 1-5 shows a curve that has been fitted to atmospheric pressure differences averaged between Easter Island and Darwin in Australia.

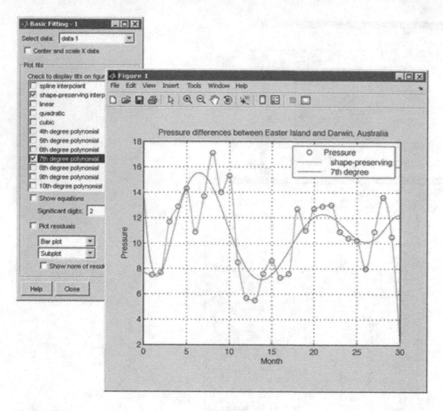

Figure 1-5.

The MATLAB platform allows efficient access to data files, other applications, databases and external devices. You can read data stored in most known formats, such as Microsoft Excel, ASCII text files or binary image, sound and video files, and scientific archives such as HDF and HDF5 files. The binary files for low level I/O functions allow you to work with data files in any format. Additional features allow you to view Web pages and XML data.

It is possible to call other applications and languages, such as C, C++, COM, DLLs, Java, FORTRAN, and Microsoft Excel objects, and access FTP sites and Web services. Using the Database Toolbox, you can even access ODBC/JDBC databases.

1.1.3 Data Visualization

All graphics functions necessary to visualize scientific and engineering data are available in MATLAB. This includes tools for two- and three-dimensional diagrams, three-dimensional volume visualization, tools to create diagrams interactively, and the ability to export using the most popular graphic formats. It is possible to customize diagrams, adding multiple axes, changing the colors of lines and markers, adding annotations, LaTeX equations and legends, and plotting paths.

Various two-dimensional graphical representations of vector data can be created, including:

- Line, area, bar and sector diagrams

- Direction and velocity diagrams

- Histograms

- Polygons and surfaces

- Dispersion bubble diagrams

- Animations

Figure 1-6 shows linear plots of the results of several emission tests of a motor, with a curve fitted to the data.

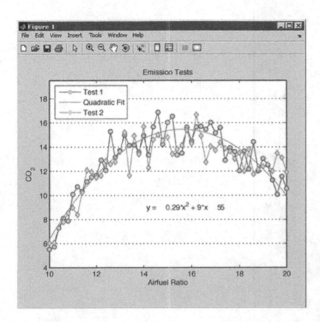

Figure 1-6.

MATLAB also provides functions for displaying two-dimensional arrays, three-dimensional scalar data and three-dimensional vector data. It is possible to use these functions to visualize and understand large amounts of complex multi-dimensional data. It is also possible to define the characteristics of the diagrams, such as the orientation of the camera, perspective, lighting, light source and transparency. Three-dimensional diagramming features include:

- Surface, contour and mesh plots

- Space curves

- Cone, phase, flow and isosurface diagrams

Figure 1-7 shows a three-dimensional diagram of an isosurface that reveals the geodesic structure of a fullerene carbon-60 molecule.

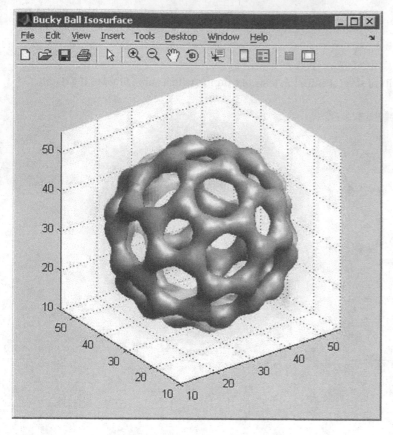

Figure 1-7.

MATLAB includes interactive tools for graphic editing and design. From a MATLAB diagram, you can perform any of the following tasks:

- Drag and drop new sets of data into the figure

- Change the properties of any object in the figure

- Change the zoom, rotation, view (i.e. panoramic), camera angle and lighting

- Add data labels and annotations

- Draw shapes

- Generate an M-file for reuse with different data

Figure 1-8 shows a collection of graphics which have been created interactively by dragging data sets onto the diagram window, making new subdiagrams, changing properties such as colors and fonts, and adding annotations.

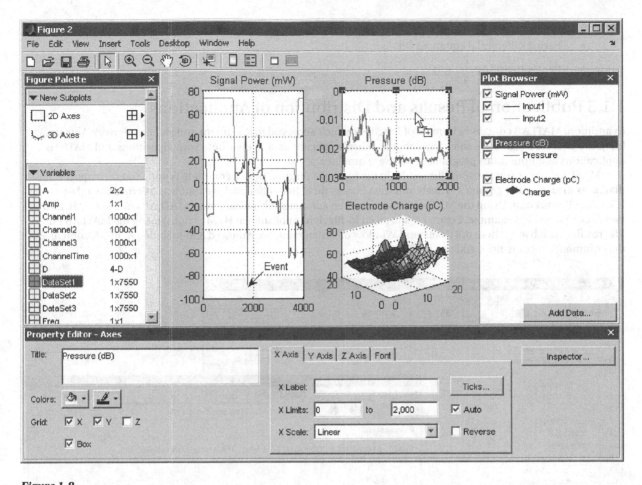

Figure 1-8.

MATLAB is compatible with all the well-known data file and graphics formats, such as GIF, JPEG, BMP, EPS, TIFF, PNG, HDF, AVI, and PCX. As a result, it is possible to export MATLAB diagrams to other applications, such as Microsoft Word and Microsoft PowerPoint, or desktop publishing software. Before exporting, you can create and apply style templates that contain all the design details, fonts, line thickness, etc., necessary to comply with the publication specifications.

1.1.4 Numerical Calculation

MATLAB contains mathematical, statistical, and engineering functions that support most of the operations carried out in those fields. These functions, developed by math experts, are the foundation of the MATLAB language. To cite some examples, MATLAB implements mathematical functions and data analysis in the following areas:

- Manipulation of matrices and linear algebra
- Polynomials and interpolation
- Fourier analysis and filters
- Statistics and data analysis
- Optimization and numerical integration

9

- Ordinary differential equations (ODEs)

- Partial differential equations (PDEs)

- Sparse matrix operations

1.1.5 Publication of Results and Distribution of Applications

In addition, MATLAB contains a number of functions which allow you to document and share your work. You can integrate your MATLAB code with other languages and applications, and distribute your algorithms and MATLAB applications as autonomous programs or software modules.

MATLAB allows you to export the results in the form of a diagram or as a complete report. You can export diagrams to all popular graphics formats and then import them into other packages such as Microsoft Word or Microsoft PowerPoint. Using the MATLAB Editor, you can automatically publish your MATLAB code in HTML format, Word, LaTeX, etc. For example, Figure 1-9 shows an M-file (left) published in HTML (right) using the MATLAB Editor. The results, which are sent to the Command Window or to diagrams, are captured and included in the document and the comments become titles and text in HTML.

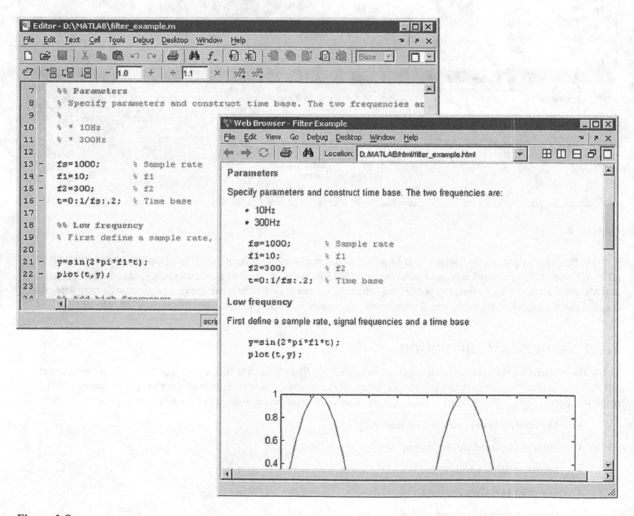

Figure 1-9.

It is possible to create more complex reports, such as mock executions and various parameter tests, using MATLAB Report Generator (available separately).

MATLAB provides functions enabling you to integrate your MATLAB applications with C and C++ code, FORTRAN code, COM objects, and Java code. You can call DLLs and Java classes and ActiveX controls. Using the MATLAB engine library, you can also call MATLAB from C, C++, or FORTRAN code.

You can create algorithms in MATLAB and distribute them to other users of MATLAB. Using the MATLAB Compiler (available separately), algorithms can be distributed, either as standalone applications or as software modules included in a project, to users who do not have MATLAB. Additional products are able to turn algorithms into a software module that can be called from COM or Microsoft Excel.

1.2 The MATLAB Working Environment

Figure 1-10 shows the primary workspace of the MATLAB environment. This is the screen in which you enter your MATLAB programs.

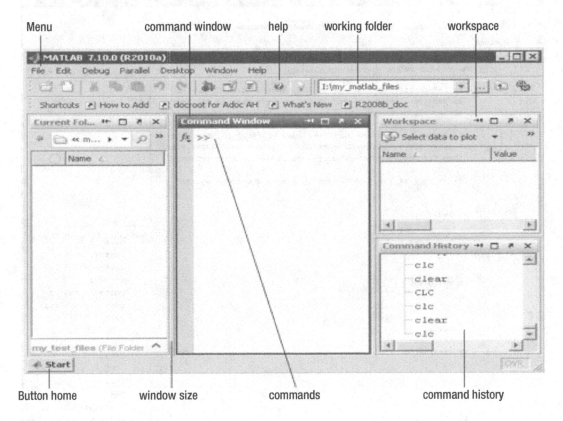

Figure 1-10.

The following table summarizes the components of the MATLAB environment.

Tool	Description
Command History	This allows you to see the commands entered during the session in the Command Window, as well as copy them and run them (lower right part of Figure 1-11)
Command Window	This is where you enter MATLAB commands (central part of Figure 1-11)
Workspace	This allows you to view the contents of the workspace (variables, etc.) (upper right part of Figure 1-11)
Help	This offers help and demos on MATLAB
Start button	This enables you to run tools and provides access to MATLAB documentation (Figure 1-12)

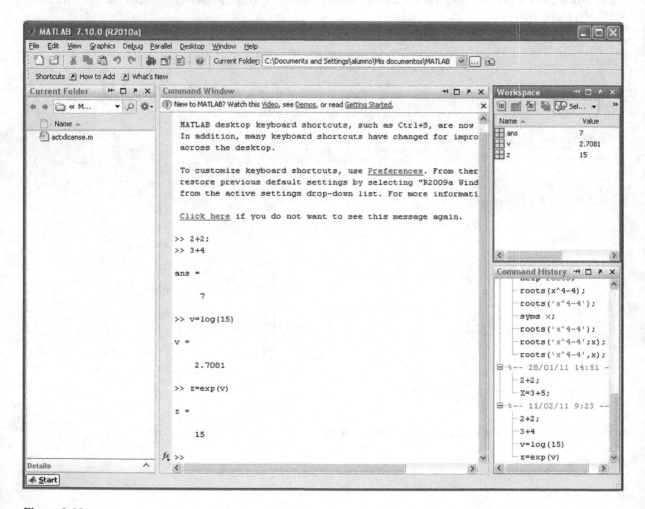

Figure 1-11.

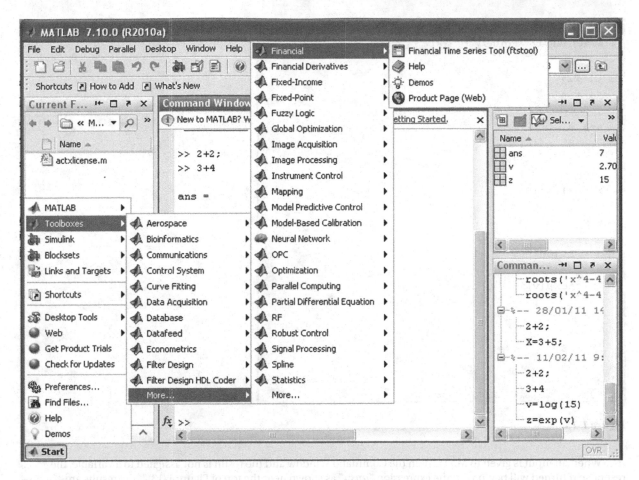

Figure 1-12.

MATLAB commands are written in the Command Window to the right of the user input prompt ">>" and the response to the command will appear in the lines immediately below. After exiting from the response, the user input prompt will re-display, allowing you to input more entries (Figure 1-13).

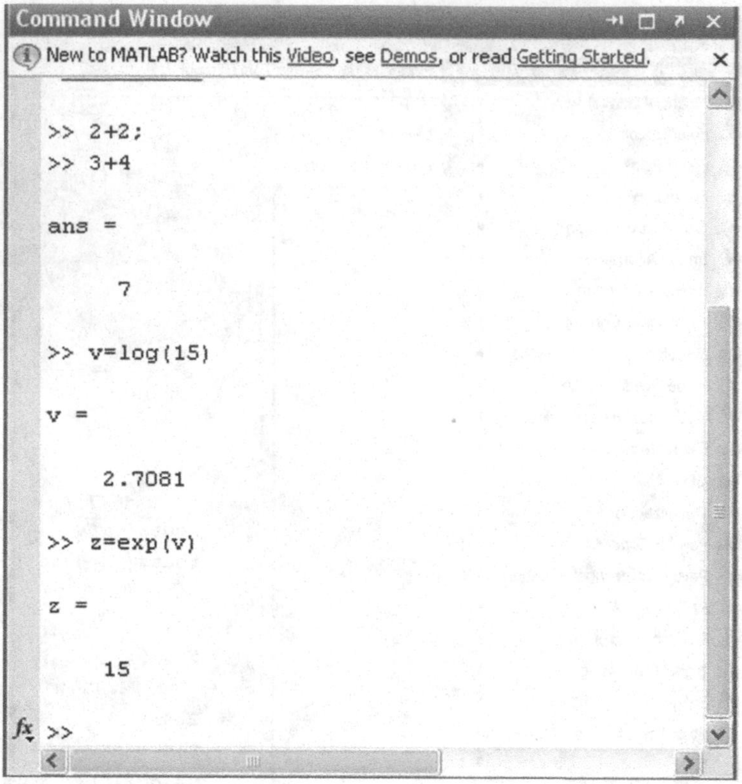

Figure 1-13.

When an input is given to MATLAB in the Command Window and the result is not assigned to a variable, the response returned will begin with the expression "*ans=*", as shown near the top of Figure 1-13. If the results are assigned to a variable, we can then use that variable as an argument for subsequent input. This is the case for the variable *v* in Figure 1-13, which is subsequently used as the input for an exponential.

To run a MATLAB command, simply type the command and press *Enter*. If at the end of the input we put a semicolon, the program runs the calculation and keeps it in memory (*Workspace*), but does not display the result on the screen (see the first entry in Figure 1-13). The input prompt ">>" appears to indicate that you can enter a new command.

Like the C programming language, MATLAB is case sensitive; for example, Sin(x) is not the same as sin(x). The names of all built-in functions begin with a lowercase character. There should be no spaces in the names of commands, variables or functions. In other cases, spaces are ignored, and they can be used to make the input more readable. Multiple entries can be entered in the same command line by separating them with commas, pressing *Enter* at the end of the last entry (see Figure 1-14). If you use a semicolon at the end of one of the entries in the line, its corresponding output will not be displayed.

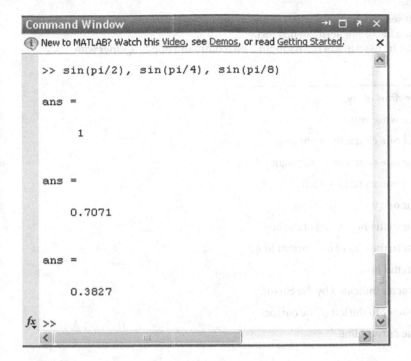

Figure 1-14.

Descriptive comments can be entered in a command input line by starting them with the "%" symbol. When you run the input, MATLAB ignores the comment and processes the rest of the code (see Figure 1-15).

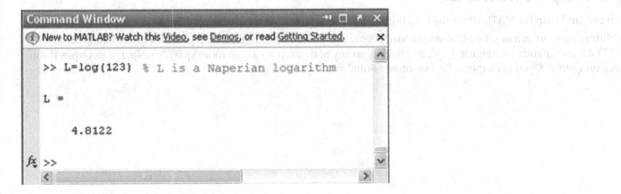

Figure 1-15.

To simplify the process of entering script to be evaluated by the MATLAB interpreter (via the Command Window prompt), you can use the arrow keys. For example, if you press the up arrow key once, you will recover the last entry you submitted. If you press the up key twice, you will recover the penultimate entry you submitted, and so on.

If you type a sequence of characters in the input area and then press the up arrow key, you will recover the last entry you submitted that begins with the specified string.

Commands entered during a MATLAB session are temporarily stored in the buffer (*Workspace*) until you end the session, at which time they can be stored in a file or are permanently lost.

Below is a summary of the keys that can be used in MATLAB's input area (command line), together with their functions:

Up arrow (Ctrl-P)	Retrieves the previous entry.
Down arrow (Ctrl-N)	Retrieves the following entry.
Left arrow (Ctrl-B)	Moves the cursor one character to the left.
Right arrow (Ctrl-F)	Moves the cursor one character to the right.
CTRL-left arrow	Moves the cursor one word to the left.
CTRL-right arrow	Moves the cursor one word to the right.
Home (Ctrl-A)	Moves the cursor to the beginning of the line.
End (Ctrl-E)	Moves the cursor to the end of the current line.
Escape	Clears the command line.
Delete (Ctrl-D)	Deletes the character indicated by the cursor.
Backspace	Deletes the character to the left of the cursor.
CTRL-K	Deletes (kills) the current line.

The command *clc* clears the command window, but does not delete the contents of the work area (the contents remain in the memory).

1.3 Help in MATLAB

You can find help for MATLAB via the help button 🔘 in the toolbar or via the *Help* option in the menu bar. In addition, support can also be obtained via MATLAB commands. The command *help* provides general help on all MATLAB commands (see Figure 1-16). By clicking on any of them, you can get more specific help. For example, if you click on *graph2d*, you get support for two-dimensional graphics (see Figure 1-17).

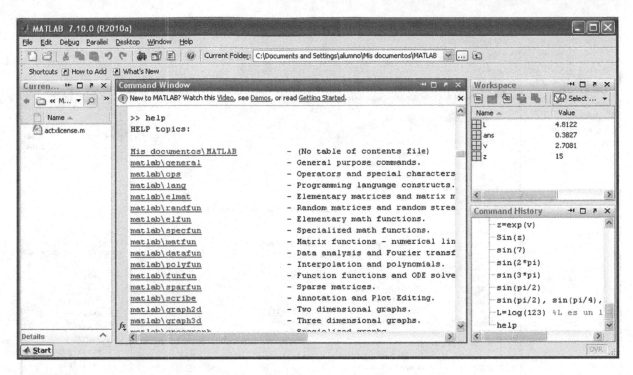

Figure 1-16.

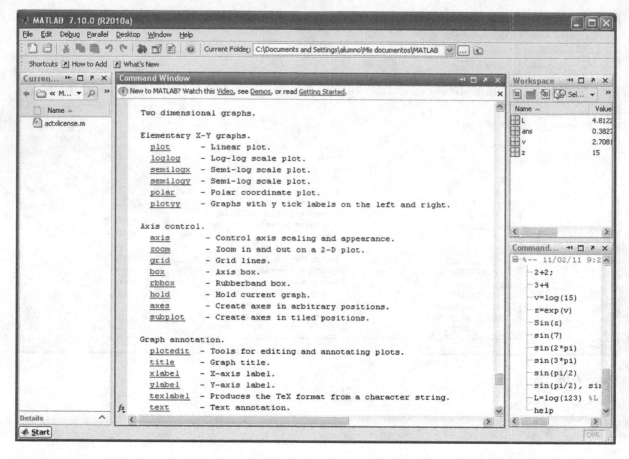

Figure 1-17.

You can ask for help about a specific command *command* (Figure 1-18) or on any topic *topic* (Figure 1-19) by using the command *help command* or *help topic*.

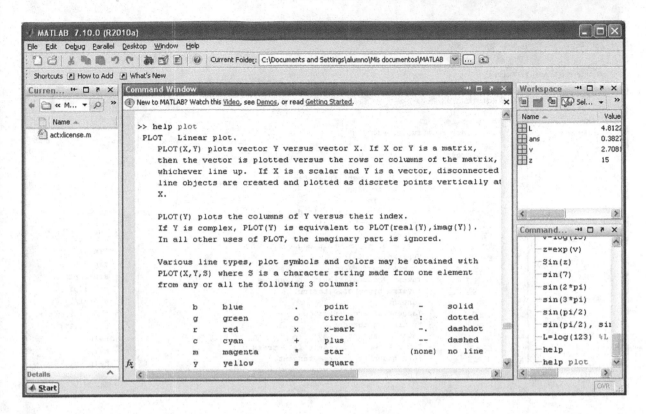

Figure 1-18.

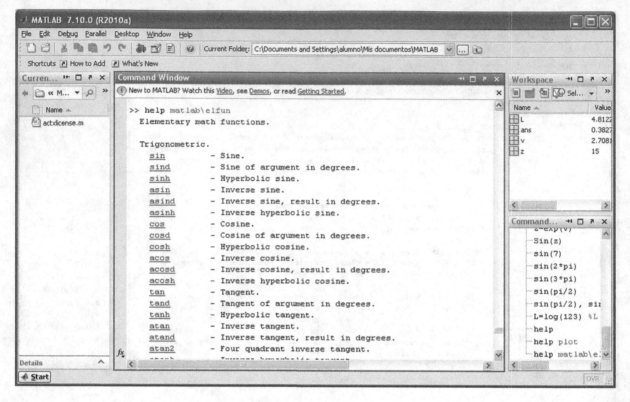

Figure 1-19.

The command *lookfor string* allows you to find all those MATLAB functions or commands that refer to or contain the string *string*. This command is very useful when there is no direct support for the specified string, or to view the help for all commands related to the given string. For example, if we want to find help for all commands that contain the sequence *inv*, we can use the command *lookfor inv* (Figure 1-20).

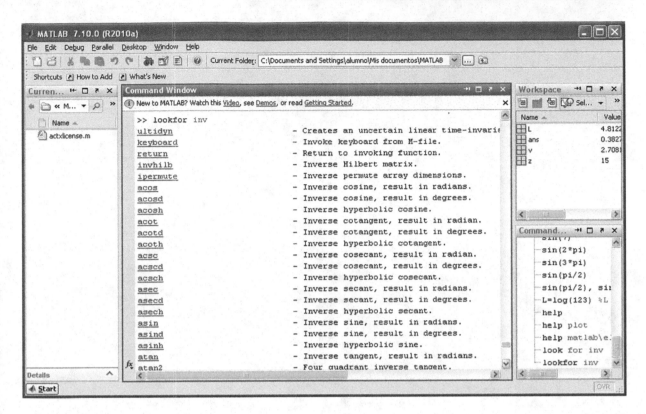

Figure 1-20.

■ ■ ■

CHAPTER 2

MATLAB Programming

2.1 MATLAB Programming

MATLAB can be used as a high-level programming language including data structures, functions, instructions for flow control, management of inputs/outputs and even object-oriented programming.

MATLAB programs are usually written into files called M-files. An M-file is nothing more than a MATLAB code (*script*) that executes a series of commands or functions that accept arguments and produce an output. The M-files are created using the text editor.

2.1.1 The Text Editor

The *Editor/Debugger* is activated by clicking on the *create a new M-file* button [icon] in the MATLAB desktop or by selecting *File* ➤ *New* ➤ *M-file* in the MATLAB desktop (Figure 2-1) or Command Window (Figure 2-2). The *Editor/Debugger* opens a file in which we create the M-file, i.e. a blank file into which we will write MATLAB programming code (Figure 2-3). You can open an existing M-file using *File* ➤ *Open* on the MATLAB desktop (Figure 2-1) or, alternatively, you can use the command *Open* in the Command Window (Figure 2-2). You can also open the *Editor/Debugger* by right-clicking on the *Current Directory* window and choosing *New* ➤ *M-file* from the resulting pop-up menu (Figure 2-4). Using the menu option *Open*, you can open an existing M-file. You can open several M-files simultaneously, each of which will appear in a different window.

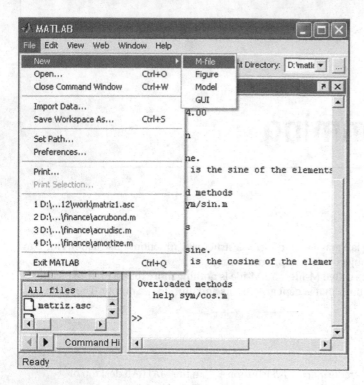

Figure 2-1.

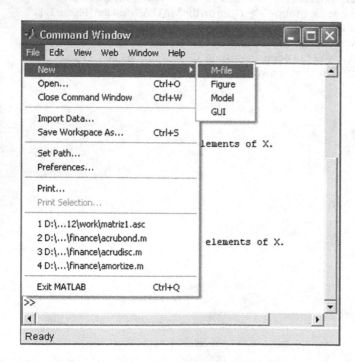

Figure 2-2.

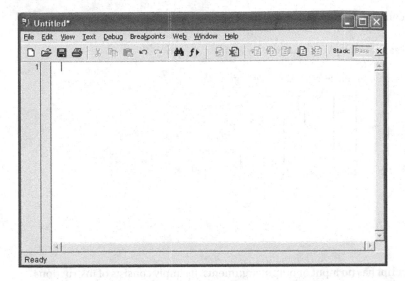

Figure 2-3.

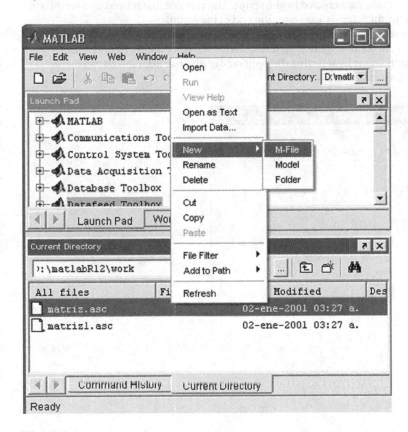

Figure 2-4.

Figure 2-5 shows the functions of the icons in the *Editor/Debugger*.

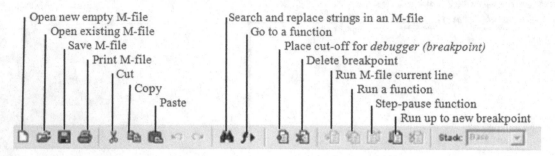

Figure 2-5.

2.1.2 Scripts

Scripts are the simplest possible M-files. A script has no input or output arguments. It simply consists of instructions that MATLAB executes sequentially and that could also be submitted in a sequence in the Command Window. Scripts operate with existing data on the workspace or new data created by the script. Any variable that is used by a script will remain in the workspace and can be used in further calculations after the end of the script.

Below is an example of a script that generates several curves in polar form, representing flower petals. Once the syntax of the script has been entered into the editor (Figure 2-6), it is stored in the work library (*work*) and simultaneously executes by clicking the button or by selecting the option *Save and run* from the *Debug* menu (or pressing F5). To move from one chart to the next press ENTER.

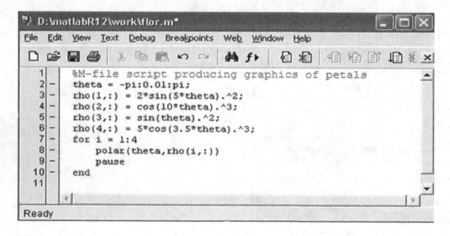

Figure 2-6.

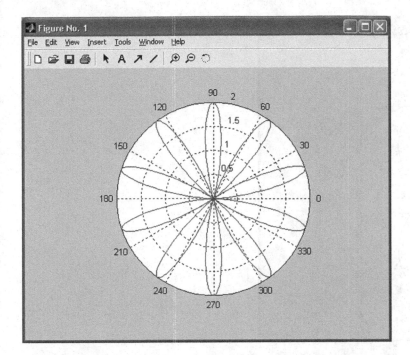

Figure 2-7.

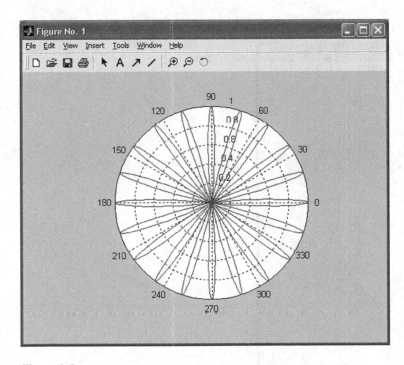

Figure 2-8.

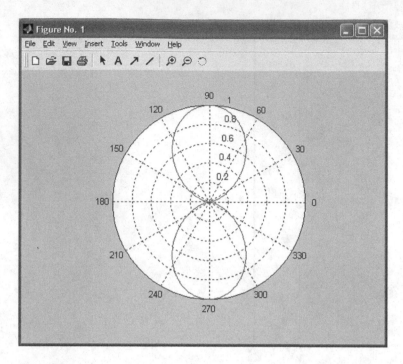

Figure 2-9.

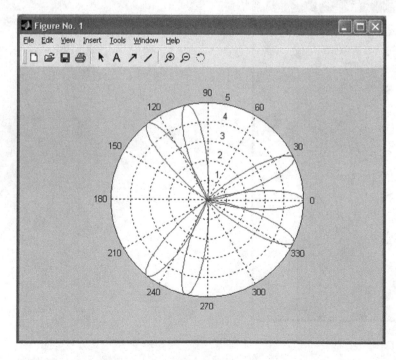

Figure 2-10.

2.1.3 Functions and M-files. Eval and Feval

We already know that MATLAB has a wide variety of functions that can be used in everyday work with the program. But, in addition, the program also offers the possibility of custom defined functions. The most common way to define a function is to write its definition to a text file, called an M-file, which will be permanent and will therefore enable the function to be used whenever required.

MATLAB is usually used in *command mode* (or *interactive mode*), in which case a command is written in a single line in the Command Window and is immediately processed. But MATLAB also allows the implementation of sets of commands in *batch* mode, in which case a sequence of commands can be submitted which were previously written in a file. This file (M-file) must be stored on disk with the extension "*.m*" in the MATLAB subdirectory, using any ASCII editor or by selecting *M-file New* from the *File* menu in the top menu bar, which opens a text editor that will allow you to write command lines and save the file with a given name. Selecting *M-File Open* from the *File* menu in the top menu bar allows you to edit any pre-existing M-file.

To run an M-file simply type its name (without extension) in interactive mode into the Command Window and press *Enter*. MATLAB sequentially interprets all commands and statements of the M-file line by line and executes them. Normally the literal commands that MATLAB is performing do not appear on screen, except when the command *echo on* is active and only the results of successive executions of the interpreted commands are displayed. Normally, work in batch mode is useful when automating large scale tedious processes which, if done manually, would be prone to mistakes. You can enter explanatory text and comments into M-files by starting each line of the comment with the symbol %. The *help* command can be used to display comments made in a particular M-file.

The command *function* allows the definition of functions in MATLAB, making it one of the most useful applications of M-files. The syntax of this command is as follows:

function output_parameters = function_name (input_parameters) the function body

Once the function has been defined, it is stored in an M-file for later use. It is also useful to enter some explanatory text in the syntax of the function (using %), which can be accessed later by using the *help* command.

When there is more than one output parameter, they are placed between square brackets and separated by commas. If there is more than one input parameter, they are separated by commas. The body of the function is the syntax that defines it, and should include commands or instructions that assign values to output parameters. Each command or instruction of the body often appears in a line that ends either with a comma or, when variables are being defined, by a semicolon (in order to avoid duplication of outputs when executing the function). The function is stored in the M-file named *function_name.m*.

Let us define the function $fun1(x) = x \wedge 3 - 2x + \cos(x)$, creating the corresponding M-file *fun1.m*. To define this function in MATLAB select *M-file New* from the *File* menu in the top menu bar (or click the button 🗋 in the MATLAB tool bar). This opens the *MATLAB Editor/Debugger* text editor that will allow us to insert command lines defining the function, as shown in Figure 2-11.

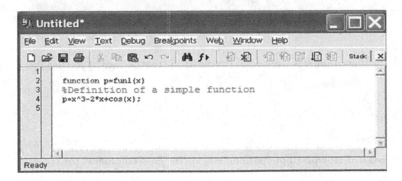

Figure 2-11.

To permanently save this code in MATLAB select the *Save* option from the *File* menu at the top of the *MATLAB Editor/Debugger*. This opens the *Save* dialog of Figure 2-12, which we use to save our function with the desired name and in the subdirectory indicated as a path in the *file name* field. Alternatively you can click on the button 🔲 or select *Save and run* from the *Debug* menu. Functions should be saved using a file name equal to the name of the function and in MATLAB's default work subdirectory *C: \MATLAB6p1\work*.

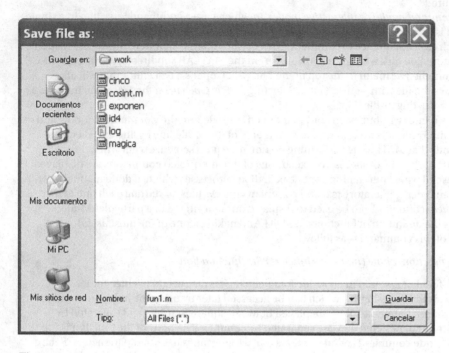

Figure 2-12.

Once a function has been defined and saved in an M-file, it can be used from the Command Window. For example, to find the value of the function at 3π-2 we write in the Command Window:

>> fun1(3*pi/2)

ans =

95.2214

For help on the previous function (assuming that comments were added to the M-file that defines it) you use the command *help*, as follows:

>> help fun1(x)

A simple function definition

A function can also be evaluated at some given arguments (input parameters) via the *feval* command, the syntax of which is as follows:

feval ('F', arg1, arg1,..., argn)

This evaluates the function F (the M-file F.m) at the specified arguments arg1, arg2,..., argn.

As an example we build an M-file named *equation2.m* which contains the function equation2, whose arguments are the three coefficients of the quadratic equation $ax^2+bx+c = 0$ and whose outputs are the two solutions (Figure 2-13).

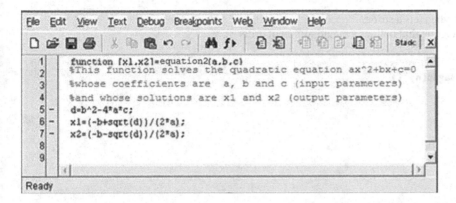

Figure 2-13.

Now if we want to solve the equation $x^2+2x+3 = 0$ using *feval*, we write the following in the Command Window:

```
>> [x 1, x 2] = feval('equation2',1,2,3)
```

x 1 =

-1.0000 + 1. 4142i

x 2 =

-1.0000 - 1. 4142i

The quadratic equation can also be solved as follows:

```
>> [x 1, x 2] = equation2(1,2,3)
```

x 1 =

-1.0000 + 1. 4142i

x 2 =

-1.0000 - 1. 4142i

If we wish to ask for help about the function equation2 we do the following:

```
>> help equation2
```

This function solves the quadratic equation ax ^ 2 + bx + c = 0

whose coefficients are a, b and c (input parameters)

and whose solutions are x 1 and x 2 (output parameters)

Evaluating a function when its arguments (input parameters) are strings is performed via the command *eval*, whose syntax is as follows:

```
eval (expression)
```

This executes the expression when it is a string.

As an example, we evaluate a string that defines a magic square of order 4.

```
>> n = 4;
>> eval(['M' num2str(n) ' = magic(n)'])

M4 =

16  2  3  13
5  11  10  8
9  7   6  12
4  14  15  1
```

2.1.4 Local and Global Variables

Typically, each function defined as an M-file contains local variables, i.e., variables that have effect only within the M-file, separate from other M-files and the base workspace. However, it is possible to define variables inside M-files which can take effect simultaneously in other M-files and in the base workspace. For this purpose, it is necessary to define global variables with the GLOBAL command whose syntax is as follows:

```
GLOBAL x y z...
```

This defines the variables x, y and z as global.

Any variables defined as global inside a function are available separately for the rest of the functions and in the base workspace command line. If a global variable does not exist, the first time it is used, it will be initialized as an empty array. If there is already a variable with the same name as a global variable being defined, MATLAB will send a warning message and change the value of that variable to match the global variable. It is convenient to declare a variable as global in every function that will need access to it, and also in the command line, in order to access it from the base workspace. The GLOBAL command is located at the beginning of a function (before any occurrence of the variable).

As an example, suppose that we want to study the effect of the interaction coefficients α and β in the Lotka–Volterra predator-prey model:

$$y_1' = y_1 - \alpha y_1 y_2$$
$$y_2' = -y_2 + \beta y_1 y_2$$

To do this, we create the function *lotka* in the M-file *lotka.m* as depicted in Figure 2-14.

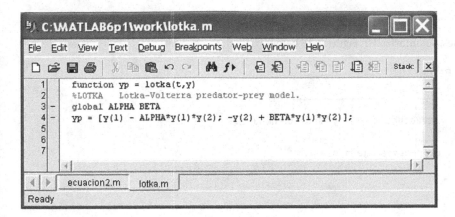

```
function yp = lotka(t,y)
%LOTKA    Lotka-Volterra predator-prey model.
global ALPHA BETA
yp = [y(1) - ALPHA*y(1)*y(2); -y(2) + BETA*y(1)*y(2)];
```

Figure 2-14.

Later, we might type the following in the command line:

```
>> global ALPHA BETA
ALPHA = 0.01
BETA = 0.02
```

These global values may then be used for α and β in the M-file *lotka.m* (without having to specify them). For example, we can generate the graph (Figure 2-15) with the following syntax:

```
>> [t, y] = ode23 ('lotka', 0.10, [1; 1]); plot(t,y)
```

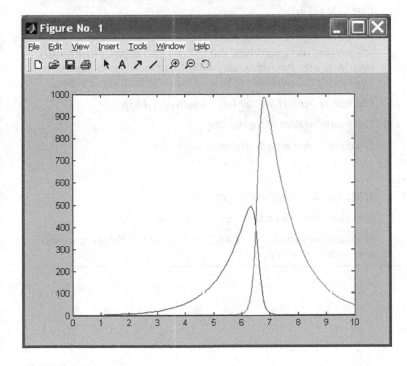

Figure 2-15.

2.1.5 Data Types

MATLAB has 14 different data types, summarized in Figure 2-16 below.

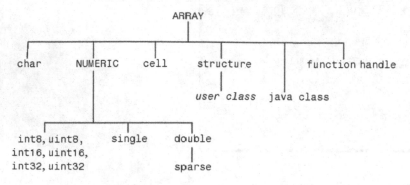

Figure 2-16.

Below are the different types of data:

Data type	Example	Description
single	3* 10 ^ 38	*Simple numerical precision. This requires less storage than double precision, but it is less precise. This type of data should not be used in mathematical operations.*
Double	3*10^300 5+6i	*Double numerical precision. This is the most commonly used data type in MATLAB*
sparse	speye(5)	*Sparse matrix with double precision.*
int8, uint8, int16, uint16, int32, uint32	UInt8(magic (3))	*Integers and unsigned integers with 8, 16, and 32 bits. These make it possible to use entire amounts with efficient memory management. This type of data should not be used in mathematical operations.*
char	'Hello'	*Characters (each character has a length of 16 bits).*
cell	{17 'hello' eye (2)}	*Cell (contains data of similar size)*

structure	a.day = 12;
	a.color = 'Red';
	a.mat = magic(3);
		Structure (contains cells of similar size)

user class	inline('sin (x)')	*MATLAB class (built with functions)*
java class	Java. awt.Frame	*Java class (defined in API or own) with Java*
function handle	@humps	*Manages functions in MATLAB. It can be last in a list of arguments and evaluated with feval.*

2.1.6 Flow Control: FOR, WHILE and IF ELSEIF Loops

The use of recursive functions, conditional operations and piecewise defined functions is very common in mathematics. The handling of loops is necessary for the definition of these types of functions. Naturally, the definition of the functions will be made via *M-files*.

FOR Loops

MATLAB has its own version of the DO statement (defined in the syntax of most programming languages). This statement allows you to run a command or group of commands repeatedly. For example:

>> for i=1:3, x(i)=0, end

X =

0

X =

0   0

X =

0 0 0

The general form of a FOR loop is as follows:

for variable = expression
    commands
end

The loop always starts with the clause *for* and ends with the clause *end*, and includes in its interior a whole set of commands that are separated by commas. If any command defines a variable, it must end with a semicolon in order to avoid repetition in the output . Typically, loops are used in the syntax of M-files. Here is an example (Figure 2-17):

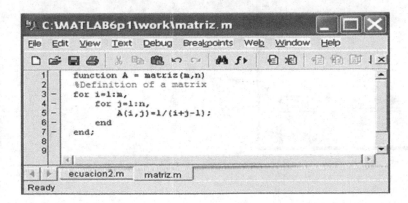

Figure 2-17.

In this loop we have defined a Hilbert matrix of order *(m, n)*. If we save it as an M-file *matriz.m*, we can build any Hilbert matrix later by running the M-file and specifying values for the variables *m* and *n* (the matrix dimensions) as shown below:

```
>> M = matriz(4,5)

M =

1.0000  0.5000  0.3333  0.2500  0.2000
0.5000  0.3333  0.2500  0.2000  0.1667
0.3333  0.2500  0.2000  0.1667  0.1429
0.2500  0.2000  0.1667  0.1429  0.1250
```

WHILE Loops

MATLAB has its own version of the WHILE structure defined in the syntax of most programming languages. This statement allows you to repeat a command or group of commands a number of times while a specified logical condition is met. The general syntax of this loop is as follows:

```
While condition
        commands
end
```

The loop always starts with the clause *while*, followed by a condition, and ends with the clause *end*, and includes in its interior a whole set of commands that are separated by commas which continually loop while the condition is met. If any command defines a variable, it must end with a semicolon in order to avoid repetition in the output. As an example, we write an M-file (Figure 2-18) that is saved as *while1.m*, which calculates the largest number whose factorial does not exceed 10^{100}.

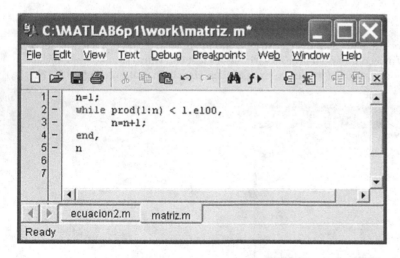

Figure 2-18.

We now run the M-file.

```
>> while1

n =

70
```

IF ELSEIF ELSE END Loops

MATLAB, like most structured programming languages, also includes the IF-ELSEIF-ELSE-END structure. Using this structure, scripts can be run if certain conditions are met. The loop syntax is as follows:

```
if condition
        commands
end
```

In this case the commands are executed if the condition is true. But the syntax of this loop may be more general.

```
if condition
        commands1
else
        commands2
end
```

In this case, the commands *commands1* are executed if the condition is true, and the commands *commands2* are executed if the condition is false.

IF statements and FOR statements can be nested. When multiple IF statements are nested using the ELSEIF statement, the general syntax is as follows:

```
if condition1
    commands1
    elseif condition2
        commands2
    elseif condition3
        commands3
.
.
    else
end
```

In this case, the commands *commands1* are executed if *condition1* is true, the commands *commands2* are executed if *condition1* is false and *condition2* is true, the commands *commands3* are executed if *condition1* and *condition2* are false and *condition3* is true, and so on.

The previous nested syntax is equivalent to the following unnested syntax, but executes much faster:

```
if condition1
    commands1
else
        if condition2
            commands2
```

```
        else
            if condition3
                commands3
            else
.
.
            end
        end
end
```

Consider, for example, the M-file *else1.m* (see Figure 2-19).

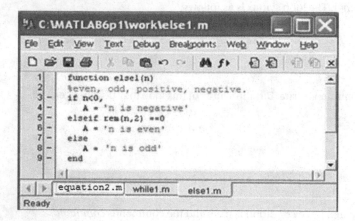

Figure 2-19.

When you run the file it returns negative, odd or even according to whether the argument *n* is negative, non-negative and odd, or non-negative and even, respectively:

>> else1(8), else1(5), else1(-10)

A =

n is even

A =

n is odd

A =

n is negative

SWITCH and CASE

The *switch* statement executes certain statements based on the value of a variable or expression. Its basic syntax is as follows:

```
switch expression (scalar or string)
    case value1
        statements % runs if expression is value1
    case value2
        statements % runs if expression is value2
.
.
.
otherwise
    statements % runs if neither case is satisfied

end
```

Below is an example of a function that returns 'minus one', 'zero', 'one', or 'another value' according to whether the input is equal to -1,0,1 or something else, respectively (Figure 2-20).

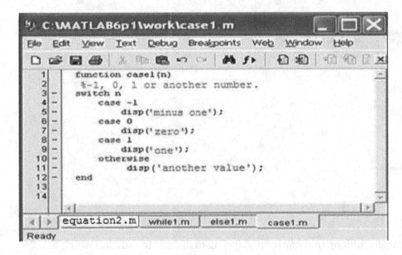

Figure 2-20.

Running the above example we get:

`>> case1(25)`

another value

`>> case1(- 1)`

minus one

CONTINUE

The *continue* statement passes control to the next iteration in a *for* loop or *while* loop in which it appears, ignoring the remaining instructions in the body of the loop. Below is an M-file *continue.m* (Figure 2-21) that counts the lines of code in the file *magic.m*, ignoring the white lines and comments.

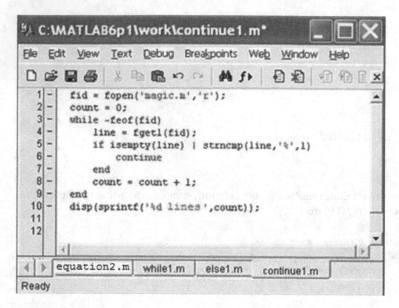

Figure 2-21.

Running the M-file, we get:

```
>> continue1

25 lines
```

BREAK

The *break* statement terminates the execution of a *for* loop or *while* loop, skipping to the first instruction which appears outside of the loop. Below is an M-file *break1.m* (Figure 2-22) which reads the lines of code in the file *fft.m*, exiting the loop as soon as it encounters the first empty line.

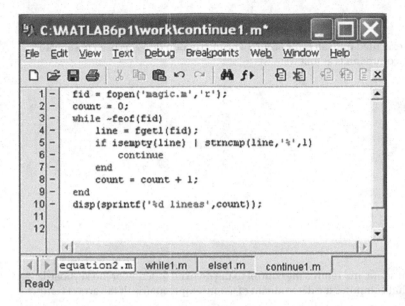

```
  1 -    fid = fopen('magic.m','r');
  2 -    count = 0;
  3 -    while ~feof(fid)
  4 -        line = fgetl(fid);
  5 -        if isempty(line) | strncmp(line,'%',1)
  6 -            continue
  7 -        end
  8 -        count = count + 1;
  9 -    end
 10 -    disp(sprintf('%d lineas',count));
 11
 12
```

equation2.m | while1.m | else1.m | continue1.m

Ready

Figure 2-22.

Running the M-file we get:

>> **break1**

```
%FFT Discrete Fourier transform.
%   FFT(X) is the discrete Fourier transform (DFT) of vector X.  For
%   matrices, the FFT operation is applied to each column. For N-D
%   arrays, the FFT operation operates on the first non-singleton
%   dimension.
%
%   FFT(X,N) is the N-point FFT, padded with zeros if X has less
%   than N points and truncated if it has more.
%
%   FFT(X,[],DIM) or FFT(X,N,DIM) applies the FFT operation across the
%   dimension DIM.
%
%   For length N input vector x, the DFT is a length N vector X,
%   with elements
%                     N
%      X(k) =        sum   x(n)*exp(-j*2*pi*(k-1)*(n-1)/N), 1 <= k <= N.
%                    n=1
%   The inverse DFT (computed by IFFT) is given by
%                     N
%      x(n) = (1/N) sum   X(k)*exp( j*2*pi*(k-1)*(n-1)/N), 1 <= n <= N.
%                    k=1
%
%   See also IFFT, FFT2, IFFT2, FFTSHIFT.
```

TRY... CATCH

The instructions between *try* and *catch* are executed until an error occurs. The instruction *lasterr* is used to show the cause of the error. The general syntax of the command is as follows:

```
try,
        instruction
        ...,
        instruction
catch,
        instruction
        ...,
        instruction
end
```

RETURN

The *return* statement terminates the current script and returns the control to the invoked function or the keyboard. The following is an example (Figure 2-23) that computes the determinant of a non-empty matrix. If the array is empty it returns the value 1.

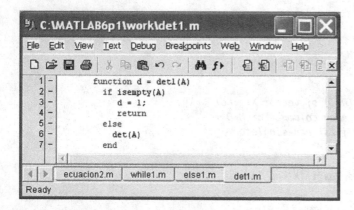

Figure 2-23.

Running the function for a non-empty array we get:

```
>> A = [- 1, - 1, - 1; 1,0,1; 1, - 1, - 1]

A =

-1 -1 -1
 1  0  1
 1 -1 -1

>> det1(A)

ans =

2
```

Now we apply the function to an empty array:

```
>> B = []

B =

[]

>> det1(B)

ans =

1
```

2.1.7 Subfunctions

M-file-defined functions can contain code for more than one function. The main function in an M-file is called a *primary function*, which is precisely the function which invokes the M-file, but subfunctions hanging from the primary function may be added which are only visible for the primary function or another subfunction within the same M-file. Each subfunction begins with its own function definition. An example is shown in Figure 2-24.

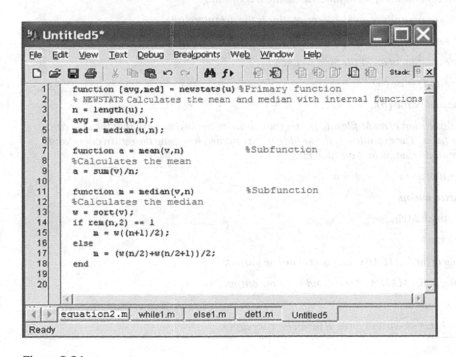

Figure 2-24.

The subfunctions *mean* and *median* calculate the arithmetic mean and the median of the input list. The primary function *newstats* determines the length n of the list and calls the subfunctions with the list as the first argument and n as the second argument. When executing the main function, it is enough to provide as input a list of values for which the arithmetic mean and median will be calculated. The subfunctions are executed automatically, as shown below.

```
>> [mean, median] = newstats([10,20,3,4,5,6])

mean =

8

median =

5.5000
```

2.1.8 Commands in M-files

MATLAB provides certain procedural commands which are often used in M-file scripts. Among them are the following:

echo on	*View on-screen commands of an M-file script while it is running.*
echo off	*Hides on-screen commands of an M-file script (this is the default setting).*
pause	*Interrupts the execution of an M-file until the user presses a key to continue.*
pause(n)	*Interrupts the execution of an M-file for n seconds.*
pause off	*Disables pause and pause (n).*
pause on	*Enables pause and pause (n).*
keyboard	*Interrupts the execution of an M-file and passes the control to the keyboard so that the user can perform other tasks. The execution of the M-file can be resumed by typing the* return *command into the Command Window and pressing Enter.*
return	*Resumes execution of an M-file after an outage.*
break	*Prematurely exits a loop.*
CLC	*Clears the Command Window.*
Home	*Hides the cursor.*
more on	*Enables paging of the MATLAB Command Window output.*
more off	*Disables paging of the MATLAB Command Window output.*
more (N)	*Sets page size to N lines.*
menu	*Offers a choice between various types of menu for user input.*

2.1.9 Functions Relating to Arrays of Cells

An array is a well-ordered collection of individual items. This is simply a list of elements, each of which is associated with a positive integer called its index, which represents the position of that element in the list. It is essential that each element is associated with a unique index, which can be zero or negative, which identifies it fully, so that to make changes to any elements of the array it suffices to refer to their indices. Arrays can be of one or more dimensions, and correspondingly they have one or more sets of indices that identify their elements. The most important commands and functions that enable MATLAB to work with arrays of cells are the following:

c = cell(n)	*Creates an n×n array whose cells are empty arrays.*
c = cell(m,n)	*Creates an m×n array whose cells are empty arrays.*
c = cell([m n])	*Creates an m×n array whose cells are empty arrays.*
c = cell(m,n,p,...)	*Creates an m×n×p×... array of empty arrays.*
c = cell([m n p ...])	*Creates an m×n×p×... array of empty arrays.*
c = cell(size(A))	*Creates an array of empty arrays of the same size as A.*
D = cellfun('f',C)	*Applies the function f (isempty, islogical, isreal, length, ndims, or prodofsize) to each element of the array C.*
D = cellfun('size',C,k)	*Returns the size of each element of dimension k in C.*
D = cellfun('isclass',C,class)	*Returns true for each element of C corresponding to class.*
C = cellstr(S)	*Places each row of the character array S into separate cells of C.*
S = cell2struct(C,fields,dim)	*Converts the array C to a structure array S incorporating field names 'fields' and the dimension 'dim' of C.*
celldisp (C)	*Displays the contents of the array C.*
celldisp(C, name)	*Assigns the contents of the array C to the variable name.*
cellplot(C)	*Shows a graphical representation of the array C.*
cellplot(C,'legend')	*Shows a graphical representation of the array C and incorporates a legend.*
C = num2cell(A)	*Converts a numeric array A to the cell array C*
C = num2cell(A,dims)	*Converts a numeric array A to a cell array C placing the given dimensions in separate cells.*

As a first example, we create an array of cells of the same size as the unit square matrix of order two.

```
>> A = ones(2,2)

A =

1     1
1     1

>> c = cell(size(A))

c =

[]    []
[]    []
```

We then define and present a 2 × 3 array of cells element by element, and apply various functions to the cells.

```
>> C{1,1} = [1 2; 4 5];
C{1,2} = 'Name';
C{1,3} = pi;
C{2,1} = 2 + 4i;
C{2,2} = 7;
C{2,3} = magic(3);
```

```
>> C
```

```
C =
```

```
[2x2 double]        'Name'     [    3.1416]
[2.0000+ 4.0000i]   [    7]    [3x3 double]
```

```
>> D = cellfun('isreal',C)
```

```
D =
```

```
1    1    1
0    1    1
```

```
>> len = cellfun('length',C)
```

```
len =
```

```
2    4    1
1    1    3
```

```
>> isdbl = cellfun('isclass',C,'double')
```

```
isdbl =
```

```
1    0    1
1    1    1
```

The contents of the cells in the array C defined above are revealed using the command *celldisp*.

```
>> celldisp(C)
```

```
C{1,1} =
```

```
1    2
4    5
```

```
C{2,1} =
```

```
2.0000 + 4.0000i
```

C{1,2} =

Name

C{2,2} =

7

C{1,3} =

3.1416

C{2,3} =

```
8    1    6
3    5    7
4    9    2
```

The following displays a graphical representation of the array C (Figure 2-25).

```
>> cellplot(C)
```

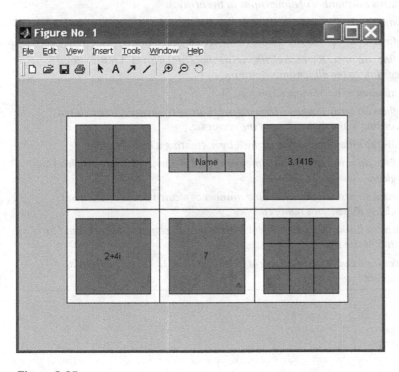

Figure 2-25.

2.1.10 Multidimensional Array Functions

The following group of functions is used by MATLAB to work with multidimensional arrays:

C = cat(dim,A,B)	*Concatenates arrays A and B according to the dimension dim.*
C = cat(dim,A1,A2,A3,A4...)	*Concatenates arrays A1, A2,... according to the dimension dim.*
B = flipdim (A, dim)	*Flips the array A along the specified dimension dim.*
[I,J] = ind2sub(*siz*,IND)	*Returns the matrices I and J containing the equivalent row and column subscripts corresponding to each index in the matrix IND for a matrix of size siz.*
[I1,I2,I3,...,In] = ind2sub(*siz*,IND)	*Returns matrices I1, I2,...,In containing the equivalent row and column subscripts corresponding to each index in the matrix IND for a matrix of size siz.*
A = ipermute(B,*order*)	*Inverts the dimensions of the multidimensional array D according to the values of the vector order.*
[X1, X2, X3,...] = ndgrid(x1,x2,x3,...)	*Transforms the domain specified by vectors x1, x2,... into the arrays X1, X2,... which can be used for evaluation of functions of several variables and interpolation.*
[X 1, X 2,...] = ndgrid (x)	*Equivalent to ndgrid(x,x,x,...).*
n = ndims(A)	*Returns the number of dimensions in the array A.*
B = permute(A,order)	*Swaps the dimensions of the array A specified by the vector order.*
B = reshape(A,m,n)	*Defines an m×n matrix B whose elements are the columns of a.*
B = reshape(A,m,n,p,...)	*Defines an array B whose elements are those of the array A restructured according to the dimensions m×n×p×...*
B = reshape(A,[m n p...])	*Equivalent to B = reshape(A,m,n,p,....)*
B = reshape(A,siz)	*Defines an array B whose elements are those of the array A restructured according to the dimensions of the vector siz.*
B = shiftdim(X,n)	*Shifts the dimensions of the array X by n, creating a new array B.*
[B,nshifts] = shiftdim(X)	*Defines an array B with the same number of elements as X but with leading singleton dimensions removed.*
B = squeeze(A)	*Creates an array B with the same number of elements as A but with all singleton dimensions removed.*
IND = sub2ind(siz,I,J)	*Gives the linear index equivalent to the row and column indices I and J for a matrix of size siz.*
IND = sub2ind(siz,I1,I2,...,In)	*Gives the linear index equivalent to the n indices I1, I2,..., in a matrix of size siz.*

As a first example we concatenate a magic square and Pascal matrix of order 3.

```
>> A = magic(3); B = pascal(3);
>> C = cat(4, A, B)
```

$C(:,:,1,1) =$

```
8    1    6
3    5    7
4    9    2
```

$C(:,:,1,2) =$

```
1    1    1
1    2    3
1    3    6
```

The following example flips the Rosser matrix.

```
>> R = rosser
```

$R =$

```
 611   196  -192   407    -8   -52   -49    29
 196   899   113  -192   -71   -43    -8   -44
-192   113   899   196    61    49     8    52
 407  -192   196   611     8    44    59   -23
  -8   -71    61     8   411  -599   208   208
 -52   -43    49    44  -599   411   208   208
 -49    -8     8    59   208   208    99  -911
  29   -44    52   -23   208   208  -911    99
```

```
>> flipdim(R,1)
```

$ans =$

```
  29   -44    52   -23   208   208  -911    99
 -49    -8     8    59   208   208    99  -911
 -52   -43    49    44  -599   411   208   208
  -8   -71    61     8   411  -599   208   208
 407  -192   196   611     8    44    59   -23
-192   113   899   196    61    49     8    52
 196   899   113  -192   -71   -43    -8   -44
 611   196  -192   407    -8   -52   -49    29
```

Now we define an array by concatenation and permute and inverse permute its elements.

```
>> a = cat(3,eye(2),2*eye(2),3*eye(2))
```

a(:,:,1) =

```
1     0
0     1
```

a(:,:,2) =

```
2     0
0     2
```

a(:,:,3) =

```
3     0
0     3
```

```
>> B = permute(a,[3 2 1])
```

B(:,:,1) =

```
1     0
2     0
3     0
```

B(:,:,2) =

```
0     1
0     2
0     3
```

```
>> C = ipermute(B,[3 2 1])
```

C(:,:,1) =

```
1     0
0     1
```

C(:,:,2) =

```
2     0
0     2
```

C(:,:,3) =

```
3     0
0     3
```

The following example evaluates the function $f(x_1,x_2) = x_1 e^{-x_1^2 - x_2^2}$ in the square $[-2, 2] \times [-2, 2]$ and displays it graphically (Figure 2-26).

```
>> [X 1, X 2] = ndgrid(-2:.2:2,-2:.2:2);
Z = X 1. * exp(-X1.^2-X2.^2);
mesh (Z)
```

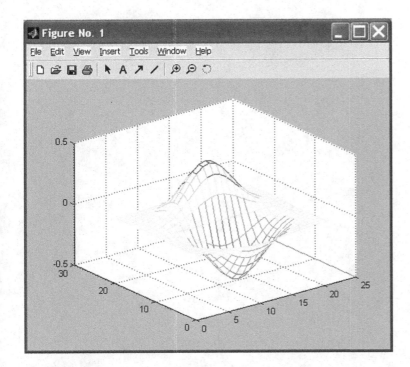

Figure 2-26.

In the following example we resize a 3 × 4 random matrix to a 2 × 6 matrix.

```
>> A = rand(3,4)
```

A =

```
0.9501    0.4860    0.4565    0.4447
0.2311    0.8913    0.0185    0.6154
0.6068    0.7621    0.8214    0.7919
```

```
>> B = reshape(A,2,6)
```

B =

```
0.9501 0.6068 0.8913 0.4565 0.8214 0.6154
0.2311 0.4860 0.7621 0.0185 0.4447 0.7919
```

CHAPTER 3

■ ■ ■

Basic MATLAB Functions for Linear and Non-Linear Optimization

3.1 Solutions of Equations and Systems of Equations

MATLAB allows you to solve equations and systems of equations using the commands below:

solve('equation' , 'x')	*Solves the equation in the variable x.*
syms x; solve(equ(x), x)	*Solves the equation equ (x) in the variable x.*
solve('eq1,eq2,...,eqn' , 'x1, x2,...,xn')	*Solves n simultaneous equations eq1,..., eqn (in the variables x1,..., xn).*
X = linsolve (A, B)	*Solves A * X = B for a square matrix A, where B and X are matrices.*
x = nnls (A, b)	*Solves A * x = b in the sense of least squares, where x is a vector ($x \geq 0$).*
x = lscov(A,b,V)	*Solves A * x = B in the least squares sense with covariance matrix proportional to V, i.e. x minimizes (b - A*x)'*inv(V)*(b - A*x).*
roots (V)	*Returns the roots of the polynomial whose coefficients are given by the vector V (from highest to lowest order).*
X = A\B	*Solves the system A * X = B.*
X = A/B	*Solves the system X * A = B.*
poly (V)	*Returns the coefficients of the polynomial whose roots are given by the vector V.*
x = lscov(A,b,V)	*Solves A * x = b in the least squares sense with covariance matrix proportional to V, i.e. x minimizes (b - A*x)'*inv(V)*(b - A*x).*
[x,dx] = lscov(A,b,V)	*In addition gives the standard error of x (dx).*

(continued)

x = bicg(A,b)	*Tries to solve the system Ax = b by the method of biconjugate gradients.*
bicg(A,b,tol)	*Solves Ax = b by specifying tolerance.*
bicg(A,b,tol,maxit)	*Solves Ax = b by specifying the tolerance and the maximum number of iterations.*
bicg(A,b,tol,maxit,M)	*Solves the system inv(M) * A * x = inv (M) * b.*
bicg(A,b,tol,maxit,M1,M2)	*Solves the system inv(M) * A * x = inv (M) * b with M = M1 * M2.*
bicg(A,b,tol,maxit,M1,M2,x0)	*Solves the system inv(M) * A * x = inv (M) * b with M = M1 * M2 and initial value x0.*
[x,f] = bicg(A,b,...)	*Tries to solve the system and also returns a convergence indicator f (0 = convergence, 1 = no-convergence, 2 = ill-conditioned, 3 = stagnation and 4 = very extreme numbers).*
x = bicgstab(A,b)	*Tries to solve the system Ax = b by the method of stabilized biconjugate gradients.*
bicgstab(A,b,tol)	*Solves Ax = b by specifying tolerance.*
bicgstab(A,b,tol,maxit)	*Solve Ax = b by specifying the tolerance and the maximum number of iterations*
bicgstab(A,b,tol,maxit,M)	*Solves the system inv(M) * A * x = inv (M) * b.*
bicgstab(A,b,tol,maxit,M1,M2)	*Solves the system inv(M) * A * x = inv (M) * b with M = M1 * M2.*
bicgstab(A,b,tol,maxit,M1,M2,x0)	*Solves the system inv(M) * A * x = inv (M) * b with M = M1 * M2 and initial value x0.*
[x,f] = bicgstab(A,b,...)	*Tries to solve the system and returns a convergence indicator f (0 = convergence, 1 = no-convergence, 2 =ill-conditioned, 3 = stagnation and 4 = very extreme numbers).*
[x,f,relres] = bicgstab(A,b,...)	*Also returns the relative residual norm(b-A*x) /norm (b).*
[x,f,relres,iter] = bicgstab(A,b,...)	*Also returns the number of iterations.*
x = cqs(A,b)	*Tries to solve the system Ax = b by the quadratic conjugate gradients method.*
cqs(A,b,tol)	*Solves Ax = b, specifying tolerance*
cqs(A,b,tol,maxit)	*Solves Ax = b, specifying the tolerance and the maximum number of iterations.*
cqs(A,b,tol,maxit,M)	*Solves the inv system (M) * A * x = inv (M) * b.*
cqs(A,b,tol,maxit,M1,M2)	*Solves the inv system (M) * A * x = inv (M) * b with M = M1 * M2.*
cqs(A,b,tol,maxit,M1,M2,x0)	*Solves the inv system (M) * A * x = inv (M) * b with M = M1 * M2 and initial value x0.*
[x,f] = cqs(A,b,...)	*Solves the system where f indicates the result (0 = convergence, 1 = no-convergence, 2 = conditional convergence, 3 = stagnation and 4 = very extreme numbers).*
[x,f,relres] = cqs(A,b,...)	*Also returns the relative residual norm(b-A*x) /norm (b).*
[x,f,relres,iter] = cqs(A,b,...)	*Also returns the number of iterations.*

(continued)

x = pcg(A,b)	*Tries to solve the system Ax = b by the pre-conditioned conjugate gradients method.*
pcg(A,b,tol)	*Solves Ax = b by specifying tolerance.*
pcg(A,b,tol,maxit)	*Solves Ax = b by specifying the tolerance and the maximum number of iterations.*
pcg(A,b,tol,maxit,M)	*Solves the system inv(M) * A * x = inv (M) * b.*
pcg(A,b,tol,maxit,M1,M2)	*Solves the system inv(M) * A * x = inv (M) * b with M = M1 * M2.*
pcg(A,b,tol,maxit,M1,M2,x0)	*Solves the system inv(M) * A * x = inv (M) * b with M = M1 * M2 and initial value x0.*
[x,f] = pcg(A,b,...)	*Tries to solve the system and returns a convergence indicator f (0 = convergence, 1 = no-convergence, 2 = ill-conditioned, 3 = stagnation and 4 = very extreme numbers).*
[x,f,relres] = pcg(A,b,...)	*Also returns the relative residual norm (b-A*x) /norm (b).*
[x,f,relres,iter] = pcg(A,b,...)	*Also returns the number of iterations.*
x = qmr(A,b)	*Tries to solve the system Ax = b by the quasi-minimal residual method.*
qmr(A,b,tol)	*Solves Ax = b by specifying tolerance.*
qmr(A,b,tol,maxit)	*Solves Ax = b by specifying the tolerance and the maximum number of iterations.*
qmr(A,b,tol,maxit,M)	*Solves the system inv(M) * A * x = inv (M) * b.*
qmr(A,b,tol,maxit,M1,M2)	*Solves the system inv(M) * A * x = inv (M) * b with M = M1 * M2.*
qmr(A,b,tol,maxit,M1,M2,x0)	*Solves the system inv(M) * A * x = inv (M) * b with M = M1 * M2 and initial value x0.*
[x,f] = qmr(A,b,...)	*Tries to solve the system and returns a convergence indicator f (0 = convergence, 1 = no-convergence, 2 = ill-conditioned, 3 = stagnation and 4 = very extreme numbers).*
[x,f,relres] = qmr(A,b,...)	*Also returns the residual waste norm (b-A*x) /norm (b).*
[x,f,relres,iter] = qmr(A,b,...)	*Also returns the number of iterations.*
x = gmres(A,b)	*Tries to solve the system Ax = b by the generalized minimum residual method.*
gmres(A,b,tol)	*Solves Ax = b by specifying tolerance.*
gmres(A,b,tol,maxit)	*Solves Ax = b by specifying the tolerance and the maximum number of iterations.*
gmres(A,b,tol,maxit,M)	*Solves the system inv(M) * A * x = inv (M) * b.*
gmres(A,b,tol,maxit,M1,M2)	*Solves the system inv(M) * A * x = inv (M) * b with M = M1 * M2.*
gmres(A,b,tol,maxit,M1,M2,x0)	*Solves the system inv(M) * A * x = inv (M) * b with M = M1 * M2 and initial value x0.*
[x,f] = gmres(A,b,...)	*Tries to solve the system and returns a convergence indicator f (0 = convergence, 1 = no-convergence, 2 = ill-convergence, 3 = stagnation and 4 = very extreme numbers).*
[x,f,relres] = gmres(A,b,...)	*Also returns the relative residual norm(b-A*x) /norm (b).*
[x,f,relres,iter] = gmres(A,b,...)	*Also returns the number of iterations.*

(continued)

x = lsqr(A,b)	*Tries to solve the system Ax = b by the LSQR method.*
lsqr(A,b,tol)	*Solves Ax = b by specifying tolerance.*
lsqr(A,b,tol,maxit)	*Solves Ax = b by specifying the tolerance and the maximum number of iterations.*
lsqr(A,b,tol,maxit,M)	*Solves the system inv(M) * A * x = inv (M) * b.*
lsqr(A,b,tol,maxit,M1,M2)	*Solves the system inv(M) * A * x = inv (M) * b with M = M1 * M2.*
lsqr(A,b,tol,maxit,M1,M2,x0)	*Solves the system inv(M) * A * x = inv (M) * b with M = M1 * M2 and initial value x0.*
[x,f] = lsqr(A,b,...)	*Tries to solve the system and returns a convergence indicator f (0 = convergence, 1 = no-convergence, 2 = ill-conditioned, 3 = stagnation and 4 = very extreme numbers).*
[x,f,relres] = lsqr(A,b,...)	*Also returns the relative residual norm (b-A*x) /norm (b).*
[x,f,relres,iter] = lsqr(A,b,...)	*Also returns the number of iterations.*
x = minres(A,b)	*Tries to solve the system Ax = b by the minimum residual method.*
minres(A,b,tol)	*Solves Ax = b by specifying tolerance.*
minres(A,b,tol,maxit)	*Solves Ax = b by specifying the tolerance and the maximum number of iterations.*
minres(A,b,tol,maxit,M)	*Solves the system inv(M) * A * x = inv (M) * b.*
minres(A,b,tol,maxit,M1,M2)	*Solves the system inv(M) * A * x = inv (M) * b with M = M1 * M2.*
minres(A,b,tol,maxit,M1,M2,x0)	*Solves the system inv(M) * A * x = inv (M) * b with M = M1 * M2 and initial value x0.*
[x,f] = minres(A,b,...)	*Tries to solve the system and returns a convergence indicator f(0 = convergence, 1 = no-convergence, 2 =ill-conditioned, 3 = stagnation and 4 = very extreme numbers).*
[x,f,relres] = minres(A,b,...)	*Also returns the relative residual norm (b-A*x) /norm (b).*
[x,f,relres,iter] = minres(A,b,...)	*Also returns the number of iterations.*
x = symmlq(A,b)	*Tries to solve the system Ax = b by the symmetric LQ method.*
symmlq(A,b,tol)	*Solves Ax = b by specifying the tolerance.*
symmlq(A,b,tol,maxit)	*Solves Ax = b by specifying the tolerance and the maximum number of iterations.*
symmlq(A,b,tol,maxit,M)	*Solves the system inv(M) * A * x = inv (M) * b.*
symmlq(A,b,tol,maxit,M1,M2)	*Solves the system inv(M) * A * x = inv (M) * b with M = M1 * M2.*
symmlq(A,b,tol,maxit,M1,M2,x0)	*Solves the system inv(M) * A * x = inv (M) * b with M = M1 * M2 and initial value x0.*
[x,flag] = symmlq(A,b,...)	*Tries to solve the system and returns a convergence indicator (0 = convergence, 1 = no-convergence, 2 = ill-conditioned, 3 = stagnation and 4 = very extreme numbers).*
[x,flag,relres] = symmlq(A,b,...)	*Also returns the relative residual norm (b-A*x) /norm (b).*
[x,flag,relres,iter] = symmlq(A,b,...)	*Also returns the number of iterations.*

(continued)

x = lsqnonneg(C,d)	*Returns the vector x that minimizes norm(C*x–d) subject to x >=0. C and d must be real.*
x = lsqnonneg(C,d,x0) **x = lsqnonneg(C,d,x0,opt)**	*Uses x0 ≥ 0 as the initial value and a possible option. The options are TolX for termination tolerance on x and Display to show the output ('off' does not display output, 'final' shows just the final output and 'notify' shows the output only if there is no convergence).*
[x,resnorm] = lsqnonneg(...) **[x,resnorm,residual] = lsqnonneg(...)**	*Returns the value of the squared 2-norm of the residual: norm(C*x–d)^2. In addition returns the residual C * x-d.*
[x,resnorm,residual,f] = lsqnonneg(...)	*In addition gives a convergence indicator f (positive indicates convergence, 0 indicates non-convergence).*
[x,resnorm,residual,f,out, lambda] = lsqnonneg(...)	*In addition to the above, returns output data describing the algorithm used, iterations taken and exit message, and also the vector of Lagrange multipliers lambda.*
x = fzero x0 (function)	*Returns a zero of the function near x0.*
[x, feval] = fzero x0 (fun)	*Also gives the objective value of the function at x.*
[x, feval, f] = fzero x0 (fun)	*Returns f > 0 if a zero x was found and F<0 otherwise.*
S = spaugment (A, c)	*Creates the sparse, square symmetric indefinite matrix S = [c*I A; A' 0]. The matrix S is related to the least squares problem.*

As a first example we find the roots of the equation $2x^3 + 11x^2 + 12x - 9 - 0$. Since it is a polynomial we use the function *roots* as follows:

```
>> roots([2, 11, 12, - 9])
```

ans =

-3.0000
-3.0000
 0.5000

The above equation also can be solved as follows:

```
>> solve('2*x^3+11*x^2+12*x-9','x')
```

ans =

[1/2]
[-3]
[-3]

The equation $xsin(x) = 1/2$ can be solved in neighborhoods of 2, 4 and 6 as follows:

```
>> [fzero('x * sin (x) - 1/2 ', 2), fzero('x * sin (x) - 1/2 ', 4), fzero('x * sin (x) - 1/2 ', 6)]
```

ans =

0.7408 2.9726 6.3619

The system of equations $x+y+z= 1$, $3x+y= 3$, $x-2y-z= 0$ can be solved as follows:

```
>> [x, y, z] = solve('x+y+z=1', '3*x+y=3', 'x-2*y-z=0','x','y','z')
```

x =

4/5

y =

3/5

z =

-2/5

The following alternative syntax could have been used:

```
>> [x, y, z] = solve('x+y+z=1, 3*x+y=3, x-2*y-z=0','x,y,z')
```

x =

4/5

y =

3/5

z =

-2/5

It is also possible to use the following syntax:

```
>> A = [1,1,1;3,1,0;1,-2,-1]; B = [1,3,0]'; linsolve (A, B)
```

ans =

[4/5]
[3/5]
[-2/5]

Or even the following:

```
>> A\B

ans =

 0.8000
 0.6000
-0.4000
```

The system can also be solved using approximation methods (however, in this case this is not necessary). For example, we could try to use the least squares method. The syntax is as follows:

```
>> lsqr(A,B)

lsqr stopped at iteration 3 without converging to the desired tolerance 1e-006
because the maximum number of iterations was reached.
The iterate returned (number 3) has relative residual 0.084

ans =

 0.8558
 0.3542
-0.0448
```

3.2 Working with Polynomials

MATLAB implements specific commands for working with polynomials, such as finding their roots, differentiation and interpolation. The following table shows the syntax of the most important of these commands.

q = conv(u,v)	*Gives the coefficients of the polynomial product of two polynomials whose coefficients are given by the vectors u and v.*
[q, r] = deconv(v,u)	*Gives the polynomial quotient and remainder of the division between polynomials u and v, so that v = conv (u, q) + r.*
p = poly (r)	*Gives the coefficients of the polynomial p whose roots are specified by the vector r.*
k = polyder(p)	*Gives the coefficients k of the derivative of the polynomial p.*
k = polyder(a,b)	*Gives the coefficients k of the derivative of the product of polynomials a and b.*
[q,d] = polyder(a,b)	*Gives the numerator q and denominator d of the derivative of a/b.*
p = (x, y, n) polyfit	*Finds the polynomial of degree n which is the best fit of the set of points (x, y).*
[p,S] = polyfit(x,y,n)	*Finds the polynomial of degree n which is the best fit of the set of points (x, y) and also returns structure data S of the fit.*
[p, S, u] = polyfit (x, y, n)	*Finds the coefficients of the polynomial in $\hat{x} = (x - m) / s$ which best fits the data, and also returns the structure data S and the row vector u=[m,s], where m is the mean and s is the standard deviation of the data x.*

(continued)

y = polyval(p,x)	*Evaluates the polynomial p at x.*
y = polyval(p,x,[],u)	*If u=[m,s], evaluates the polynomial p at $\hat{x}=(x-m)/s$.*
[y, delta] = polyval (p, x, S)	*Uses the optional output structure S generated by polyfit to generate error estimates delta.*
[y, delta] = polyval(p,x,S,u)	*Does the above with $\hat{x}=(x-m)/s$ in place of x, where u[m,s].*
Y = polyvalm (p, X)	*For a polynomial p and a matrix X, evaluates p(X) in the matrix sense.*
[r,p,k] = residue(b,a)	*Finds the residues, poles and direct term of the rational expansion of b/a.*

$$\frac{b(s)}{a(s)} = \frac{r_1}{s-p_1} + \frac{r_2}{s-p_2} + \cdots + \frac{r_n}{s-p_n} + k(s)$$

[b,a] = residue(r,p,k)	*Converts the partial fraction expansion back into a quotient of polynomials.*
r = roots (c)	*Gives the column vector r of the roots of the polynomial with coefficients c.*

As a first example, we calculate the roots of the polynomial $x^3 - 6x^2 - 72x - 27$.

```
>> p = [1 -6 -72 -27]; r = roots(p)
```

r =

12.1229
-5.7345
-0.3884

Next we evaluate the polynomial $x^3 - 6x^2 - 72x - 27$ first at the Pascal matrix of order 4 and then at the integer 10.

```
>> Y = polyval (p, pascal(4))
```

Y =

```
-104   -104  -104  -104
-104   -187  -270  -347
-104   -270  -459  -347
-104   -347  -347  -4133
```

```
>> polyval(p,10)
```

ans =

-347

In the following example we define a vector x of equally spaced points in the interval $[0, 2.5]$, evaluate the function $erf(x)$ at these points and find the approximate coefficients of the polynomial of degree 6 which best fits the points $(x, erf(x))$.

```
>> x = (0: 0.1: 2.5)'; y = erf(x), p = polyfit(x,y,6)

p =

0.0084 -0.0983 0.4217 -0.7435 0.1471 1.1064 0.0004
```

We then calculate the derivative of both the product and the quotient of the polynomials $(3x^2 + 6x + 9)$ and $(x^2 + 2x)$.

```
>> a = [3 6 9];
b = [1 2 0];
k = polyder(a,b)

k =

12 36 42 18
```

The derivative of the product is therefore the polynomial $12x^3 + 36x^2 + 42x + 18$.

```
>> [q,d] = polyder(b,a)

q =

18 18

d =

9 36 90 108 81
```

The derivative of the quotient is therefore $\dfrac{18x+18}{9x^4 + 36x^3 + 90x^2 + 108x + 81}$.

EXERCISE 3-1

Solve the following equations:

$$x^{3/2} \, log(x) = x \, log(x^{3/2}), \ sqrt[1-x] + sqrt[1+x] = a, \ x^4 - 1 = 0 \ and \ sin(z) = 2.$$

```
>> s1 = solve('x^(3/2)*log(x) = x*log(x)^(3/2)')

s1 =

[ -lambertw(-1)]
[            1]
```

```
>> s2 = solve('sqrt(1-x)+sqrt(1+x) = a','x')
```

s2 =

```
[  1/2*a*(-a^2+4)^(1/2)]
[ -1/2*a*(-a^2+4)^(1/2)]
```

```
>> s3 = solve('x^4-1=0')
```

s3 =

```
[  1]
[ -1]
[  i]
[ -i]
```

```
>> s4=solve('sin(z)=2')
```

S4 =

asin(2)

The solution of the first equation is better interpreted by passing it to numeric format as follows:

```
>> numeric(s1)
```

ans =

```
0.3181 - 1.3372i
1.0000
```

EXERCISE 3-2

Solve the following system of two equations:

$$\cos(x/12) \,/\exp(x^2/16) = y$$

$$-5/4 + y = \sin(x^{3/2})$$

```
>> [x, y] = solve('cos(x/12) /exp(x^2/16) = y','-5/4 + y = sin(x ^(3/2))')
```

x =

*-.18864189802267887925036526820236.-. 34569744170126319331033283636228 * i*

y =

*5/4+sin((-.14259332915370291604677691198415-.51515304994330991250882243014347e-2*i)*3^(1/2))*

EXERCISE 3-3

Study and solve the system:

$$x + 2y + 3z = 6$$
$$x + 3y + 8z = 19$$
$$2x + 3y + z = -1$$
$$5x + 6y + 4z = 5$$

```
>> A = [1,2,3;1,3,8;2,3,1;5,6,4]
```

A =

```
1    2    3
1    3    8
2    3    1
5    6    4
```

```
>> B = [1,2,3,6;1,3,8,19;2,3,1,-1;5,6,4,5]
```

B =

```
1    2    3    6
1    3    8    19
2    3    1    -1
5    6    4    5
```

```
>> [rank(A), rank(B)]
```

ans =

3 3

```
>> b = [6, 19, -1, 5]
```

b =

19 -6 -5 -1

We see that the ranks of *A* and *B* coincide and their common value is 3, which is equal to the number of unknowns in the system. Therefore, the system will have a unique solution. We can find this solution with the command *linsolve*:

```
>> X = linsolve(A,b')
```

X =

[1]
[-2]
[3]

We can also solve the system in the following way:

```
>> A\b'
```

ans =

 1.0000
-2.0000
 3.0000

EXERCISE 3-4

Study and solve the system:

$$2x + y + z + t = 1$$

$$x + 2y + z + t = 1$$

$$x + y + z + 2t = 1$$

$$x + y + z + 2t = 1$$

```
>> A = [2,1,1,1;1,2,1,1;1,1,2,1;1,1,1,2];
>> B = [2,1,1,1,1;1,2,1,1,1;1,1,2,1,1;1,1,1,2,1];
>> [rank(A), rank(B)]
```

ans =

4 4

```
>> b = [1,1,1,1]';
```

We see that the matrices *A* and *B* (the augmented matrix) both have rank 4, which also coincides with the number of unknowns. Thus the system has a unique solution. To calculate the solution we can use any of the commands shown below.

```
>> x = nnls(A,b)

x =

0.2000
0.2000
0.2000
0.2000

>> x = bicg(A,b)
bicg converged at iteration 1 to a solution with relative residual 0

x =

0.2000
0.2000
0.2000
0.2000

>> x = bicgstab(A,b)
bicgstab converged at iteration 0.5 to a solution with relative residual 0

x =

0.2000
0.2000
0.2000
0.2000

>> x = pcg(A,b)
pcg converged at iteration 1 to a solution with relative residual 0

x =

0.2000
0.2000
0.2000
0.2000

>> gmres(A,b)
gmres converged at iteration 1 to a solution with relative residual 0

ans =

0.2000
0.2000
0.2000
0.2000
```

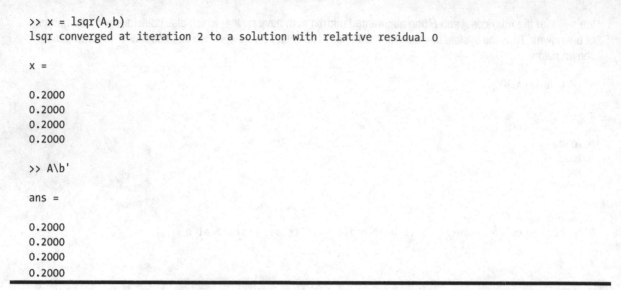

```
>> x = lsqr(A,b)
lsqr converged at iteration 2 to a solution with relative residual 0

x =

0.2000
0.2000
0.2000
0.2000

>> A\b'

ans =

0.2000
0.2000
0.2000
0.2000
```

■ ■ ■

CHAPTER 4

Optimization by Numerical Methods: Solving Equations

4.1 Non-Linear Equations

MATLAB is able to implement a number of algorithms which provide numerical solutions to certain problems which play a central role in the solution of non-linear equations. Such algorithms are easy to construct in MATLAB and are stored as M-files. From previous chapters we know that an M-file is simply a sequence of MATLAB commands or functions that accept arguments and produces output. The M-files are created using the text editor.

4.1.1 The Fixed Point Method for Solving x = g(x)

The fixed point method solves the equation $x = g(x)$, under certain conditions on the function g, using an iterative method that begins with an initial value p_0 (a first approximation to the solution) and defines $p_{k+1} = g(p_k)$. The fixed point theorem ensures that, in certain circumstances, this sequence will converges to a solution of the equation $x = g(x)$. In practice the iterative process will stop when the absolute or relative error corresponding to two consecutive iterations is less than a preset value (*tolerance*). The smaller this value, the better the approximation to the solution of the equation.

This simple iterative method can be implemented using the M-file shown in Figure 4-1.

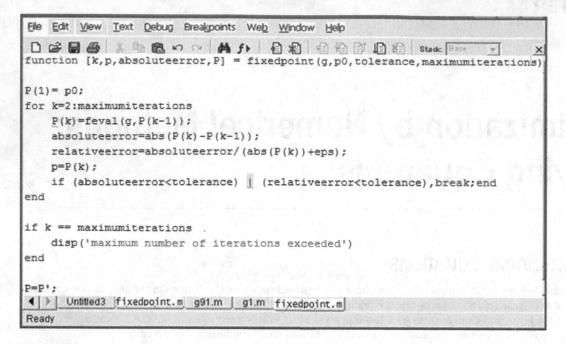

```
File  Edit  View  Text  Debug  Breakpoints  Web  Window  Help
function [k,p,absoluteerror,P] = fixedpoint(g,p0,tolerance,maximumiterations)

P(1)= p0;
for k=2:maximumiterations
    P(k)=feval(g,P(k-1));
    absoluteerror=abs(P(k)-P(k-1));
    relativeerror=absoluteerror/(abs(P(k))+eps);
    p=P(k);
    if (absoluteerror<tolerance) | (relativeerror<tolerance),break;end
end

if k == maximumiterations
    disp('maximum number of iterations exceeded')
end

P=P';
    Untitled3  fixedpoint.m  g91.m  g1.m  fixedpoint.m
Ready
```

Figure 4-1.

As an example we solve the following non-linear equation:

$$x - 2^{-x} = 0.$$

In order to apply the fixed point algorithm we write the equation in the form $x = g(x)$ as follows:

$$x - 2^{-x} = g(x).$$

We will start by finding an approximate solution which will be the first term p_0. To plot the x axis and the curve defined by the given equation on the same graph we use the following syntax (see Figure 4-2):

```
>> fplot('[x-2^(-x), 0]',[0, 1])
```

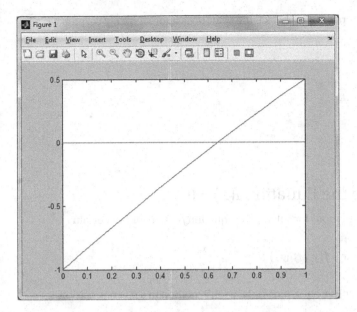

Figure 4-2.

The graph shows that one solution is close to $x = 0.6$. We can take this value as the initial value. We choose $p_0 = 0.6$. If we consider a tolerance of 0.0001 for a maximum of 1000 iterations, we can solve the problem once we have defined the function $g(x)$ in the M-file *g1.m* (see Figure 4-3).

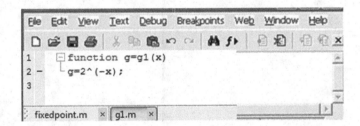

Figure 4-3.

We can now solve the equation using the MATLAB syntax:

```
>> [k, p] = fixedpoint('g1',0.6,0.0001,1000)

k =

10

p =

0.6412
```

We obtain the solution $x = 0.6412$ at the 1000th iteration. To check if the solution is approximately correct, we must verify that g1(0.6412) is close to 0.6412.

```
>> g1 (0.6412)

ans =

0.6412
```

Thus we observe that the solution is acceptable.

4.1.2 Newton's Method for Solving the Equation f(x) = 0

Newton's method (also called the Newton–Raphson method) for solving the equation $f(x) = 0$, under certain conditions on f, uses the iteration

$$x_{r+1} = x_r - f(x_r)/f'(x_r)$$

for an initial value x_0 close to a solution.

The M-file in Figure 4-4 shows a program which solves equations by Newton's method to a given precision.

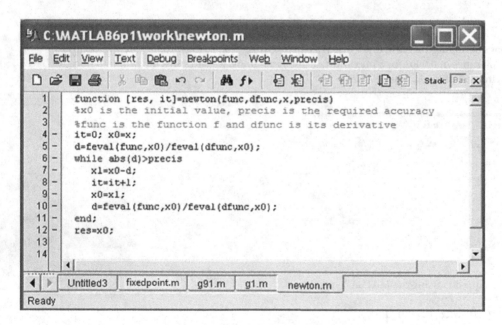

```
function [res, it]=newton(func,dfunc,x,precis)
%x0 is the initial value, precis is the required accuracy
%func is the function f and dfunc is its derivative
it=0; x0=x;
d=feval(func,x0)/feval(dfunc,x0);
while abs(d)>precis
    x1=x0-d;
    it=it+1;
    x0=x1;
    d=feval(func,x0)/feval(dfunc,x0);
end;
res=x0;
```

Figure 4-4.

As an example we solve the following equation by Newton's method:

$$x^2 - x - \sin(x + 0.15) = 0.$$

The function $f(x)$ is defined in the M-file *f1.m* (see Figure 4-5), and its derivative $f'(x)$ is given in the M-file *derf1.m* (see Figure 4-6).

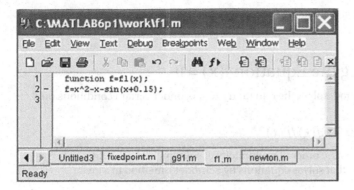

Figure 4-5.

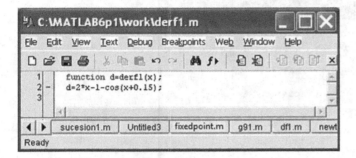

Figure 4-6.

We can now solve the equation up to an accuracy of 0.0001 and 0.000001 using the following MATLAB syntax, starting with an initial estimate of 1.5:

```
>> [x,it] = newton('f1','derf1',1.5,0.0001)

x =

1.6101


it =

2

>> [x,it] = newton('f1','derf1',1.5,0.000001)

x =

1.6100

it =

3
```

Thus we have obtained the solution $x = 1.61$ in just 2 iterations with a precision of 0.0001 and in just 3 iterations with a precision of 0.000001.

4.1.3 Schröder's Method for Solving the Equation f(x) = 0

Schröder's method, which is similar to Newton's method, solves the equation $f(x) = 0$, under certain conditions on f, via the iteration

$$x_{r+1} = x_r - mf(x_r) / f'(x_r)$$

for an initial value x_0 close to a solution, and where m is the order of multiplicity of solution being sought.

The M-file shown in Figure 4-7 gives the function that solves equations by Schröder's method to a given precision.

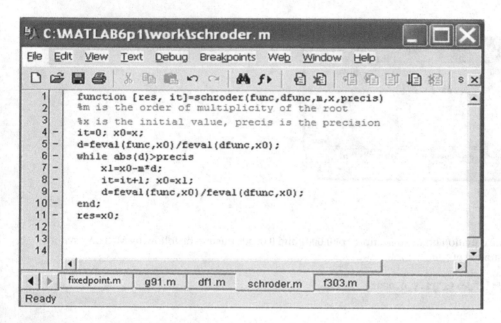

Figure 4-7.

4.2 Systems of Non-Linear Equations

As for differential equations, it is possible to implement algorithms with MATLAB that solve systems of non-linear equations using classical iterative numerical methods.

Among a diverse collection of existing methods we will consider the Seidel and Newton–Raphson methods.

4.2.1 The Seidel Method

The Seidel method for solving systems of equations is a generalization of the fixed point iterative method for single equations.

In the case of a system of two equations $x = g_1(x, y)$ and $y = g_2(x, y)$ the terms of the iteration are defined as:

$$p_{k+1} = g_1(p_k, q_k) \text{ and } q_{k+1} = g_2(p_k, q_k).$$

Similarly, in the case of a system of three equations $x = g_1(x, y, z)$, $y = g_2(x, y, z)$ and $y = g_3(x, y, z)$ the terms of the iteration are defined as:

$$p_{k+1} = g_1(p_k, q_k, r_k), \ q_{k+1} = g_2(p_k, q_k, r_4) \text{ and } r_{k+1} = g_3(p_k, q_k, r_4).$$

The M-file shown in Figure 4-8 gives a function which solves systems of equations using Seidel's method up to a specified accuracy.

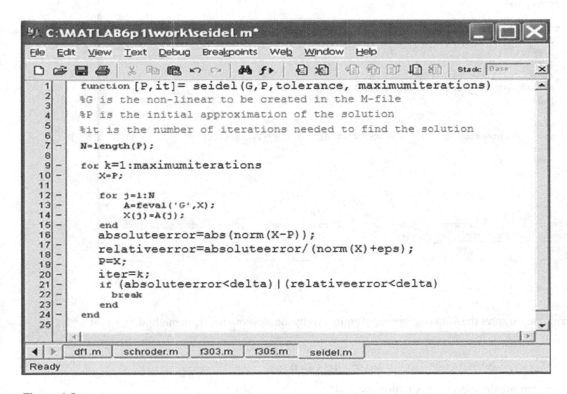

```
function [P,it]= seidel(G,P,tolerance, maximumiterations)
%G is the non-linear to be created in the M-file
%P is the initial approximation of the solution
%it is the number of iterations needed to find the solution

N=length(P);

for k=1:maximumiterations
    X=P;

    for j=1:N
        A=feval('G',X);
        X(j)=A(j);
    end
    absoluteerror=abs(norm(X-P));
    relativeerror=absoluteerror/(norm(X)+eps);
    P=X;
    iter=k;
    if (absoluteerror<delta)|(relativeerror<delta)
       break
    end
end
```

Figure 4-8.

4.2.2 The Newton-Raphson Method

The Newton–Raphson method for solving systems of equations is a generalization of Newton's method for single equations.

The idea behind the algorithm is familiar. The solution of the system of non-linear equations $F(X) = 0$ is obtained by generating from an initial approximation P_0 a sequence of approximations P_k which converges to the solution. Figure 4-9 shows the M-file containing the function which solves systems of equations using the Newton–Raphson method up to a specified degree of accuracy.

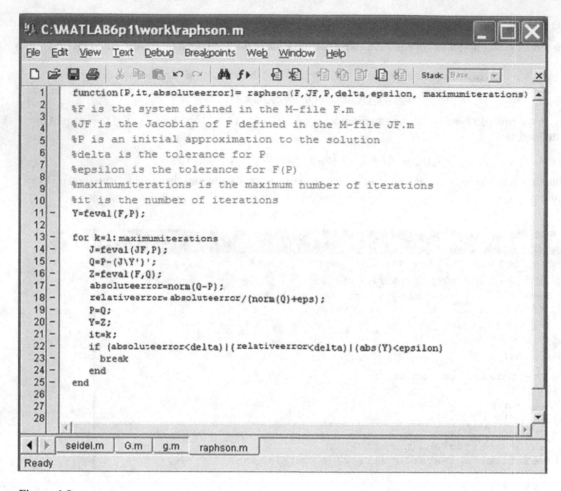

```
function[P,it,absoluteerror]= raphson(F,JF,P,delta,epsilon, maximumiterations)
%F is the system defined in the M-file F.m
%JF is the Jacobian of F defined in the M-file JF.m
%P is an initial approximation to the solution
%delta is the tolerance for P
%epsilon is the tolerance for F(P)
%maximumiterations is the maximum number of iterations
%it is the number of iterations
Y=feval(F,P);

for k=1:maximumiterations
    J=feval(JF,P);
    Q=P-(J\Y')';
    Z=feval(F,Q);
    absoluteerror=norm(Q-P);
    relativeerror= absoluteerror/(norm(Q)+eps);
    P=Q;
    Y=Z;
    it=k;
    if (absoluteerror<delta)|(relativeerror<delta)|(abs(Y)<epsilon)
        break
    end
end
```

Figure 4-9.

As an example we solve the following system of equations by the Newton–Raphson method:

$$x^2 - 2x - y = -0.5$$

$$x^2 + 4y^2 - 4 = 0$$

taking as an initial approximation to the solution $P = [2\ 3]$.

We start by defining the system $F(X) = 0$ and its Jacobian matrix JF according to the M-files *F.m* and *JF.m* shown in Figures 4-10 and 4-11.

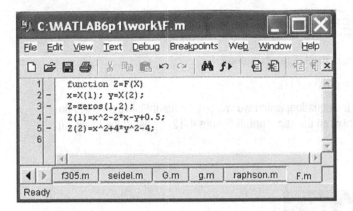

Figure 4-10.

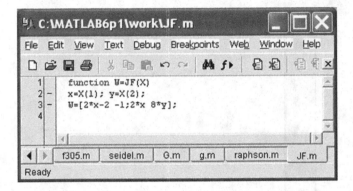

Figure 4-11.

Then the system is solved with a tolerance of 0.00001 and with a maximum of 100 iterations using the following MATLAB syntax:

```
>> [P,it,absoluteerror] = raphson('F','JF',[2 3],0.00001,0.00001,100)

P =

1.9007 0.3112

it =

6

absoluteerror =

8. 8751e-006
```

The solution obtained in 6 iterations is $x = 1.9007$, $y = 0.3112$, with an absolute error of 8.8751e- 006.

EXERCISE 4-1

Solve the following non-linear equation using the fixed point iterative method:

$$x = \cos(\sin(x))$$

We will start by finding an approximate solution to the equation, which we will use as the initial value p_0. To do this we show the x axis and the curve $y = x-\cos(\sin(x))$ on the same graph (Figure 4-12) by using the following command:

```
>> fplot([x-cos (sin (x)), 0], [- 2, 2])
```

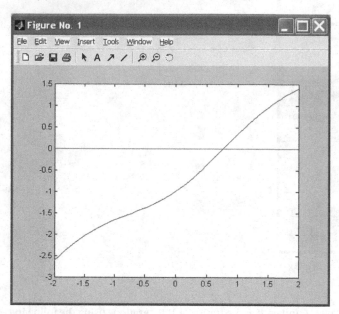

Figure 4-12.

The graph indicates that there is a solution close to $x = 1$, which is the value that we shall take as our initial approximation to the solution, i.e. $p_0 = 1$. If we consider a tolerance of 0.0001 for a maximum number of 100 iterations, we can solve the problem once we have defined the function $g(x) = \cos(\sin(x))$ via the M-file *g91.m* shown in Figure 4-13.

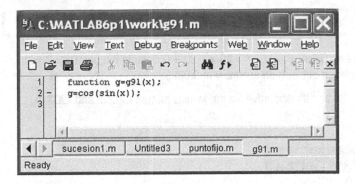

Figure 4-13.

We can now solve the equation using the MATLAB command:

```
>> [k, p, absoluteerror, P] = fixedpoint('g91',1,0.0001,1000)

k =

13

p =

0.7682

absoluteerror =

6. 3361e-005

P =

1.0000
0.6664
0.8150
0.7467
0.7781
0.7636
0.7703
0.7672
0.7686
0.7680
0.7683
0.7681
0.7682
```

The solution is *x* = 0.7682, which has been found in 13 iterations with an absolute error of 6.3361 *e*- 005. Thus, the convergence to the solution is particularly fast.

EXERCISE 4-2

Using Newton's method calculate the root of the equation $x^3 - 10\,x^2 + 29\,x - 20 = 0$ close to the point $x = 7$ with an accuracy of 0.00005. Repeat the same calculation but with an accuracy of 0.0005.

We define the function $f(x) = x^3 - 10x^2 + 29x - 20$ and its derivative via the M-files named *f302.m* and *f303.m* shown in Figures 4-14 and 4-15.

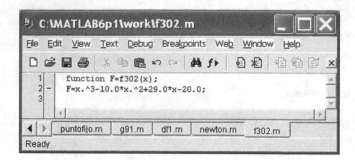

Figure 4-14.

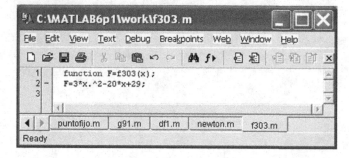

Figure 4-15.

To run the program that solves the equation, type:

```
>> [x, it] = newton('f302','f303',7,.00005)

x =

5.0000

it =

6
```

In 6 iterations and with an accuracy of 0.00005 the solution $x = 5$ has been obtained. In 5 iterations and with an accuracy of 0.0005 we get the solution $x = 5.0002$:

```
>> [x, it] = newton('f302','f303',7,.0005)

x =

5.0002

it =

5
```

EXERCISE 4-3

Write a program that calculates a root with multiplicity 2 of the equation $(e^{-x} - x)^2 = 0$ close to the point $x = -2$ to an accuracy of 0.00005.

We define the function $f(x)=(e^x - x)^2$ and its derivative via the M-files *f304.m* and *f305.m* shown in Figures 4-16 and 4-17:

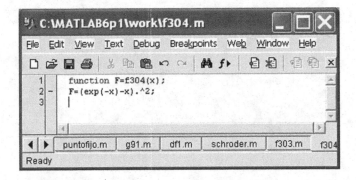

Figure 4-16.

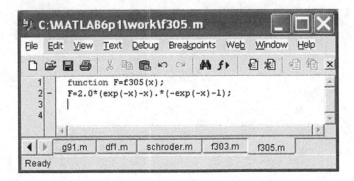

Figure 4-17.

We solve the equation using Schröder's method. To run the program we enter the command:

```
>> [x,it] = schroder('f304','f305',2,-2,.00005)

x =

0.5671

it =

5
```

In 5 iterations we have found the solution $x = 0.56715$.

CHAPTER 5

■ ■ ■

Optimization Using Symbolic Computation

5.1 Symbolic Equations and Systems of Equations

The following commands can be used for the solution of symbolic equations and systems of equations:

solve('equation', 'x')	*Solves the equation in the variable x.*
syms x; solve(equation,x)	*Solves the equation in the variable x.*
solve('e1,e2,...,en', 'x1,x2,...,xn')	*Solves the system of equations e1,..., en in the variables x1,..., xn.*
syms x1 x2... xn; solve(e1,e2,...,en, x1,x2,...,xn)	*Solve the system of equations e1,..., en in the variables x1,..., xn.*

As a first example we solve the equation $3ax - 7x^2 + x^3 = 0$ in terms of x, where a is a parameter.

```
>> solve('3*a*x-7*x^2+x^3=0','x')

ans =

[                  0]
[7/2 + 1/2 *(49-12*a) ^(1/2)]
[7/2-1/2 *(49-12*a) ^(1/2)]
```

Next we solve the above equation where a is the variable and x is the parameter.

```
>> pretty(solve('3*a*x-7*x^2+x^3=0','a'))

-1/3 x (- 7 + x)
```

In the following example, we calculate the fourth roots of –1 and 1.

```
>> S = solve('x^4+1=0')

S =

[   1/2*2^(1/2)+1/2*i*2^(1/2)]
[ -1/2*2^(1/2)-1/2*i*2^(1/2)]
[   1/2*2^(1/2)-1/2*i*2^(1/2)]
[ -1/2*2^(1/2)+1/2*i*2^(1/2)]

>> numeric(S)

ans =

 0.70710678118655 + 0.70710678118655i
-0.70710678118655 - 0.70710678118655i
 0.70710678118655 - 0.70710678118655i
-0.70710678118655 + 0.70710678118655i

>> S1 = solve('x^4-1=0')

S1 =

[  1]
[ -1]
[  i]
[ -i]
```

Next we calculate the fifth roots of the complex number $2 + 2i$.

```
>> numeric(solve('x^5-(2+2*i)=0'))

ans =

 1.21598698264961 + 0.19259341768888i
 0.19259341768888 + 1.21598698264961i
-1.09695770450838 + 0.55892786746601i
-0.87055056329612 - 0.87055056329612i
 0.55892786746601   1.09695770450838i
```

In the following example we solve the equation $\sin(x)\cos(x)=a$ in the variable x:

```
>> simple(solve('sin (x) * cos (x) = a', 'x'))
```

ans =

```
pi/2 - asin(2*a)/2
       asin(2*a)/2
```

```
>> pretty(ans)
```

```
+-                  -+
|  pi    asin(2 a)  |
|  -- - ----------  |
|  2        2       |
|                   |
|       asin(2 a)   |
|       ---------   |
|           2       |
+-                  -+
```

If we solve the above equation for the particular case $a=0$ we get:

```
>> solve('sin (x) * cos (x) = 0', 'x')
```

ans =

```
[         0]
[1/2 * pi]
[-1/2 * pi]
```

In the following example we solve the system $u + v + w = a$, $3u + v = b$, $u - 2v - w = 0$, where u, v and w are variables and a, b and c parameters.

```
>> syms u v w a b c
>> [u, v, w] = solve('u+v+w=a,3*u+v=b,u-2*v-w=c',u,v,w)
```

u =

```
1/5 * b + 1/5 * + 1/5 * c
```

v =

```
2/5 * b-3/5 * a-3/5 * c
```

w =

```
-3/5 * b + 7/5 * + 2/5 * c
```

EXERCISE 5-1

Find the intersection of the hyperbolas with equations $x^2 - y^2 = 1$ and $y^2x^2 - b^2y^2 = 16$ with the parabola $z^2 = 2x$.

We solve the system of three equations as follows:

```
>> [x, y, z] = solve('a^2*x^2-b^2*y^2=16','x^2-y^2=1','z^2=2*x', 'x,y,z')
```

x =

```
[  1/2*(((b^2-16)/(a^2-b^2))^(1/4)+i*((b^2-16)/(a^2-b^2))^(1/4))^2]
[  1/2*(((b^2-16)/(a^2-b^2))^(1/4)+i*((b^2-16)/(a^2-b^2))^(1/4))^2]
[ 1/2*(-((b^2-16)/(a^2-b^2))^(1/4)+i*((b^2-16)/(a^2-b^2))^(1/4))^2]
[ 1/2*(-((b^2-16)/(a^2-b^2))^(1/4)+i*((b^2-16)/(a^2-b^2))^(1/4))^2]
[  1/2*(((b^2-16)/(a^2-b^2))^(1/4)-i*((b^2-16)/(a^2-b^2))^(1/4))^2]
[  1/2*(((b^2-16)/(a^2-b^2))^(1/4)-i*((b^2-16)/(a^2-b^2))^(1/4))^2]
[ 1/2*(-((b^2-16)/(a^2-b^2))^(1/4)-i*((b^2-16)/(a^2-b^2))^(1/4))^2]
[ 1/2*(-((b^2-16)/(a^2-b^2))^(1/4)-i*((b^2-16)/(a^2-b^2))^(1/4))^2]
```

y =

```
[  1/(a^2-b^2)*(-(a^2-b^2)*(a^2-16))^(1/2)]
[ -1/(a^2-b^2)*(-(a^2-b^2)*(a^2-16))^(1/2)]
[  1/(a^2-b^2)*(-(a^2-b^2)*(a^2-16))^(1/2)]
[ -1/(a^2-b^2)*(-(a^2-b^2)*(a^2-16))^(1/2)]
[  1/(a^2-b^2)*(-(a^2-b^2)*(a^2-16))^(1/2)]
[ -1/(a^2-b^2)*(-(a^2-b^2)*(a^2-16))^(1/2)]
[  1/(a^2-b^2)*(-(a^2-b^2)*(a^2-16))^(1/2)]
[ -1/(a^2-b^2)*(-(a^2-b^2)*(a^2-16))^(1/2)]
```

z =

```
[  ((b^2-16)/(a^2-b^2))^(1/4)+i*((b^2-16)/(a^2-b^2))^(1/4)]
[  ((b^2-16)/(a^2-b^2))^(1/4)+i*((b^2-16)/(a^2-b^2))^(1/4)]
[ -((b^2-16)/(a^2-b^2))^(1/4)+i*((b^2-16)/(a^2-b^2))^(1/4)]
[ -((b^2-16)/(a^2-b^2))^(1/4)+i*((b^2-16)/(a^2-b^2))^(1/4)]
[  ((b^2-16)/(a^2-b^2))^(1/4)-i*((b^2-16)/(a^2-b^2))^(1/4)]
[  ((b^2-16)/(a^2-b^2))^(1/4)-i*((b^2-16)/(a^2-b^2))^(1/4)]
[ -((b^2-16)/(a^2-b^2))^(1/4)-i*((b^2-16)/(a^2-b^2))^(1/4)]
[ -((b^2-16)/(a^2-b^2))^(1/4)-i*((b^2-16)/(a^2-b^2))^(1/4)]
```

■ ■ ■

CHAPTER 6

Optimization Techniques Via The Optimization Toolbox

6.1 The Optimization Toolbox

The Optimization Toolbox provides algorithms for solving a wide range of optimization problems. It contains routines that put into practice the most widely used methods for minimization and maximization.

The toolbox includes state-of-the-art algorithms for constrained and restricted non-linear minimization, minimax optimization, objective achievement, semi-infinitely constrained minimization, quadratic and linear programming, non-linear least-squares optimization, the solution of non-linear equations and constrained linear least-squares systems.

The toolbox also contains algorithms for large-scale specialized scattering problems and data curve fitting. The environment works with scalar, vector or matrix entries. Optimization functions can be written as interactive functions or saved in the MATLAB command line.

6.1.1 Standard Algorithms

The toolbox implements the current state of the art in optimization algorithms. The main algorithms for non-limited minimization are the BFGS quasi-Newton method and the Nelder-Mead direct search method. Sequential quadratic programming (SQP) variations are used for minimization with boundaries, achievement of objectives and semi-infinitely constrained optimization. Non-linear least-squares problems are solved using the Gauss–Newton or Levenberg-Marquardt methods. Routines to solve linear and quadratic programming problems use an active-set method combined with imaging techniques. The routines provide a range of algorithms and linear research strategies. Linear research strategies are protected methods of quadratic and cubic interpolation and extrapolation.

6.1.2 Large Scale Algorithms

The Optimization Toolbox also includes algorithms for problems with dispersion or structure. Large scale methods make use of MATLAB's treatment of sparse matrices. The toolbox includes algorithms to solve linear programming problems, non-linear least squares with limits, non-linear unconstrained minimization, non-linear minimization with constrained limits, non-linear minimization with linear equalities, solving non-linear systems of equations, quadratic minimization with limits restrictions, quadratic minimization with linear equalities and limit-constrained linear least squares optimization. Is also implements a new large scale linear programming algorithm. This algorithm is based on Zhang Yin's method 1 LIPSOL (*Linear programming Interior-Point SOLver*), a primal-dual interior point algorithm based on Mahrota's method of prediction-correction. There are also large scale methods available for some formulations of quadratic programming and non-linear objectives with linear constraints or limit restrictions. These methods are trust region algorithms, developed by Thomas F. Coleman, and reflective and projective Newton methods used to manage restrictions.

6.2 Minimization Algorithms

Most multivariate minimization techniques (with and without restriction) are implemented as specific functions in MATLAB's Optimization Toolbox.

The minimization functions provided by the Optimization Toolbox are summarized in the following table.

fgoalattain	*Solves multiobjective goal attainment problems*
fminbnd	*Finds the minimum of a single-variable function on fixed interval*
fmincon	*Finds the minimum of a constrained non-linear multivariable function*
fminimax	*Solves minimax constraint problems*
fminsearch	*Finds the minimum of an unconstrained multivariable function using a derivative-free method*
fminunc	*Finds the minimum of an unconstrained multivariable function*
fseminf	*Finds the minimum of a semi-infinitely constrained multivariable non-linear function*
linprog	*Solves linear programming problems*
quadprog	*Quadratic programming*

6.2.1 Multiobjective Problems

A general multiobjective problem may be defined as follows:

$$\underset{x,\gamma}{\text{minimize}} \quad \gamma$$

subject to the following restrictions:

$$F(x) - weight. \, \gamma \le goal$$
$$c(x) \le 0$$
$$ceq(x) = 0$$
$$A \cdot x \le b$$
$$Aeq \cdot x = beg$$
$$lb \le x \le ub$$

where '*x*', '*weight*', '*goal*', '*b*', '*beq*', '*lb*', and '*ub*', are *vectors*, *A* and *Aeq* are matrices, and *c* (*x*), *ceq* (*x*), and *F* (*x*) are functions that return vectors. *F* (*x*), *c(x)* and *ceq* (*x*) may be non-linear functions.

The function *fgoalattain* solves such problems with the following syntax:

```
x = fgoalattain(fun,x0,goal,weight)
x = fgoalattain(fun,x0,goal,weight,A,b)
x = fgoalattain(fun,x0,goal,weight,A,b,Aeq,beq)
x = fgoalattain(fun,x0,goal,weight,A,b,Aeq,beq,lb,ub)
x = fgoalattain(fun,x0,goal,weight,A,b,Aeq,beq,lb,ub,nonlcon)
x = fgoalattain(fun,x0,goal,weight,A,b,Aeq,beq,...
                lb,ub,nonlcon,options)
x = fgoalattain(fun,x0,goal,weight,A,b,Aeq,beq,...
                lb,ub,nonlcon,options,P1,P2,...)
```

```
[x,fval] = fgoalattain(...)
[x,fval,attainfactor] = fgoalattain(...)
[x,fval,attainfactor,exitflag] = fgoalattain(...)
[x,fval,attainfactor,exitflag,output] = fgoalattain(...)
[x,fval,attainfactor,exitflag,output,lambda] = fgoalattain(...)
```

The various different forms of the syntax above cover particular cases of the general problem. It begins by considering the problem in its simplest form and then gradually extends it to wider generalizations. The solution of the problem is *x*, and *fval* is the objective value of the function at *x*. The amount of over- or underachievement of the goals is indicated by *attainfactor*, *exitflag* is an indicator of output, *output* provides information about the optimization process and *lambda* contains information concerning Lagrange multipliers.

As an example, we consider a driver *K* that produces a closed-loop system:

$$x = (A+BKC)x + Bu$$
$$y = Cx$$

The eigenvalues of the system are determined by the matrices *A, B, C, K* using *eig(A+B*K*C)*. The eigenvalues should be on the real axis or in the complex plane. In addition, to avoid saturating the entries of *K*, elements must be between – 4 and 4. This is an unstable system with two inputs and two outputs with an open loop and the following state space matrices:

$$A = \begin{bmatrix} -0.5 & 0 & 0 \\ 0 & -2 & 10 \\ 0 & 1 & -2 \end{bmatrix} \quad B = \begin{bmatrix} 1 & 0 \\ -2 & 2 \\ 0 & 1 \end{bmatrix} \quad C = \begin{bmatrix} 1 & 0 & 0 \\ 0 & 0 & 1 \end{bmatrix}$$

The target values set for the eigenvalues of the closed cycle are initialized as [– 5, – 3, – 1].

We begin by defining the controller in the M-file *eigfun.m* with *K*= [– 1, – 1, – 1, – 1] as shown in Figure 6-1.

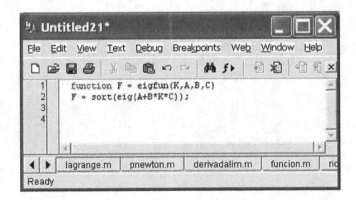

Figure 6-1.

Then the matrix system is introduced and the optimization routine is invoked.

```
>> A = [- 0.5 0 0; 0 - 10-2, 0-1 - 2];
B = [1 0; - 2 2; 0 1];
C = [1 0 0, 0 0 1];
K0 = [- 1 - 1; - 1 - 1]; % Initializes the array controller
goal = [- 5 - 3 - 1];    % Set target values of eigenvalues
weight = abs (goal)      % puts weights
```

```
lb = - 4 * ones (size (KO)); % Located lower on the driver dimensions
UB = 4 * ones (size (KO));   % Located in the driver dimensions
options = optimset('Display','iter');
[K,fval,attainfactor] = fgoalattain(@eigfun,KO,...
    goal,weight,[],[],[],[],lb,ub,[],options,A,B,C)

weight =

5     3     1
```

Iter	F-count	Attainment factor	Step-size	Directional derivative	Procedure
1	6	1.885	1	1.03	
2	13	1.061	1	-0.679	
3	20	0.4211	1	-0.523	Hessian modified
4	27	-0.06352	1	-0.053	Hessian modified twice
5	34	-0.1571	1	-0.133	
6	41	-0.3489	1	-0.00768	Hessian modified
7	48	-0.3643	1	-4.25e-005	Hessian modified
8	55	-0.3645	1	-0.00303	Hessian modified twice
9	62	-0.3674	1	-0.0213	Hessian modified
10	69	-0.3806	1	0.00266	
11	76	-0.3862	1	-2.73e-005	Hessian modified twice
12	83	-0.3863	1	-1.25e-013	Hessian modified twice

```
Optimization terminated successfully: Search direction less than 2*options.TolX and maximum
constraint violation is less than options.TolCon

Active Constraints:

    1
    2
    4
    9
    10

K =

-4.0000    -0.2564
-4.0000    -4.0000

fval =

-6.9313
-4.1588
-1.4099

attainfactor =

-0.3863
```

6.2.2 Non-Linear Scalar Minimization With Boundary Conditions

A general problem of this type can be defined as follows:

$$\min_{x} \ f(x)$$

subject to the restriction:

$$x_1 < x < x_2$$

where x, x_1 and x_2 are scalars and $f(x)$ is a function that returns a scalar.

This problem is solved using the function *fminbd,* whose syntax is as follows:

```
x = fminbnd(fun,x1,x2)
x = fminbnd(fun,x1,x2,options)
x = fminbnd(fun,x1,x2,options,P1,P2,...)
[x,fval] = fminbnd(...)
[x,fval,exitflag] = fminbnd(...)
[x,fval,exitflag,output] = fminbnd(...)
```

As an example, we minimize the function $sin(x)$ in $[0,2\pi]$.

```
>> x = fminbnd(@sin,0,2*pi)

x =

4.7124
```

6.2.3 Non-Linear Minimization with Restrictions

A general problem of this type can be defined as follows:

$$\min_{x} \ f(x)$$

subject to the constraints:

$$c(x) \le 0$$
$$ceq(x) = 0$$
$$A \cdot x \le b$$
$$Aeq \cdot x = beg$$
$$lb \le x \le ub$$

where x, b, beq, lb and ub are vectors, A and Aeq are matrices and $c(x)$, $ceq(x)$ and $F(x)$ are functions that return vectors. $F(x)$, $c(x)$ and $ceq(x)$ can be non-linear functions.

This problem is solved using the function *mincon,* whose syntax is as follows:

```
x = fmincon (fun, x 0, A, b)
x = fmincon(fun,x0,A,b,Aeq,beq)
x = fmincon (fun, x 0, A, b, Aeq, beq, lb, ub)
x = fmincon (fun, x 0, A, b, Aeq, beq, lb, ub, nonlcon)
x = fmincon (fun, x 0, A, b, Aeq, beq, lb, ub, nonlcon, options)
```

```
x = fmincon(fun,x0,A,b,Aeq,beq,lb,ub,nonlcon,options,P1,P2, ...)
[x, fval] = fmincon (...)
[x, fval, exitflag] = fmincon (...)
[x,fval,exitflag,output] = fmincon(...)
[x,fval,exitflag,output,lambda] = fmincon(...)
[x,fval,exitflag,output,lambda,grad] = fmincon(...)
[x,fval,exitflag,output,lambda,grad,hessian] = fmincon(...)
```

As an example, we minimize the function $f(x) = -x_1 * x_2 * x_3$ subject to restriction $0 \le x_1 + 2x_2 + 2x_3 \le 72$ starting at the point $x_0 = [10; 10; 10]$.

Rewriting the constraint as:

$$-x_1 - 2x_2 - 2x_3 \le 0$$
$$x_1 + 2x_2 + 2x_3 \le 72$$

we can use the matrices

$$A = \begin{bmatrix} -1 & -2 & -2 \\ 1 & 2 & 2 \end{bmatrix} \quad b = \begin{bmatrix} 0 \\ 72 \end{bmatrix}$$

to consider the restriction in the form $A * x \le b$.

We define the objective function by means of the M-file shown in Figure 6-2.

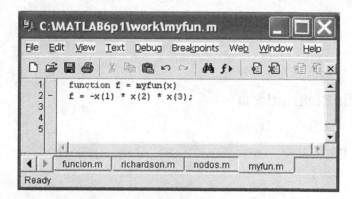

Figure 6-2.

Now we can solve the problem by using the syntax:

```
>> A = [-1 -2 -2; 1 2 2];
>> b = [0 72]';
>> x0 = [10; 10; 10];
>> [x,fval] = fmincon(@myfun,x0,A,b)
```

Optimization terminated successfully: Magnitude of directional derivative in search direction less than 2*options.TolFun and maximum constraint violation is less than options.TolCon

Active Constraints:

2

```
x =

    24.0000
    12.0000
    12.0000

FVal =

    -3456
```

6.2.4 Minimax Optimization: fminimax and fminuc

A general problem of this type can be defined as follows:

$$\min_{x} \max_{\{F_i\}} \{F_i(x)\}$$

subject to the constraints:

$$c(x) \leq 0$$
$$ceq(x) = 0$$
$$A \cdot x \leq b$$
$$Aeq \cdot x = beg$$
$$lb \leq x \leq ub$$

where x, b, beq, lb and ub are vectors, A and Aeq are matrices and $c(x)$, $ceq(x)$ and $F(x)$ are functions that return vectors. $F(x)$, $c(x)$ and $ceq(x)$ can be non-linear functions.

This problem is solved using the function *fminimax*, whose syntax is as follows:

```
x = fminimax (fun, x 0)
x = fminimax(fun,x0,A,b)
x = fminimax(fun,x0,A,b,Aeq,beq)
x = fminimax (fun, x 0, A, b, Aeq, beq, lb, ub)
x = fminimax(fun,x0,A,b,Aeq,beq,lb,ub,nonlcon)
x = fminimax(fun,x0,A,b,Aeq,beq,lb,ub,nonlcon,options)
x = fminimax(fun,x0,A,b,Aeq,beq,lb,ub,nonlcon,options,P1,P2,...)
[x, fval] = fminimax (...)
[x, fval, maxfval] = fminimax (...)
[x, fval, maxfval, exitflag] = fminimax (...)
[x, fval, maxfval, exitflag, output] = fminimax (...)
[x, fval, maxfval, exitflag, output, lambda] = fminimax (...)
```

This minimizes the functions defined on the basis of the initial value $x0$ subject to the constraint $A * x < = b$ or $Aeq * x = beq$ or solutions x in the range $lb < = x < = ub$. The value *maxfval* is the maximum value of the function. The function *fminuc* finds the minimum of a multivariate function without restrictions

$$\min_{x} f(x)$$

where x is a vector and $f(x)$ is a function that returns a scalar.

The syntax is as follows:

```
x = fminunc(fun,x0)
x = fminunc(fun,x0,options)
x = fminunc(fun,x0,options,P1,P2,...)
[x, fval] = fminunc (...)
[x, fval, exitflag] = fminunc (...)
[x,fval,exitflag,output] = fminunc(...)
[x,fval,exitflag,output,grad] = fminunc(...)
[x,fval,exitflag,output,grad,hessian] = fminunc(...)
```

6.2.5 Minimax Optimization

A general problem of this type can be defined as follows:

$$\min_{x} \max_{\{F_i\}} \{F_i(x)\}$$

subject to the constraints:

$$c(x) \leq 0$$
$$ceq(x) = 0$$
$$A \cdot x \leq b$$
$$Aeq \cdot x = beg$$
$$lb \leq x \leq ub$$

where x, b, beq, lb and ub are vectors, A and Aeq are matrices and $c(x)$, $ceq(x)$ and $F(x)$ are functions that return vectors. $F(x)$, $c(x)$ and $ceq(x)$ can be non-linear functions.

This problem is solved using the function *fminimax*, whose syntax is as follows:

```
x = fminimax (fun, x 0)
x = fminimax(fun,x0,A,b)
x = fminimax(fun,x0,A,b,Aeq,beq)
x = fminimax(fun,x0,A,b,Aeq,beq,lb,ub)
x = fminimax(fun,x0,A,b,Aeq,beq,lb,ub,nonlcon)
x = fminimax(fun,x0,A,b,Aeq,beq,lb,ub,nonlcon,options)
x = fminimax(fun,x0,A,b,Aeq,beq,lb,ub,nonlcon,options,P1,P2,...)
[x, fval] = fminimax (...)
[x, fval, maxfval] = fminimax (...)
[x, fval, maxfval, exitflag] = fminimax (...)
[x, fval, maxfval, exitflag, output] = fminimax (...)
[x, fval, maxfval, exitflag, output, lambda] = fminimax (...)
```

This minimizes the functions defined on the basis of the initial value $x0$ subject to the constraint $A * x <= b$ or $Aeq * x = beq$ or solutions x in the range $lb <= x <= ub$. The value *maxfval* is the maximum value of the function.

6.2.6 Minimum Optimization: fminsearch and fminuc

The function *fminsearch* finds the minimum of a multivariate function without restrictions

$$\min_{x} \ f(x)$$

where x is a vector and $f(x)$ is a function that returns a scalar.

The syntax is as follows:

```
x = fminsearch(fun,x0)
x = fminsearch(fun,x0,options)
x = fminsearch(fun,x0,options,P1,P2,...)
[x,fval] = fminsearch(...)
[x,fval,exitflag] = fminsearch(...)
[x,fval,exitflag,output] = fminsearch(...)
```

As an example, we minimize the function $f(x) = sin(x) + 3$ as follows:

```
>> x = fminsearch('sin(x)+3',2)

x =

4.7124
```

Function *fminuc* finds the minimum of a multivariate function without restrictions

$$\min_{x} \ f(x)$$

where x is a vector and $f(x)$ is a function that returns a scalar.

The syntax is as follows:

```
x = fminunc(fun,x0)
x = fminunc(fun,x0,options)
x = fminunc(fun,x0,options,P1,P2,...)
[x, fval] = fminunc (...)
[x, fval, exitflag] = fminunc (...)
[x,fval,exitflag,output] = fminunc(...)
[x,fval,exitflag,output,grad] = fminunc(...)
[x,fval,exitflag,output,grad,hessian] = fminunc(...)
```

6.2.7 Semi-Infinitely Constrained Minimization

A general problem of this type requires us to find the minimum of a semi-infinitely constrained multivariate function with restrictions:

$$\min_{x} \ f(x)$$

subject to the constraints:

$$c(x) \leq 0$$
$$ceq(x) = 0$$
$$A \cdot x \leq b$$
$$Aeq \cdot x = beg$$
$$lb \leq x \leq ub$$
$$K_1(x,w_1) \leq 0$$
$$K_2(x,w_2) \leq 0$$
$$\dots$$
$$K_n(x,w_n) \leq 0$$

where *x, b, beq, lb* and *ub* are vectors, *A* and *Aeq* are matrices and *c(x)*, *ceq(x)* and *F(x)* are functions that return vectors. *F(x)*, *c(x)* and *ceq(x)* can be non-linear functions. K_i and (x, w_i) are functions that return vectors and w_i are vectors of length at least 2.

This problem is solved using the function *fseminf,* whose syntax is as follows:

```
x = fseminf(fun,x0,ntheta,seminfcon)
x = fseminf (fun, x 0, ntheta, seminfcon, A, b)
x = fseminf(fun,x0,ntheta,seminfcon,A,b,Aeq,beq)
x = fseminf (fun, x 0, ntheta, seminfcon, A, b, Aeq, beq, lb, ub)
x = fseminf (fun, x 0, ntheta, seminfcon, A, b, Aeq, beq, lb, ub, options)
x = fseminf(fun,x0,ntheta,seminfcon,A,b,Aeq,beq,...)
              lb,ub,options,P1,P2,...)
[x,fval] = fseminf(...)
[x,fval,exitflag] = fseminf(...)
[x,fval,exitflag,output] = fseminf(...)
[x,fval,exitflag,output,lambda] = fseminf(...)
```

6.2.8 Linear Programming

A general problem of this type can be defined as follows:

$$\min_{x} f^T x$$

subject to the constraints:

$$A \cdot x \leq b$$
$$Aeq \cdot x = beg$$
$$lb \leq x \leq ub$$

where *f, x, b, beq, lb* and *ub* are vectors and *A* and *Aeq* are matrices.

This problem is solved using the function *linprog,* whose syntax is as follows:

```
x = linprog(f,A,b)
x = linprog(f,A,b,Aeq,beq)
x = linprog(f,A,b,Aeq,beq,lb,ub)
x = linprog(f,A,b,Aeq,beq,lb,ub,x0)
x = linprog(f,A,b,Aeq,beq,lb,ub,x0,options)
```

```
[x,fval] = linprog(...)
[x,fval,exitflag] = linprog(...)
[x,fval,exitflag,output] = linprog(...)
[x,fval,exitflag,output,lambda] = linprog(...)
```

This minimizes f'^*x subject to the constraint $A * x <= b$ or $Aeq * x = beq$ or so that x is in the range $lb <= x <= ub$ where we use an initial value $x0$.

As an example, we minimize the function:

$$f(x) = -5x_1 - 4x_2 - 6x_3$$

subject to the constraints:

$$x_1 - x_2 + x_3 \le 20$$
$$3x_1 + 2x_2 + 4x_3 \le 42$$
$$3x_1 + 2x_2 \le 30$$
$$0 \le x_1, 0 \le x_2, 0 \le x_3$$

We use the following syntax:

```
>> f = [- 5, - 4, - 6]
A = [1 -1 -1]
     3 -2 -4
     3  2  0];
b = [20; 42; 30];
lb = zeros (3.1);

f =

-5
-4

>> [x,fval,exitflag,output,lambda] = linprog(f,A,b,[],[],lb)

Optimization terminated successfully.

x =

 0.0000
15.0000
 3.0000

fval =

-78.0000

exitflag =

1
```

```
output =

  iterations: 6
cgiterations: 0
  algorithm: 'lipsol'

lambda =

ineqlin: [3x1 double]
  eqlin: [0x1 double]
  upper: [3x1 double]
  lower: [3x1 double]
```

>> lambda.ineqlin

```
ans =

0.0000
1.5000
0.5000
```

>> lambda.lower

```
ans =

1.0000
0.0000
0.0000
```

6.2.9 Quadratic programming

A general problem of this type can be defined as follows:

$$\min_{x} \quad \frac{1}{2}x^{\tau}Hx + f^{T}x$$

subject to the constraints:

$$A \cdot x \le b$$
$$Aeq \cdot x = be_{\cdot}$$
$$lb \le x \le ub$$

where f, x, b, beq, lb and ub are vectors and H, A and Aeq are matrices.

This problem is solved using the function *quadprog*, whose syntax is as follows:

```
x = quadprog(H,f,A,b)
x = quadprog(H,f,A,b,Aeq,beq)
x = quadprog(H,f,A,b,Aeq,beq,lb,ub)
x = quadprog(H,f,A,b,Aeq,beq,lb,ub,x0)
x = quadprog(H,f,A,b,Aeq,beq,lb,ub,x0,options)
x = quadprog(H,f,A,b,Aeq,beq,lb,ub,x0,options,p1,p2,...)
```

```
[x,fval] = quadprog(...)
[x,fval,exitflag] = quadprog(...)
[x,fval,exitflag,output] = quadprog(...)
[x,fval,exitflag,output,lambda] = quadprog(...)
```

This minimizes $1/2*x'*H*x+f'*x$ subject to the constraint $A*x <= b$ or $Aeq*x = beq$ or so that x is in the range $lb <= x <= ub$ where we use an initial value $x0$.

As an example, we minimize the function:

$$f(x) = \frac{1}{2}x_1^2 + x_2^2 - x_1 x_2 - 2x_1 - 6x_2$$

subject to the constraints:

$$x_1 + x_2 \leq 2$$
$$-x_1 + 2x_2 \leq 2$$
$$2x_1 + x_2 \leq 3$$
$$0 \leq x_1, \ 0 \leq x_2$$

We begin by writing the function as:

$$f(x) = \frac{1}{2}x^T H x + f^T x$$

where:

$$H = \begin{bmatrix} 1 & -1 \\ -1 & 2 \end{bmatrix}, \quad f = \begin{bmatrix} -2 \\ -6 \end{bmatrix}, \quad x = \begin{bmatrix} x_1 \\ x_2 \end{bmatrix}$$

```
>> H = [1 -1; -1 2] ;
f = [-2; -6];
A = [1 1; -1 2; 2 1];
b = [2; 2; 3];
lb = zeros(2,1);

>> [x,fval,exitflag,output,lambda] = quadprog(H,f,A,b,[],[],lb);

Optimization terminated successfully.

x =

0.6667
1.3333

fval =

-8.2222

exitflag =

1
```

```
output =

    iterations: 3
      algorithm: 'medium-scale: active-set'
  firstorderopt: []
   cgiterations: []

lambda =

    lower: [2x1 double]
    upper: [2 x 1 double]
    eqlin: [0 x 1 double]
  ineqlin: [3 x 1 double]
```

6.3 Equation Solving Algorithms

The Optimization Toolbox provides the following functions for the solution of equations and systems of equations.

fsolve	*Solves equations and non-linear systems of equations*
fzero	*Solves non-linear scalar equations*

6.3.1 Solving Equations and Systems of Equations

The function *fsolve* solves systems of non-linear equations $F(x) = 0$ where x is a vector and $F(x)$ is a function that returns a vector value. Its syntax is as follows:

```
x = fsolve (fun, x 0)
x = fsolve(fun,x0,options)
x = fsolve(fun,x0,options,P1,P2, ... )
[x,fval] = fsolve(...)
[x,fval,exitflag] = fsolve(...)
[x,fval,exitflag,output] = fsolve(...)
[x,fval,exitflag,output,jacobian] = fsolve(...)
```

As an example, we solve the system:

$$2x_1 - x_2 = e^{-x_1}$$
$$-x_1 + 2x_2 = e^{-x_2}$$

with initial conditions [- 5 5].

We begin by writing the system in the form:

$$2x_1 - x_2 - e^{-x_1} = 0$$
$$-x_1 + 2x_2 - e^{-x_2} = 0$$

We build the equations in the M-file shown in Figure 6-3.

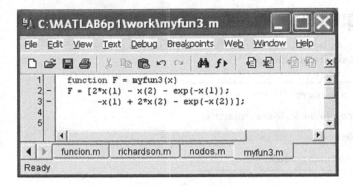

Figure 6-3.

The system is solved by using the syntax:

```
>> x0 = [-5; -5];
>> [x,fval] = fsolve(@myfun3,x0)
```

```
Optimization terminated successfully: Relative function value changing by less than OPTIONS.TolFun

x =

0.5671
0.5671

FVal =

1.0E-008 *

-0.5319
-0.5319
```

The function *fzero* solves non-linear equations by using the following syntax:

```
x = fzero x 0 (fun)
x = fzero(fun,x0,options)
x = fzero(fun,x0,options,P1,P2,...)
[x, fval] = fzero (...)
[x, fval, exitflag] = fzero (...)
[x,fval,exitflag,output] = fzero(...)
```

As an example we solve the equation $x^3 - 2x - 5$ in a neighborhood of $x = 2$.

```
>> z = fzero (inline('x^3-2*x-5'), 2)

z =

2.0946
```

6.4 Fitting Curves by Least Squares

MATLAB adjusts curves by least squares with restrictions, by non-linear least squares and non-negative linear least-squares. The functions implemented for these tasks are as follows:

lsqlin	*Solves constrained linear least-squares problems*
lsqcurvefit	*Solves non-linear curve-fitting problems in the least-squares sense*
lsqnonlin	*Solves non-linear least-squares problems*
lsqnonneg	*Solves non-negative least-squares constraints problem*

6.4.1 Conditional Least Squares Problems

A conditional least squares problem has the following structure:

$$\min_{x} \frac{1}{2}\|Cx - d\|_2^2$$

subject to the constraints:

$$A \cdot x \leq b$$
$$Aeq \cdot x = beg$$
$$lb \leq x \leq ub$$

where *d, x, b, beq, lb* and *ub* are vectors, and *C, A* and *Aeq* are matrices.

This problem is solved using the function *lsqlin,* whose syntax is as follows:

```
x = lsqlin(C,d,A,b)
x = lsqlin(C,d,A,b,Aeq,beq)
x = lsqlin(C,d,A,b,Aeq,beq,lb,ub)
x = lsqlin(C,d,A,b,Aeq,beq,lb,ub,x0)
x = lsqlin(C,d,A,b,Aeq,beq,lb,ub,x0,options)
x = lsqlin(C,d,A,b,Aeq,beq,lb,ub,x0,options,p1,p2,...)
[x,resnorm] = lsqlin(...)
[x,resnorm,residual] = lsqlin(...)
[x,resnorm,residual,exitflag] = lsqlin(...)
[x,resnorm,residual,exitflag,output] = lsqlin(...)
[x,resnorm,residual,exitflag,output,lambda] = lsqlin(...)
```

This solves $C*x = d$ subject to the constraint $A * x <= b$ or $Aeq * x = beq$ or so that x is in the range $lb <= x <= ub$ where we use an initial value $x0$.

6.4.2 Non- Linear Least Squares Problems

The function *lscurvefit* is used to fit non-linear curves by least squares. Given a set of input data *xdata* and a set of observed output data *ydata*, we seek the coefficients x that best fit the function $F(x, xdata)$:

$$\min_{x} \frac{1}{2}\|F(x,xdata) - ydata\|_2^2 = \frac{1}{2}\sum \left(F(x,xdata_i) - ydata_i\right)^2$$

The syntax is as follows:

```
x = lsqcurvefit(fun,x0,xdata,ydata)
x = lsqcurvefit(fun,x0,xdata,ydata,lb,ub)
x = lsqcurvefit(fun,x0,xdata,ydata,lb,ub,options)
x = lsqcurvefit(fun,x0,xdata,ydata,lb,ub,options,P1,P2,...)
[x,resnorm] = lsqcurvefit(...)
[x,resnorm,residual] = lsqcurvefit(...)
[x,resnorm,residual,exitflag] = lsqcurvefit(...)
[x,resnorm,residual,exitflag,output] = lsqcurvefit(...)
[x,resnorm,residual,exitflag,output,lambda] = lsqcurvefit(...)
[x,resnorm,residual,exitflag,output,lambda,jacobian] =
    lsqcurvefit (...)
```

The function *lsqnonlin* solves the following non-linear least squares problem:

$$\min_{x} f(x) = f_1(x)^2 + f_2(x)^2 + f_3(x)^2 + \dots f_m(x)^2 + L$$

by using the syntax:

```
x = lsqnonlin (fun, x 0)
x = lsqnonlin(fun,x0,lb,ub)
x = lsqnonlin(fun,x0,lb,ub,options)
x = lsqnonlin(fun,x0,eb,ub,options,P1,P2, ... )
[x,resnorm] = lsqnonlin(...)
[x,resnorm,residual] = lsqnonlin(...)
[x,resnorm,residual,exitflag] = lsqnonlin(...)
[x,resnorm,residual,exitflag,output] = lsqnonlin(...)
[x,resnorm,residual,exitflag,output,lambda] = lsqnonlin(...)
[x,resnorm,residual,exitflag,output,lambda,jacobian] =
    lsqnonlin (...)
```

6.4.3 Linear Non- Negative Least Squares Problems

The function *lsqnonneg* solves the following non-negative least squares problem:

$$\min_{x} \frac{1}{2}\|Cx - d\|_2^2.$$
$$x \geq 0$$

where the matrix *C* and the vector *d* are the coefficients of the objective function. Its syntax is as follows:

```
x = lsqnonneg (C, d)
x = lsqnonneg (C, d, x 0)
x = lsqnonneg(C,d,x0,options)
[x,resnorm] = lsqnonneg(...)
[x,resnorm,residual] = lsqnonneg(...)
[x,resnorm,residual,exitflag] = lsqnonneg(...)
[x,resnorm,residual,exitflag,output] = lsqnonneg(...)
[x,resnorm,residual,exitflag,output,lambda] = lsqnonneg(...)
```

The following example compares the solutions to the 4×2 problem defined by C and d using the normal method and *lsqnonneg*.

```
>> C = [

        0.0372 0.2869
        0.6861 0.7071
        0.6233 0.6245
        0.6344 0.6170];

d = [

    0.8587
    0.1781
    0.0747
    0.8405];

[C\d, lsqnonneg (C, d)]

ans =

-2.5627         0
 3.1108    0.6929

>> [norm(C*(C\d)-d), norm(C*lsqnonneg(C,d)-d)]

ans =

0.6674 0.9118
```

EXERCISE 6-1

Minimize the function $f(x) = (x-3)^2 - 1$ in the interval $(0,5)$.

```
>> x = fminbnd(inline('(x-3)^2-1'),0,5)

x =

3
```

EXERCISE 6-2

Find the value of x that minimizes the maximum value of:

$$[f_1(x), f_2(x), f_3(x), f_4(x), f_5(x)]$$

where the functions $f_i(x)$ are defined below.

$$f_1(x) = 2x_1^2 + x_2^2 - 48x_1 - 40x_2 + 304$$
$$f_2(x) = -x_2^2 - 3x_2$$
$$f_3(x) = x_1 + 3x_2 - 18$$
$$f_4(x) = -x_1 - x_2$$
$$f_5(x) = x_1 + x_2 - 8$$

We begin by building the M-file *myfun1* which defines the functions (Figure 6-4).

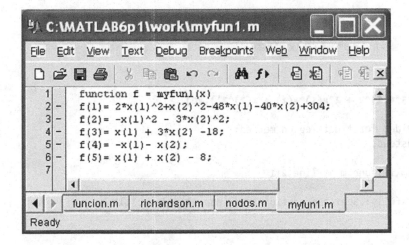

Figure 6-4.

Using as baseline [0.1 0.1] we solve the problem by using the following syntax:

```
>> x0 = [0.1; 0.1];
>> [x,fval] = fminimax(@myfun1,x0)
```

Optimization terminated successfully: Magnitude of directional derivative in search direction less than 2*options.TolFun and maximum constraint violation is less than options.TolCon

```
Active Constraints:

    1
    5

X =

4.0000
4.0000

FVal =

0.0000 - 64.0000 - 2.0000 - 8.0000 - 0.0000
```

EXERCISE 6-3

Minimize the following function:

$$f(x) = 3 * x_1^2 + 2 * x1 * x2 + x_2^2$$

using as initial values [1,1].

>> [x,fval] = fminunc(inline('3*x(1)^2 + 2*x(1)*x(2) + x(2)^2'),x0)

```
Warning: Gradient must be provided for trust-region method;
    using line-search method instead.

> In C:\MATLAB6p1\toolbox\optim\fminunc.m at line 211

Optimization terminated successfully: Search direction less than 2*options.TolX

X =

 1.0E-008 *

-0.7591 0.2665

FVal =

1. 3953e-016
```

EXERCISE 6-4

Find the values of x that minimize the function f(x) subject to restrictions $k_1(x, w_1)$ and $k_2(x, w_2)$ for w_1 and w_2 in [1, 100]. The function and the constraints are defined in the problem and the starting point is (0.5 0.2 0.3).

$$f(x) = (x_1 - 0.58)^2 + (x_2 - 0.5)^2 + (x_3 - 0.5)^2$$

$$K_1(x, w_1) = \sin(w_1 x_1)\cos(w_1 x_2) - \frac{1}{1000}(w_1 - 50)^2 - \sin(w_1 x_3) - x_3 \le 1$$

$$K_2(x, w_2) = \sin(w_2 x_2)\cos(w_2 x_1) - \frac{1}{1000}(w_2 - 50)^2 - \sin(w_2 x_3) - x_3 \le 1$$

We start by creating an M-file with restrictions (Figure 6-5).

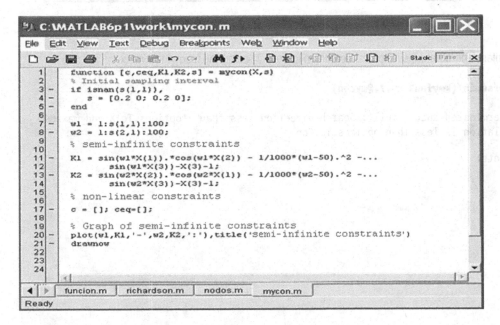

Figure 6-5.

We also create a target file for the function (Figure 6-6).

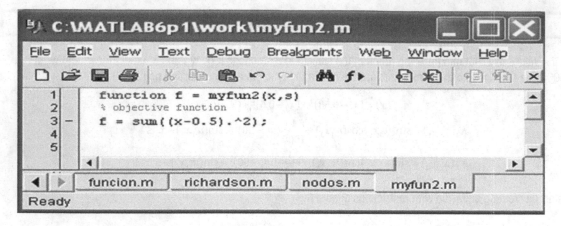

Figure 6-6.

We solve the problem and obtain the graphical solution (Figure 6-7) using the following syntax:

>> [x,fval] = fseminf(@myfun2,x0,2,@mycon)

Optimization terminated successfully: Search direction less than 2*options.TolX and maximum constraint violation is less than options.TolCon

Check Constraints:

      7
     10

x =

0.6673
0.3013
0.4023

FVal =

0.0770

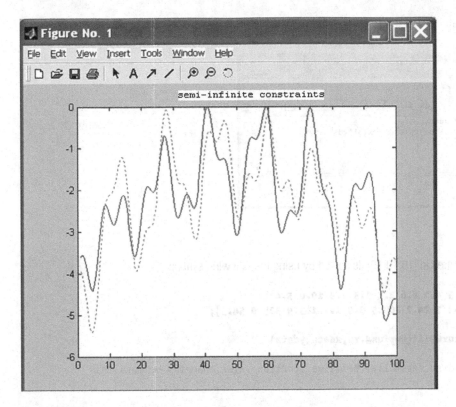

Figure 6-7.

EXERCISE 6-5

Given the data sets:

xdata = [3.6 7.7 9.3 4.1 8.6 2.8 1.3 7.9 10.0 5.4];
ydata = [16.5 150.6 263.1 24.7 208.5 9.9 2.7 163.9 325,0 54.3];

find the x coefficients that minimize the function ydata (i) defined in the problem below.

$$ydata(i) = x(1) \cdot xdata(i)^2 + x(2) \cdot \sin(xdata(i)) + x(3) \cdot xdata(i)^3$$

Our problem can be written as:

$$\min_{X} \frac{1}{2} \sum_{i=1}^{n} \left(F(x, xdata_i) - ydata_i \right)^2$$

We start by defining the function F in the M-file shown in Figure 6-8:

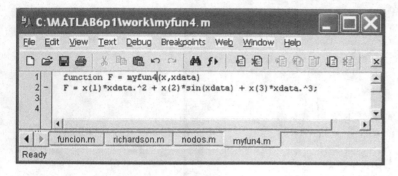

Figure 6-8.

The problem, with initial values in [10,10,10], is solved by using the following syntax:

```
>> xdata = [3.6 7.7 9.3 4.1 8.6 2.8 1.3 7.9 10.0 5.4];
ydata = [16.5 150.6 263.1 24.7 208.5 9.9 2.7 163.9 325,0 54.3];
>> x 0 = [10, 10, 10];
>> [x, resnorm] = lsqcurvefit(@myfun4,x0,xdata,ydata)

Optimization terminated successfully: Relative function value changing by less than
OPTIONS.TolFun

x =

0.2269 0.3385 0.3021

resnorm =

6.2950
```

CHAPTER 7

■ ■ ■

Differentiation in one and Several Variables. Applications to Optimization

7.1 Derivatives

The derivative of a real function at a point is the instantaneous rate of change of that function in a neighborhood of the point; i.e., it is a measure of how the dependent variable changes as a result of a small change in the independent variable.

Geometrically, the derivative of a function at a point represents the gradient of the tangent to the function at the point. The origin of the idea of the derivative comes precisely from the attempt to draw the tangent line at a given point on a curve.

A function $f(x)$ defined in a neighborhood of a point $x = a$ is *differentiable* at a if the following limit exists:

$$\lim_{h \to 0} \frac{f(a+h) - f(a)}{h}$$

The value of the limit, if it exists, is denoted by $f'(a)$, and *is called the derivative of the function f at the point a*. If f is differentiable at every point of its domain, it is simply said to be differentiable.

The continuity of a function is a necessary condition for its differentiablity, and all differentiable functions are continuous.

The following table shows the basic commands that enables MATLAB to work with derivatives.

diff('f', 'x')	*Differentiates the function f with respect to x*
	`>> diff('sin(x^2)','x')`
	`ans =`
	`2 * x * cos(x^2)`
syms x, diff(f,x)	*Differentiates the function f with respect to x*
	`>> syms x` `>> diff(sin(x^2),x)`
	`ans =`
	`2 * x * cos(x^2)`

(*continued*)

diff('f', 'x', n)   *Finds the nth derivative of the function f with respect to x*

```
>> diff('sin(x^2)','x',2)
```

```
ans =
```

```
2 * cos(x^2) - 4 * x ^ 2 * sin(x^2)
```

syms x, diff(f, x, n)   *Finds the nth derivative of the function f with respect to x*

```
>> syms x
>> diff(sin(x^2),x,2)
```

```
ans =
```

```
2 * cos(x^2) - 4 * x ^ 2 * sin(x^2)
```

R = jacobian(w,v)   *Returns the Jacobian matrix of w with respect to v*

```
>> syms x y z
>> jacobian([x*y*z; y; x+z],[x y z])
```

```
ans =
```

```
[y * z, x * z, x * y]
[   0,     1,     0]
[   1,     0,     1]
```

Y = diff(X)   *Calculates the successive differences between elements of the vector X: [X(2) - X (1), X(3) - X (2),..., X(n) - X (n-1)]. If X is an m×n matrix, then diff (X) returns the array of differences by rows: [X(2:m,:)-X(1:m-1,:)]*

```
x = [1 2 3 4 5];
y = diff (x)
y =
1 1 1 1
```

Y = diff(X,n)   *Find differences of order n, for example: diff(X,2) = diff (diff (X))*

```
x = [1 2 3 4 5];
z = diff(x,2)
z =
0 0 0
```

As a first example, we consider the function $f(x) = x^5 - 3x^4 - 11x^3 + 27x^2 + 10x - 24$ and graph it in the interval $[-4,5]$.

```
>> x=-4:0.1:5;
>> f=x.^5-3*x.^4-11*x.^3+27*x.^2+10*x-24;
>> df=diff(f)./diff(x);
>> plot(x,f)
```

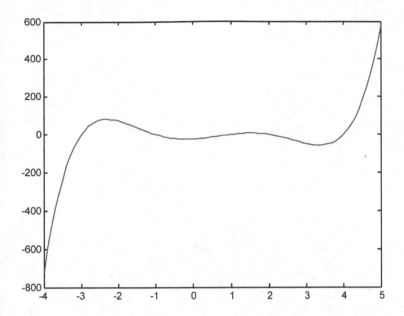

As a second example, we calculate the derivative of the function $log(sin(2x))$, simplifying the result.

```
>> pretty(simplify(diff('log(sin(2*x))','x')))

  2 cot(2 x)
```

As a third example, we calculate the first four derivatives of $f(x) = 1/x^2$

```
>> f = '1/x^2'

f =
1/x^2

>> [diff(f),diff(f,2),diff(f,3),diff(f,4)]

ans =

[-2/x ^ 3, 6/x ^ 4, - 24/x ^ 5, 120/x ^ 6]
```

7.2 Partial Derivatives

The MATLAB commands for differentiation described above can also be used for partial differentiation.

As an example, given the function $f(x, y) = sin(xy) + cos(xy^2)$, we calculate the following:

$$\frac{\partial f}{\partial x},\ \frac{\partial f}{\partial y},\ \frac{\partial^2 f}{\partial x^2},\ \frac{\partial^2 f}{\partial y^2},\ \frac{\partial^2 f}{\partial x \partial y},\ \frac{\partial^2 f}{\partial y \partial x} \cdots \text{ and } \cdots \frac{\partial^4 f}{\partial^2 x \partial^2 y}$$

```
>> syms x y
>> f = sin(x*y) + cos(x*y^2)

f =

sin(x*y) + cos(x*y^2)

>> diff(f,x)

ans =

cos(x*y)*y-sin(x*y^2)*y^2

>> diff(f,y)

ans =

cos(x*y)*x-2*sin(x*y^2)*x*y

>> diff(diff(f,x),x)

ans =

-sin(x*y)*y^2-cos(x*y^2)*y^4

>> diff (diff(f,y), y)

ans =

-sin(x*y)*x^2-4*cos(x*y^2)*x^2*y^2-2*sin(x*y^2)*x

>> diff(diff(f,x),y)

ans =

-sin(x*y)*x*y + cos(x*y)-2*cos(x*y^2)*x*y^3-2*sin(x*y^2)*y

>> diff(diff(f,y),x)

ans =

-sin(x*y)*x*y+cos(x*y)-2*cos(x*y^2)*x*y^3-2*sin(x*y^2)*y

>> diff(diff(diff(diff(f,x),x),y,y))

ans =

sin(x*y)*y^3*x-3*cos(x*y)*y^2+2*cos(x*y^2)*y^7*x+6*sin(x*y^2)*y ^ 5
```

7.3 Applications of Derivatives. Tangents, Asymptotes, Extreme Points and Turning Points

By calculating the derivative of a function we can find the tangent to a function at a point, find the asymptotes (horizontal, vertical or oblique) of a function, study the growth and concavity of functions and determine maxima, minima and turning points of functions on intervals.

With this information it is possible to give a fairly complete study of curves.

If f is a function for which $f'(x_0)$ exists, then $f'(x_0)$ is the slope of the tangent line to the function f at the point $(x_0, f(x_0))$. The equation of the tangent will be y-$f(x_0)$ = $f'(x_0)$ (x-x_0).

The horizontal asymptotes of the curve $y = f(x)$ are limit tangents, as $x_0 \to \infty$, which are horizontal. They are defined by the equation $y = \lim_{x_0 \to \infty} f(x_0)$.

The vertical asymptotes of the curve $y = f(x)$ are limit tangents, as $f(x_0) \to \infty$, which are vertical. They are defined by the equation $x = x_0$, where x_0 is a value such that $\lim_{x \to x_0} f(x) = \infty$.

The oblique asymptotes to the curve $y = f(x)$ at the point $x = x_0$ have the equation $y = mx+n$, where

$$m = \lim_{x \to \infty} \frac{y}{x} \text{ and } n = \lim_{x \to \infty}(y - mx).$$

If f is a function for which $f'(x_0)$ and $f''(x_0)$ both exist, then, if $f'(x_0) = 0$ and $f''(x_0) < 0$, the function f has a local maximum at the point $(x_0, f(x_0))$.

If f is a function for which $f'(x_0)$ and $f''(x_0)$ both exist, then, if $f'(x_0) = 0$ and $f''(x0) > 0$, the function f has a local minimum at the point $(x0, f(x0))$.

If f is a function for which $f'(x_0), f''(x_0)$ and $f'''(x_0)$ exist, then, if $f'(x_0) = 0$ and $f''(x_0) = 0$ and $f'''(x_0) \neq 0$, the function f has a turning point at the point $(x_0, f(x_0))$.

If f is differentiable, then the values of x for which the function f is increasing are those for which $f'(x)$ is greater than zero.

If f is differentiable, then the values of x for which the function f is decreasing are those for which $f'(x)$ is less than zero.

If f is twice differentiable, then the values of x for which the function f is concave are those for which $f''(x)$ is greater than zero.

If f is twice differentiable, then the values of x for which the function f is convex are those for which $f''(x)$ is less than zero.

As an example, we conduct a full study of the function:

$$f(x) = \frac{x^3}{x^2 - 1}$$

calculating the asymptotes, maxima, minima, inflection points, intervals of growth and decrease and intervals of concavity and convexity.

```
>> f='x^3/(x^2-1)'

f =

x^3/(x^2-1)

>> syms x, limit(x^3/(x^2-1),x,inf)

ans =

NaN
```

Therefore, there are no horizontal asymptotes. To see if there are vertical asymptotes, let's look at the values of x that make y infinite:

```
>> solve('x^2-1')

ans =

[1]
[-1]
```

The vertical asymptotes will be the straight lines $x = 1$ and $x = -1$. Now let's see if there are any oblique asymptotes:

```
>> limit(x^3/(x^2-1)/x,x,inf)

ans =

1

>> limit(x^3/(x^2-1)-x,x,inf)

ans =

0
```

The straight line $y = x$ is an oblique asymptote. Now, we will analyze the maximum and minimum, inflection points and intervals of concavity and growth:

```
>> solve (diff (f))

ans =

[       0]
[       0]
[3 ^(1/2)]
[^(1/2) - 3]
```

The first derivative vanishes at $x = 0$, $x = \sqrt{3}$ and $x = -\sqrt{3}$. These include maximum and minimum candidates. To verify if they are minima or maxima, we find the value of the second derivative at those points:

```
>> [numeric(subs(diff(f,2),0)),numeric(subs(diff(f,2),sqrt(3))),
   numeric(subs(diff(f,2),-sqrt(3)))]

ans =

0    2.5981   -2.5981
```

Therefore, at the point with abscissa $x = -\sqrt{3}$ there is a maximum and at the point with abscissa $x = \sqrt{3}$ there is a minimum. At $x = 0$ we know nothing:

```
>> [numeric (subs (f, sqrt (3))), numeric (subs (f, - sqrt (3)))]

ans =

2.5981    -2.5981
```

Therefore, the maximum point is $(-\sqrt{3}, -2.5981)$ and the minimum point is $(\sqrt{3}, 2.5981)$.
We will now analyze the points of inflection:

```
>> solve(diff(f,2))

ans =

[          0]
[ i*3^(1/2)]
[-i * 3 ^(1/2)]
```

The only possible turning point occurs at $x = 0$, and as $f(0) = 0$, this point is $(0,0)$:

```
>> subs (diff(f,3), 0)

ans =

-6
```

As the third derivative at $x = 0$ is not zero, the origin is a turning point:

```
>> pretty(simple(diff(f)))
                 2    2
               x  (x  - 3)
               -----------
                  2    2
               (x  - 1)
```

The curve is increasing when $y' > 0$, i.e., in the intervals $(-\infty, -\sqrt{3})$ and $(\sqrt{3}, \infty)$.
The curve is decreasing when $y' < 0$, i.e., in the intervals $(-\sqrt{3}, -1)$, $(-1, 0)$, $(0, 1)$ and $(1, \sqrt{3})$.

```
>> pretty(simple(diff(f,2)))

                     2
                   x (x + 3)
               2 -----------
                   2    3
                 (x - 1)
```

The curve will be concave when $y'' > 0$, i.e., in the intervals $(-1, 0)$ and $(1, \infty)$.
The curve is convex when $y'' > 0$, i.e. in the intervals $(0, 1)$ and $(-\infty, -1)$.
The curve has a horizontal tangent at the three points at which the first derivative is zero. The equations of the horizontal tangents are $y = 0$, $y = 2.5981$, and $y = -2.5981$.

The curve has a vertical tangent at the points where the first derivative is infinite. These include $x = 1$ and $x = -1$. Therefore the vertical tangents coincide with two vertical asymptotes.

Next we represent the curve along with its asymptotes:

```
>> fplot('[x^3/(x^2-1),x]',[-5,5,-5,5])
```

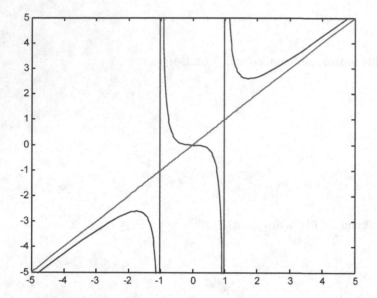

We can also represent the curve, its asymptotes and the horizontal and vertical tangents in the same graph.

```
>> fplot('[x^3/(x^2-1),x,2.5981,-2.5981]',[-5,5,-5,5])
```

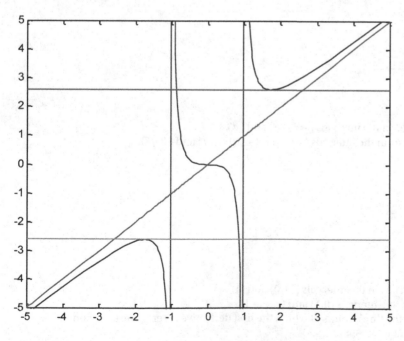

7.4 Differentiation of Functions of Several Variables

The notion of the derivative of a function generalizes to functions of several variables. Below we discuss the concept in the two variable case.

Given a function $f: R^2 \to R$, the *partial derivative of f* with respect to the variable x at the point (a, b) is defined as follows:

$$\frac{\partial f}{\partial x}(a,b) = \lim_{h \to 0} \frac{f(a+h,b) - f(a,b)}{h}$$

Similarly, the partial derivative of f with respect to the variable y at the point (a, b) is defined as:

$$\frac{\partial f}{\partial y}(a,b) = \lim_{h \to 0} \frac{f(a,b+h) - f(a,b)}{h}$$

Generally speaking, we can define the partial derivative with respect to any variable for a function of n variables.

Given the function $f: R^n \to R$, the partial derivative of f with respect to the variable x_i ($i = 1, 2,..., n$) at the point $(a_1, a_2,..., a_n)$ is defined as follows:

$$\frac{\partial f}{\partial x_i}(a_1, a_2,..., a_n) = \lim_{h \to 0} \frac{f(a_1, a_2,..., a_i + h,..., a_n) - f(a_1, a_2,..., a_n)}{h}$$

The function f is differentiable if all partial derivatives with respect to x_i ($i = 1, 2,..., n$) exist and are continuous. All differentiable functions are continuous, and if a function is not continuous, it cannot be differentiable.

The *directional derivative of the function f* with respect to the vector $v = (v_1, v_2,..., v_n)$ is defined as the following scalar product:

$$(Df)v = \left(\frac{\partial f}{\partial x_1}, \frac{\partial f}{\partial x_2},..., \frac{\partial f}{\partial x_n} \right) \bullet (v_1, v_2,..., v_n) = (\nabla f) \bullet v$$

$$\nabla f = \left(\frac{\partial f}{\partial x_1}, \frac{\partial f}{\partial x_2},..., \frac{\partial f}{\partial x_n} \right) \quad \text{is called the } \textit{gradient vector of f.}$$

The directional derivative of the function f with respect to the vector $v = (dx_1, dx_2,..., dx_n)$ is called the *total differential of f*. Its value is:

$$Df = \left(\frac{\partial f}{\partial x_1} dx_1 + \frac{\partial f}{\partial x_2} dx_2 +...+ \frac{\partial f}{\partial x_n} dx_n \right)$$

Derivatives of functions of several variables can be found by MATLAB using the following commands.

---

diff(f(x,y,z,...),x)	*Returns the partial derivative of f with respect to x*

```
>> syms x and z
>> diff(x^2+y^2+z^2+x*y-x*z-y*z+1,z)

ans =

2*z - y - x
```

diff (f(x,y,z,...), x, n)	*Returns the nth partial derivative of f with respect to x*

```
>> diff(x^2+y^2+z^2+x*y-x*z-y*z+1,z,2)

ans =

2
```

diff(f(x1,x2,x3,...),xj)	*Returns the partial derivative of f with respect to xj*

```
>> diff(x^2+y^2+z^2+x*y-x*z-y*z+1,y)

ans =

x + 2*y - z
```

diff(f(x1,x2,x3,...),xj,n)	*Returns the nth partial derivative of f with respect to xj*

```
>> diff(x^2+y^2+z^2+x*y-x*z-y*z+1,y,2)

ans =

2
```

diff(diff(f(x,y,z,...),x),y))	*Returns the second partial derivative of f with respect to x and y*

```
>> diff (diff(x^2+y^2+z^2+x*y-x*z-y*z+1,x), y)

ans =

1
```

As a first example, we study the differentiability and continuity of the function:

$$f(x,y) = \frac{2xy}{\sqrt{x^2+y^2}} \text{ if } (x,y) \neq (0,0) \text{ and } f(0,0)=0$$

To determine if the function is differentiable, we need to show that it has continuous partial derivatives at every point. We consider any point other than the origin and calculate the partial derivative with respect to the variable x:

```
>> syms x y
>> pretty (simplify (diff ((2*x*y) /(x^2+y^2) ^(1/2), x)))

            3
      2 y
    ----------

            3
            -
            2
      2   2
    (x + y )
```

Now, let's see if this partial derivative is continuous at the origin. When calculating the iterated limits at the origin, we observe that they do not coincide.

```
>> limit (limit (2 * y ^ 3 /(x^2+y^2) ^(3/2), x, 0), y, 0)

ans =

NaN

>> limit (limit (2 * y ^ 3 /(x^2+y^2) ^(3/2), y, 0), x, 0)

ans =

0
```

The limit of the partial derivative does not exist at $(0,0)$, and so we conclude that the function is not differentiable at the origin.

However, the function is continuous, since the only problematic point is the origin, and the limit of the function tends to $0 = f(0,0)$:

```
>> limit (limit ((2*x*y) /(x^2+y^2) ^(1/2), x, 0), y, 0)

ans =

0

>> limit (limit ((2*x*y) /(x^2+y^2) ^(1/2), y, 0), x, 0)

ans =

0
```

```
>> m = sym('m', 'positive')
>> limit((2*x*(m*x))/(x^2+(m*x)^2)^(1/2),x,0)

ans =

0


>> a = sym('a', 'real');
>> f =(2*x*y) /(x^2+y^2) ^(1/2);
>> limit (subs (f, {x, y}, {r * cos (a), r * sin (a)}), r, 0)

ans =

0
```

The iterated limits and the directional limits are all zero, and by changing the function to polar coordinates, the limit at the origin turns out to be zero, which coincides with the value of the function at the origin.

This is therefore an example of a non-differentiable continuous function.

The following graph helps to interpret the result.

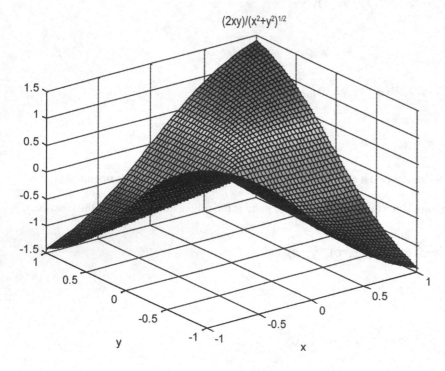

$(2xy)/(x^2+y^2)^{1/2}$

As a second example we consider the function:

$$f(x,y,z) = \frac{1}{\sqrt{x^2+y^2+z^2}}$$

We check the equation:

$$\frac{\partial^2 f}{\partial x^2} + \frac{\partial^2 f}{\partial y^2} + \frac{\partial^2 f}{\partial z^2} = 0$$

```
>> syms x y z
>> f = 1 /(x^2+y^2+z^2) ^(1/2)

f =

1/(x^2 + y^2 + z^2)^(1/2)

>> diff(f,x,2)+diff(f,y,2)+diff(f,z,2)

ans =

(3 * x ^ 2) /(x^2 + y^2 + z^2) ^(5/2) - 3 /(x^2 + y^2 + z^2) ^(3/2) + (3 * y ^ 2)
/(x^2 + y^2 + z^2) ^(5/2) + (3 * z ^ 2) /(x^2 + y^2 + z^2) ^(5/2)

>> simplify(diff(f,x,2)+diff(f,y,2)+diff(f,z,2))

ans =

0
```

As a third example, we calculate the directional derivative of the function:

$$f(x,y,z) = \frac{1}{\sqrt{x^2 + y^2 + z^2}}$$

at the point $(2,1,1)$ in the direction of the vector $v = (1,1,0)$. We also find the gradient vector of f.

Recall that the *directional derivative of the function f* with respect to the vector $v = (v_1, v_2, ..., v_n)$ is defined as the following scalar product:

$$(Df)v = \left(\frac{\partial f}{\partial x_1}, \frac{\partial f}{\partial x_2}, ..., \frac{\partial f}{\partial x_n} \right) \bullet (v_1, v_2, ..., v_n) = (\nabla f) \bullet v$$

$$\nabla f = \left(\frac{\partial f}{\partial x_1}, \frac{\partial f}{\partial x_2}, ..., \frac{\partial f}{\partial x_n} \right) \quad \text{is called the } gradient \; vector \; of f.$$

First we calculate the gradient of the function f.

```
>> syms x y z
>> f = 1 /(x^2+y^2+z^2) ^(1/2)

f =

1 /(x^2 + y^2 + z^2) ^(1/2)
```

```
>> Gradient_f = simplify ([diff(f,x), diff(f,y), diff (f, z)])

Gradient_f =

[-x /(x^2 + y^2 + z^2) ^(3/2),- y /(x^2 + y^2 + z^2) ^(3/2),-z /(x^2 + y^2 + z^2) ^(3/2)]
```

We then calculate the gradient vector at the point $(2,1,1)$.

```
>> Gradient_f_p = subs(Gradient_f,{x,y,z},{2,1,1})

Gradient_f_p =

  -0.1361 - 0.0680 - 0.0680
```

Finally, we calculate the directional derivative.

```
>> Directional_derivative_p = dot (Gradient_f_p, [1,1,0])

Directional_derivative_p =

  -0.2041
```

7.5 Maxima and Minima of Functions of Several Variables

MATLAB allows you to easily calculate maxima and minima of functions of several variables.

A function f: $R^n{\rightarrow}R$, which maps the point $(x_1, x_2,..., x_n) \in R$ to $f(x_1,x_2,...,x_n) \in R$, has an extreme point at $(a_1,a_2,...,a_n)$ if the gradient vector $\nabla f = \left(\dfrac{\partial f}{\partial x_1}, \dfrac{\partial f}{\partial x_2},..., \dfrac{\partial f}{\partial x_n} \right)$ is zero at $(a_1,a_2,...,a_n)$.

By setting all the first order partial derivatives equal to zero and solving the resulting system, we can find the possible maxima and minima.

To determine the nature of the extreme point, it is necessary to construct the **Hessian matrix**, which is defined as follows:

$$H = \begin{bmatrix} \dfrac{\partial^2 f}{\partial x_1^2} & \dfrac{\partial^2 f}{\partial x_1 \partial x_2} & .... & \dfrac{\partial^2 f}{\partial x_1 \partial x_n} \\ \dfrac{\partial^2 f}{\partial x_1 \partial x_2} & \dfrac{\partial^2 f}{\partial x_2^2} & .... & \dfrac{\partial^2 f}{\partial x_2 \partial x_n} \\ .... & .... & .... & .... \\ \dfrac{\partial^2 f}{\partial x_1 \partial x_n} & \dfrac{\partial^2 f}{\partial x_2 \partial x_n} & .... & \dfrac{\partial^2 f}{\partial x_n^2} \end{bmatrix}$$

First, suppose that the determinant of H is non-zero at the point $(a_1,a_2,...,a_n)$. In this case, we say that the point is non-degenerate and, in addition, we can determine the nature of the extreme point via the following conditions:

If the Hessian matrix at the point $(a_1,a_2,...,a_n)$ is positive definite, then the function has a minimum at that point.

If the Hessian matrix at the point $(a_1,a_2,...,a_n)$ is negative definite, then the function has a maximum at that point.

In any other case, the function has a saddle point at $(a_1,a_2,...,a_n)$.

If the determinant of H is zero at the point $(a_1,a_2,...,a_n)$, we say that the point is degenerate.

As an example we find and classify the extreme points of the function:

$$f(x,y,z) = x^2 + xy + y^2 + z^2$$

We start by finding the possible extreme points. To do so, we equate all of the partial derivatives of *f* with respect to each of its variables (i.e. the components of the gradient vector of *f*) to zero and solve the resulting system in three variables:

```
>> syms x y z
>> f = x ^ 2 + y ^ 2 + z ^ 2 + x * y

f =

x ^ 2 + x * y + y ^ 2 + z ^ 2

>> [x y z] = solve (diff(f,x), diff(f,y), diff (f, z), x, y , z)

x =

0

y =

0

z =

0
```

The single extreme point is the origin (0,0,0). We will analyze what kind of extreme it is. To do this, we calculate the Hessian matrix and express it as a function of *x*, *y* and *z*:

```
>> clear all
>> syms x y z
>> f = x ^ 2 + y ^ 2 + z ^ 2 + x * y

f =

x ^ 2 + x * y + y ^ 2 + z ^ 2

>> diff(f,x)

ans =

2*x + y

>> H=simplify([diff(f,x,2),diff(diff(f,x),y),diff(diff(f,x),z);
              diff(diff(f,y),x),diff(f,y,2),diff(diff(f,y),z);
              diff(diff(f,z),x),diff(diff(f,z),y),diff(f,z,2)])

H =

[2, 1, 0]
[1, 2, 0]
[0, 0, 2]
```

```
>> det(H)

ans =

6
```

We have seen that the Hessian matrix is constant (i.e. it does not depend on the point at which applies), therefore its value at the origin has already been found. The determinant is non-zero, so there are no degenerate extrema.

```
>> eig(H)

ans =

1
2
3
```

We see that the Hessian matrix at the origin is positive definite, because all its eigenvalues are positive. Thus, we conclude that the origin is a minimum of the function.

In addition, MATLAB incorporates specific commands for optimizing and finding zeros of functions of several variables. The most important of these are shown in the following table.

---

g = inline(expr)	*Constructs an inline function from the string expr*
	``` >> g = inline('t^2') g = Inline function: g(t) = t^2 ```
g = inline(expr,arg1,arg2, ...)	*Constructs an inline function from the string expr with the given input arguments*
	``` >> g = inline('sin(2*pi*f + theta)', 'f', 'theta') g = Inline function: g(f,theta) = sin(2*pi*f + theta) ```
g = inline(expr,n)	*Constructs an inline function from the string expr with n input arguments*
	``` >> g = inline('x^P1', 1) g = Inline function: g(x,P1) = x^P1 ```

(*continued*)

f = @function	*Enables the function to be evaluated*
	`>> f=@cos`
	`f =`
	`@cos`
	`>> ezplot(f, [-pi,pi])`
x = fminbnd(fun,x1,x2)	*Minimizes the function on the interval (x1, x2)*
	`>> x=fminbnd(@cos,3,4)`
	`x =`
	`3.1416`
x = fminbnd(fun,x1,x2,options)	*Minimizes the function on the interval (x1, x2) according to the option given by optimset (...). This last command is explained later.*
	`>> x = fminbnd (@cos, 3, 4, optimset ('TolX', 1e-12,` `'Display', 'off'))`
	`x =`
	`3.1416`
x = fminbnd(fun,x1,x2, options,P1,P2,...)	*Specifies additional parameters P1, P2, to pass to the target function fun(x,P1,P2,...)*
[x, fval] = fminbnd (...)	*Evaluates the objective function at x*
	`>> [x,fval] = fminbnd(@cos,3,4)`
	`x =`
	`3.1416`
	`fval =`
	`-1.0000`

(*continued*)

[x, fval, f] = fminbnd (...)	*In addition, returns an indicator of convergence f (f > 0 indicates convergence to the solution, f < 0 no convergence and f = 0 exceeded number of steps)*

```
>> [x,fval,f] = fminbnd(@cos,3,4)

x =

3.1416

fval =

-1.0000

f =

1
```

[x,fval,f,output] = fminbnd(...)	*Gives further information on optimization (output.algorithm gives the algorithm used, output.funcCount gives the number of evaluations of fun and output.iterations gives the number of iterations)*

```
>> [x,fval,f,output] = fminbnd(@cos,3,4)

x =

3.1416

fval =

-1.0000

f =

1

output =

iterations: 7
funcCount: 8
algorithm: 'golden section search, parabolic interpolation'
message: [1x112 char]
```

(continued)

x = fminsearch(fun,x0)
x = fminsearch(fun,x0,options)
x = fminsearch(fun,x0,options,P1
,P2,...)
[x,fval] = fminsearch(...)
[x,fval,f] = fminsearch(...)
[x,fval,f,output] = fminsearch(...)

Identical to the previous command to minimize function of several variables with initial values given by x0. Here x0 can be an interval [a, b] in which a solution is sought. Thus, to minimize fun in [a, b] we use x = fminsearch (fun, [a, b]).

```
>> x = fminsearch(inline('(100*(1-x^2)^2+(1-x)^2)'),3)

x =

1.0000
>> [x,feval] = fminsearch(inline('(100*(1-x^2)^2 +(1-x)^2)'),3)

x =

1.0000

feval =

2.3901e-007

>> [x,feval,f] = fminsearch(inline('(100*(1-x^2)^2 +(1-x)^2)'),3)

x =

1.0000

feval =

2.3901e-007

f =

1
>> [x,feval,f,output] = fminsearch(inline('(100*(1-x^2)^2+(1-x)^2)'),3)

x =

1.0000

feval =

2.3901e-007

f =

1

output =

iterations: 18
funcCount: 36
algorithm: 'Nelder-Mead simplex direct search'
message: [1x196 char]
```

(continued)

x = fzero x0 (fun)
x = fzero(fun,x0,options)
x = fzero(fun,x0,options,P1,P2,...)
[x, fval] = fzero (...)
[x, fval, exitflag] = fzero (...)
[x,fval,exitflag,output] = fzero(...)

Identical to the previous command to find zeros of functions. Here x0 can be an interval [a, b] in which a solution is sought. Then, to find a zero of fun in [a, b] we use x = fzero (fun, [a, b]), where fun has opposite signs at a and b.

```
>> x = fzero(@cos,[1 2])

x =

1.5708

>> [x, fval] = fzero(@cos,[1 2])

x =

1.5708

fval =

6. 1232e-017

>> [x, fval, exitflag] = fzero(@cos,[1 2])

x =

1.5708

fval =

6. 1232e-017

exitflag =

1

>> [x, fval, exitflag, output] = fzero(@cos,[1 2])

x =

1.5708

fval =

6. 1232e-017

exitflag =

1

output =

intervaliterations: 0
iterations: 5
funcCount: 7
algorithm:'bisection, interpolation'
message: 'Zero found in the interval [1, 2]'
```

(continued)

options = optimset('p1','v1','p2','v2,...)	*Creates optimization options parameters p1, p2,... with values v1, v2... The possible parameters are* Display *(with possible values 'off', 'iter', 'final', 'notify' to hide the output, display the output of each iteration, display only the final output and show a message if there is no convergence);* MaxFunEvals, *whose value is an integer indicating the maximum number of evaluations;* MaxIter *whose value is an integer indicating the maximum number of iterations;* TolFun, *whose value is an integer indicating the tolerance in the value of the function, and* TolX, *whose value is an integer indicating the tolerance in the value of x*
val = optimget (options, 'param')	*Returns the value of the parameter specified in the optimization options structure*

As a first example we minimize the function *cos(x)* in the interval (3,4).

```
>> x = fminbnd(inline('cos(x)'),3,4)

x =

3.1416
```

In the following example we conduct the same minimization with a tolerance of 8 decimal places and find both the value of *x* that minimizes the cosine in the range given and the minimum value of the cosine function in that interval, presenting information relating to all iterations of the process.

```
>> [x, fval, f] = fminbnd (@cos, 3, 4, optimset('TolX',1e-8,...)) (( 'Display', 'iter'));

Func-count      x          f(x)         Procedure
   1         3.38197    -0.971249        initial
   2         3.61803    -0.888633        golden
   3         3.23607    -0.995541        golden
   4         3.13571    -0.999983        parabolic
   5         3.1413         -1           parabolic
   6         3.14159        -1           parabolic
   7         3.14159        -1           parabolic
   8         3.14159        -1           parabolic
   9         3.14159        -1           parabolic

Optimization terminated successfully:
the current x satisfies the termination criteria using OPTIONS.TolX of 1.000000e-008
```

In the following example, taking as initial values (- 1.2, 1), we minimize and find the target value of the function of two variables:

$$f(x)=100(x_2 - x_1^2)^2 +(1-x_1)^2$$

```
>> [x,fval] = fminsearch(inline('100*(x(2)-x(1)^2)^2+...
   1-x (1)) ^ 2'), [- 1.2, 1])
```

x =

1.0000 1.0000

FVal =

8. 1777e-010

The following example computes a zero of the sine function near 3 and a zero of the cosine function between 1 and 2.

```
>> x = fzero(@sin,3)
```

x =

3.1416

```
>> x = fzero(@cos,[1 2])
```

x =

1.5708

7.6 Conditional Minima and Maxima. The Method of "Lagrange Multipliers"

Suppose we want to optimize (i.e. maximize or minimize) the function $f(x_1,x_2,...,x_n)$, called the objective function, but subject to certain restrictions given by the equations:

$g_1(x_1,x_2,...,x_n)=0$
$g_2(x_1,x_2,...,x_n)=0$
. . . .
$g_k(x_1,x_2,...,x_n)=0$

This is the setting in which the Lagrangian is introduced. The Lagrangian is a linear combination of the objective function and the constraints, and has the following form:

$$L(X_1,X_2,...X_n,\lambda)=f(X_1,X_2,...X_n)+\sum_{i=1}^{k}\lambda_i\,g_i(x_1,x_2,...,x_n)$$

The extreme points are found by solving the system by setting the components of the gradient vector of L to zero, that is, $\nabla L(x_1,x_2,...,x_n,\lambda)=(0,0,...,0)$. Which translates into:

$$\nabla L=\left(\frac{\partial L}{\partial x_1},\frac{\partial L}{\partial x_2},....,\frac{\partial L}{\partial x_n},\frac{\partial L}{\partial \lambda_1},\frac{\partial L}{\partial \lambda_2},....,\frac{\partial L}{\partial \lambda_n}\right)=(0,0,......,0)$$

By setting the partial derivatives to zero and solving the resulting system, we obtain the values of x_1, x_2,..., x_n, λ_1, λ_2,...,λ_k corresponding to possible maxima and minima.

To determine the nature of the points $(x_1, x_2,..., x_n)$ found above, the following bordered Hessian matrix is used:

$$
\begin{bmatrix}
\dfrac{\partial^2 f}{\partial x_1^2} & \dfrac{\partial^2 f}{\partial x_1 \partial x_2} & \cdots & \dfrac{\partial^2 f}{\partial x_1 \partial x_n} & \dfrac{\partial g_i}{\partial x_1} \\[2mm]
\dfrac{\partial^2 f}{\partial x_1 \partial x_2} & \dfrac{\partial^2 f}{\partial x_2^2} & \cdots & \dfrac{\partial^2 f}{\partial x_2 \partial x_n} & \dfrac{\partial g_i}{\partial x_2} \\[2mm]
\cdots & \cdots & \cdots & \cdots & \cdots \\[2mm]
\dfrac{\partial^2 f}{\partial x_1 \partial x_n} & \dfrac{\partial^2 f}{\partial x_2 \partial x_n} & \cdots & \dfrac{\partial^2 f}{\partial x_n^2} & \dfrac{\partial g_i}{\partial x_n} \\[2mm]
\dfrac{\partial g_i}{\partial x_1} & \dfrac{\partial g_i}{\partial x_2} & \cdots & \dfrac{\partial g_i}{\partial x_n} & 0
\end{bmatrix}
$$

The nature of extreme points can be determined by studying the set of bordered Hessian matrices:

$$
H1 = \begin{bmatrix} \dfrac{\partial f}{\partial x_1^2} & \dfrac{\partial g_i}{\partial x_1} \\[2mm] \dfrac{\partial g_i}{\partial x_1} & 0 \end{bmatrix} \quad
H2 = \begin{bmatrix} \dfrac{\partial^2 f}{\partial x_1^2} & \dfrac{\partial^2 f}{\partial x_1 \partial x_2} & \dfrac{\partial g_i}{\partial x_1} \\[2mm] \dfrac{\partial^2 f}{\partial x_1 \partial x_2} & \dfrac{\partial^2 f}{\partial x_2^2} & \dfrac{\partial g_i}{\partial x_2} \\[2mm] \dfrac{\partial g_i}{\partial x_1} & \dfrac{\partial g_i}{\partial x_2} & 0 \end{bmatrix} \cdots Hn = H
$$

For a single restriction g_1, if H1 < 0, H2 < 0, H3 < 0,..., H < 0, then the extreme point is a minimum.

For a single restriction g_1, if H1 > 0, H2 < 0, H3 > 0, H4 < 0, H5 > 0, ... then the extreme point is a maximum.

For a collection of restrictions $g_i(x_1,..., x_n)$ (i = 1, 2,..., k) the lower right 0 will be a block of zeros and the conditions for a mimimum will all have sign $(-1)^k$, while the conditions for a maximum will have alternating signs with H1 having sign $(-1)^{k+1}$. When considering several restrictions at the same time, it is easier to determine the nature of the extreme point by simple inspection.

As an example we find and classify the extreme points of the function:

$$f(x,y,z) = x + z$$

subject to the restriction:

$$x^2 + y^2 + z^2 = 1.$$

First we find the Lagrangian L, which is a linear combination of the objective function and the constraints:

```
>> syms x y z L p
>> f = x + z

f =

x + z
```

```
>> g = x ^ 2 + y ^ 2 + z ^ 2-1

g =

x ^ 2 + y ^ 2 + z ^ 2 - 1

>> L = f + p * g

L =

x + z + p *(x^2 + y^2 + z^2-1)
```

Then, the possible extreme points are obtained by solving the system obtained by setting the components of the gradient vector of L equal to zero, that is, $\nabla L(x_1, x_2, ..., x_n, \lambda) = (0, 0, ..., 0)$. Which translates into:

```
>> [x, y, z, p] = solve (diff(L,x), diff(L,y), diff(L,z), diff(L,p), x, y, z, p)

x =

-2 ^(1/2)/2
 2 ^(1/2)/2

y =

 2 ^(1/2)/2
-2 ^(1/2)/2

z =

0
0

p =

 2 ^(1/2)/2
-2 ^(1/2)/2
```

By matching all the partial derivatives to zero and solving the resulting system, we find the values of $x_1, x_2, ..., x_n$, $\lambda_1, \lambda_2, ..., \lambda_k$ corresponding to possible maxima and minima.

We already see that the possible extreme points are:

$$(-\sqrt{2}/2, \sqrt{2}/2, 0) \text{ and } (\sqrt{2}/2, -\sqrt{2}/2, 0)$$

Now, let us determine the nature of these extreme points. To this end, we substitute them into the objective function.

```
>> clear all
>> syms x y z
>> f=x+z

f =

x + z
```

```
>> subs(f, {x,y,z},{-sqrt(2)/2,sqrt(2)/2,0})

ans =

-0.7071

>> subs(f, {x,y,z},{sqrt(2)/2,-sqrt(2)/2,0})

ans =

0.7071
```

Thus, at the point $(-\sqrt{2}/2, \sqrt{2}/2, 0)$ the function has a maximum, and at the point $(\sqrt{2}/2, -\sqrt{2}/2, 0)$ the function has a minimum.

7.7 Vector Differential Calculus

Here we shall introduce four classical theorems of differential calculus in several variables: the chain rule or composite function theorem, the implicit function theorem, the inverse function theorem and the change of variables theorem.

Consider a function $\bar{F} : R^m \rightarrow R^n$:

$$(x_1, x_2, \ldots, x_m) \rightarrow [F_1(x_1, x_2, \ldots, x_m), \ldots, F_n(x_1, x_2, \ldots, x_m)]$$

The vector function $\bar{F}$ is said to be differentiable at the point $a = (a_1, \ldots, a_m)$ if each of the component functions $F_1, F_2, \ldots, F_n$ is differentiable.

The Jacobian matrix of the above function is defined as:

$$J = \begin{bmatrix} \dfrac{\partial F_1}{\partial x_1} & \dfrac{\partial F_1}{\partial x_2} & \cdots & \dfrac{\partial F_1}{\partial x_n} \\ \dfrac{\partial F_2}{\partial x_1} & \dfrac{\partial F_2}{\partial x_2} & \cdots & \dfrac{\partial F_2}{\partial x_n} \\ \cdots & \cdots & \cdots & \cdots \\ \dfrac{\partial F_n}{\partial x_1} & \dfrac{\partial F_n}{\partial x_2} & \cdots & \dfrac{\partial F_n}{\partial x_n} \end{bmatrix} = \dfrac{\partial(F_1, F_2, \ldots, F_n)}{\partial(x_1, x_2, \ldots, x_n)}$$

The Jacobian of a vector function is an extension of the concept of a partial derivative for a single-component function.

MATLAB has the command *Jacobian* which enables you to calculate the Jacobian matrix of a function.

As first example we calculate the Jacobian of the vector function mapping (x,y,z) to $(x*y*z, y, x+z)$.

```
>> syms x y z
>> jacobian([x*y*z; y; x+z],[x y z])

ans =

[y * z, x * z, x * y]
[    0,     1,     0]
[    1,     0,     1]
```

As second example we calculate the Jacobian of the vector function $f(x,y,z) = (e^x, \cos(y), \sin(z))$ at the point $(0, -\pi/2, 0)$.

```
>> syms x y z

>> J = jacobian ([exp(x), cos(y), sin(z)], [x, y, z])

J =

[exp(x), 0, 0]
[0,-sin(y), 0]
[0, 0, cos(z)]

>> subs(J,{x,y,z},{0,-pi/2,0})

ans =

1 0 0
0 1 0
0 0 1
```

Thus the Jacobian turns out to be the identity matrix.

7.8 The Composite Function Theorem

The chain rule or composite function theorem allows you to differentiate compositions of vector functions. The chain rule is one of the most familiar rules of differential calculus. It is often first introduced in the case of single variable real functions, and is then generalized to vector functions. It says the following:

Suppose we have two vector functions

$$\bar{g} : U \subset R^n \to R^m \ and \ \bar{f} : V \subset R^m \to R^p$$

where U and V are open and consider the composite function $\bar{f} \circ \bar{g} : R^n \to R^p$.

If $\bar{g}$ is differentiable at $\bar{x}_0$ and $\bar{f}$ is differentiable at $\bar{y}_0 = \bar{g}(\bar{x}_0)$, then $\bar{f} \circ \bar{g}$ is differentiable at $\bar{x}_0$ and we have the following:

$$D(\bar{f} \circ \bar{g})(\bar{x}_0) = D\bar{f}(\bar{y}_0) D\bar{g}(\bar{x}_0)$$

MATLAB will directly apply the chain rule when instructed to differentiate composite functions.

Let us take for example $f(x,y) = x^2 + y$ and $\bar{h}(u) = (\sin(3u), \cos(8u))$. If $g(x,y) = \bar{f}(\bar{h}(u))$ we calculate the Jacobian of g at $(0,0)$ as follows.

```
>> syms x y u
>> f = x ^ 2 + y

f =

x ^ 2 + y
```

```
>> h = [sin(3*u), cos(8*u)]

h =

[sin(3*u), cos(8*u)]

>> g = compose (h, f)

g =

[sin(3*x^2 + 3*y), cos(8*x^2 + 8*y)]

>> J = jacobian(g,[x,y])

J =

[6 * x * cos(3*x^2 + 3*y), 3 * cos(3*x^2 + 3*y)]
[- 16 * x * sin(8*x^2 + 8*y), - 8 * sin(8*x^2 + 8*y)]

>> H = subs(J,{x,y},{0,0})

H =

        0       3
        0       0
```

7.9 The Implicit Function Theorem

Consider the vector function $\bar{F}: A \subset \mathbb{R}^{n+m} \to \mathbb{R}^m$ where A is an open subset of $\mathbb{R}^{n+m}$

$$(\bar{x},\bar{y}) \xrightarrow{\bar{F}} [F_1(\bar{x},\bar{y}),...,F_m(\bar{x},\bar{y})]$$

If F_i ($i = 1, 2,..., m$) are differentiable with continuous derivatives up to order r and the Jacobian matrix $J = \partial (F_1,..., F_m) / \partial (y_1,..., y_m)$ has non-zero determinant at a point $(\bar{x}_0,\bar{y}_0)$ such that $\bar{F}(\bar{x}_0,\bar{y}_0) = 0$, then there is an open $U \subset \mathbb{R}^n$ containing $\bar{x}_0$ and an open $V \subset \mathbb{R}^m$ containing to $\bar{y}_0$ and a single-valued function $\bar{f}: U \to V$ such that $\bar{F}[\bar{x},\bar{f}(\bar{x})] = \bar{0} \ \forall x \in U$ and $\bar{f}$ is differentiable of order r with continuous derivatives.

This theorem guarantees the existence of certain derivatives of implicit functions. MATLAB allows differentiation of implicit functions and offers the results in those cases where the hypothesis of the theorem are met.

As an example we will show that near the point $(x, y, u, v) = (1,1,1,1)$ the following system has a unique solution:

$$xy + yvu^2 = 2$$
$$xu^3 + y^2v^4 = 2$$

where u and v are functions of x and y ($u = u(x, y)$, $v = v(x, y)$).

First, we check if the hypothesis of the implicit function theorem are met at the point $(1,1,1,1)$.

The functions are differentiable and have continuous derivatives. We need to show that the corresponding Jacobian determinant is non-zero at the point $(1,1,1,1)$.

```
>> clear all
>> syms x y u v
>> f = x * y + y * v * u ^ 2-2

f =

v * y * u ^ 2 + x * y - 2

>> g = x * u ^ 3 + y ^ 2 * v ^ 4-2

g =

x * u ^ 3 + v ^ 4 * y ^ 2 - 2

>> J = simplify (jacobian([f,g],[u,v]))

J =

[2 * u * v * y, u ^ 2 * y]
[3 * u ^ 2 * x, 4 * v ^ 3 * y ^ 2]

>> D = det (subs(J,{x,y,u,v},{1,1,1,1}))

D =

5
```

7.10 The Inverse Function Theorem

Consider the vector function $\overline{f}: U \subset R^n \to R^n$ where U is an open subset of R^n

$$(x_1, x_2, \ldots, x_n) \to [f_1(x_1, x_2, \ldots, x_n), \ldots, f_n(x_1, x_2, \ldots, x_n)]$$

and assume it is differentiable with continuous derivative.

If there is an $\overline{x}_0$ such that $|J| = |\partial(f_1,\ldots,f_n) / \partial(x_1,\ldots,x_n)| \neq 0$ at x_0, then there is an open set A containing $\overline{x}_0$ and an open set B containing $\overline{f}(\overline{x}_0)$ such that $\overline{f}(A) = B$ and $\overline{f}$ has an inverse function $\overline{f}^{-1}: B \to A$ that is differentiable with continuous derivative. In addition we have:

$$D\overline{f}^{-1}(y) = \left[D\overline{f}(\overline{x})\right]^{-1} \text{ and if } J = \partial (f1,\ldots, fn) / \partial (x_1,\ldots, x_n) \text{ then } |J^{-1}| = 1 / |J|.$$

MATLAB automatically performs the calculations related to the inverse function theorem, provided that the assumptions are met.

As an example, we consider the vector function $(u(x, y), v(x, y))$, where:

$$u(x,y) = \frac{x^4 + y^4}{x}, v(x,y) = \sin(x) + \cos(y).$$

We will find the conditions under which the vector function $(x(u,v), y(u,v))$ is invertible, with $x = x(u, v)$ and $y = y(u,v)$, and find the derivative and the Jacobian of the inverse transformation. We will also find its value at the point $(\pi/4, -\pi/4)$.

The conditions that must be met are those described in the hypothesis of the inverse function theorem. The functions are differentiable with continuous derivatives, except perhaps at $x = 0$. Now let us consider the Jacobian of the direct transformation $\partial (u(x, y), v(x,y)) / \partial (x, y)$:

```
>> syms x y
>> J = simple ((jacobian ([(x^4+y^4)/x, sin (x) + cos (y)], [x, y])))

J =

[3 * x ^ 2-1/x ^ 2 * y ^ 4, 4 * y ^ 3/x]
[cos(x),-sin(y)]

>> pretty (det (J))
```

$$
\frac{3 \sin(y) x^4 - \sin(y) y^4 + 4 y^3 \cos(x) x}{x^2}
$$

Therefore, at those points where this expression is non-zero, we can solve for x and y in terms of u and v. In addition, we also must have that $x^1 \neq 0$.

We calculate the derivative of the inverse function. Its value is the inverse of the initial Jacobian matrix and its determinant is the reciprocal of the determinant of the initial Jacobian matrix:

```
>> I = simple(inv(J));
>> pretty(simple(det(I)))
```

$$
\frac{x^2}{3 \sin(y) x^4 - \sin(y) y^4 + 4 y^3 \cos(x) x}
$$

Observe that the determinant of the Jacobian of the inverse vector function is indeed the reciprocal of the determinant of the Jacobian of the original function.

We now find the value of the inverse at the point $(\pi/4, -\pi/4)$:

```
>> numeric(subs(subs(determ(I),π/4,'x'),-π/4,'y'))

ans =

    0.38210611216717

>> numeric(subs(subs(symdiv(1,determ(J)),π/4,'x'),-π/4,'y'))

ans =

    0.38210611216717
```

Again these results confirm that the determinant of the Jacobian of the inverse function is the reciprocal of the determinant of the Jacobian of the function.

7.11 The Change of Variables Theorem

The change of variable theorem is another key tool in multivariable differential analysis. Its applications extend to any problem in which it is necessary to transform variables.

Suppose we have a function $f(x,y)$ that depends on the variables x and y, and that meets all the conditions of differentiation and continuity necessary for the inverse function theorem to hold. We introduce new variables u and v, relating to the above, regarding them as functions $u = u(x,y)$ and $v = v(x,y)$, so that u and v also fulfil the necessary conditions of differentiation and continuity (described by the inverse function theorem) to be able to express x and y as functions of u and v: $x = x(u,v)$ and $y = y(u,v)$.

Under the above conditions, it is possible to express the initial function f as a function of the new variables u and v using the expression:

$$f(u,v) = f(x(u,v), y(u,v))|J| \text{ where } J \text{ is the Jacobian } \partial(x(u,v), y(u,v)) / \partial(u,v).$$

The theorem generalizes to vector functions of n components.

As an example we consider the function $f(x,y) = e^{-(x+y)}$ and the transformation $u = u(x,y) = x + y$, $v = v(x,y) = x$ to finally find $f(u,v)$.

We calculate the inverse transformation and its Jacobian to apply the change of variables theorem:

```
>> syms x y u v
>> [x, y] = solve('u = x+y,v = x','x','y')

x =

v

y =

u-v

>> jacobian([v,u-v],[u,v])

ans =

[0, 1]
[1, - 1]

>> f = exp(x-y);
>> pretty (simple (subs(f,{x,y},{v,u-v}) * abs (det (jacobian ()))
   ((([v, u-v], [u, v])))
```

$$\exp(2\ v-u)$$

The requested function is $f(u,v) = e^{2v-u}$.

7.12 Series Expansions in Several Variables

The familiar concept of a power series representation of a function of one variable can be generalized to several variables. *Taylor's theorem for several variables theorem* reads as follows:

Let $f : R^n \to R$, $(x_1,...,x_n) \to f(x_1,...,x_n)$, be differentiable k times with continuous partial derivatives.

The Taylor series expansion of order k of $f(\bar{x})$ at the point $\bar{a} = (a_1, ..., a_n)$ is as follows:

$$f(\bar{x}) = f(\bar{a}) + \sum_{i=1}^{n} \frac{\partial f}{\partial x_i}(\bar{a}) t_i + \frac{1}{2!} \sum_{i=1}^{n} \sum_{j=1}^{n} \frac{\partial^2 f}{\partial x_i \partial x_j}(\bar{a}) t_i t_j +$$

$$\frac{1}{3!} \sum_{i=1}^{n} \sum_{j=1}^{n} \sum_{k=1}^{n} \frac{\partial^3 f}{\partial x_i \partial x_j \partial x_k}(\bar{a}) t_i t_j t_k + ... + R(k+1)$$

Here $\bar{x} = (x_1, x_2, ..., x_n), \vec{a} = (a_1, a_2, ..., a_n), t_i = x_i - a_i (i = 1, 2, ..., n)$.
R = remainder.
Normally, the series are given up to order 2.
As an example we find the Taylor series up to order 2 of the following function at the point (1,0):

$$f(x,y) = e^{(x-1)^2} \cos(y)$$

```
>> pretty(simplify(subs(f,{x,y},{1,0})+subs(diff(f,x),{x,y},{1,0})*(x-1)
+subs(diff(f,y),{x,y},{1,0})*(y)+1/2*(subs(diff(f,x,2),{x,y},{1,0})*
(x-1)^2+subs(diff(f,x,y),{x,y},{1,0})*(x-1)*(y)+ subs(diff(f,y,2),{x,y},{1,0})* (y)^2)))
```

```
              2
       2     y
 (x - 1)  -  --  + 1
              2
```

7.13 Vector Fields. Curl, Divergence and the Laplacian

The most common concepts used in the study of vector fields are directly treatable by MATLAB and are summarized below.

Definition of gradient: If $h = f(x,y,z)$, then the gradient of f, which is denoted by $\Delta f(x,y,z)$, is the vector:

$$Grad(f) = \Delta f(x,y,z) = \frac{\partial f(x,y,z)}{\partial x} i + \frac{\partial f(x,y,z)}{\partial y} j + \frac{\partial f(x,y,z)}{\partial z} k$$

Definition of a scalar potential of a vector field: A vector field $\bar{F}$ is called conservative if there is a differentiable function f such that $\bar{F} = \Delta f$. The function f is known as a scalar potential function for $\bar{F}$.

Definition of the curl of a vector field: The curl of a vector field $F(x,y,z) = Mi + Nj + Pk$ is the following:

$$curl\, F(x,y,z) = \Delta \times F(x,y,z) = \left(\frac{\partial P}{\partial y} - \frac{\partial N}{\partial z}\right) i - \left(\frac{\partial P}{\partial x} - \frac{\partial M}{\partial z}\right) j + \left(\frac{\partial N}{\partial x} - \frac{\partial M}{\partial y}\right) k$$

Definition of a vector potential of a vector field: A vector field F is a vector potential of another vector field G if $F = curl\,(G)$.

Definition of the divergence of a vector field: The divergence of the vector field $F(x,y,z) = Mi + Nj + Pk$ is the following:

$$diverge\, F(x,y,z) = \Lambda \bullet F(x,y,z) = \frac{\partial M}{\partial x} + \frac{\partial N}{\partial y} + \frac{\partial P}{\partial z}$$

Definition of the Laplacian: The Laplacian is the differential operator defined by:

$$Laplacian = \Delta^2 = \Delta \bullet \Delta = \frac{\partial^2}{\partial x^2} + \frac{\partial^2}{\partial y^2} + \frac{\partial^2}{\partial z^2}$$

As a first example, we calculate gradient and Laplacian of the function:

$$w = \frac{1}{\sqrt{1-x^2-y^2-z^2}}$$

```
>> gradient = simplify([diff(f,x), diff(f,y), diff(f,z)])

gradient =

[x /(-x^2-y^2-z^2 + 1) ^(3/2), y /(-x^2-y^2-z^2 + 1) ^(3/2), z /(-x^2-y^2-z^2 + 1) ^(3/2)]

>> pretty (gradient)

+-                                                                      -+
|           x                      y                      z              |
|  --------------------- ,  --------------------- ,  ---------------------  |
|            3                        3                        3         |
|            -                        -                        -         |
|            2                        2                        2         |
|     2    2    2              2    2    2              2    2    2       |
|  (- x  - y  - z  + 1)     (- x  - y  - z  + 1)     (- x  - y  - z  + 1)  |
+-                                                                      -+

>> Laplacian = simplify ([diff(f,x,2) + diff(f,y,2) + diff(f,z,2)])

Laplacian =

3 /(-x^2-y^2-z^2 + 1) ^(5/2)

>> pretty (Laplacian)

              3
   ---------------------
              5
              -
              2
      2    2    2
   (- x  - y  - z  + 1)
```

As a second example, we calculate the curl and the divergence of the vector field:

$$\overline{F}(x,y,z) = \tan^{-1}\frac{x}{y}\,\overline{i} + \ln\sqrt{x^2+y^2}\,\overline{j} + \overline{k}.$$

```
>> M = atan (x/y)

M =

atan (x/y)
```

```
>> N = log (sqrt(x^2+y^2))

N =

log ((x^2 + y^2) ^(1/2))

>> P = 1

P =
    1

>> Curl = simplify ([diff(P,y)-diff(N,z), diff(P,x)-diff(M,z), diff(N,x)-diff(M,y)])

Curl =

[0, 0, (2 * x) /(x^2 + y^2)]

>> pretty (Curl)

  +-              -+
  |         2 x    |
  |  0, 0, ------- |
  |         2  2   |
  |        x  + y  |
  +-              -+

>> Divergence = simplify (diff(M,x) + diff(N,y) + diff(P,z))

Divergence =

(2 * y) /(x^2 + y^2)

>> pretty (divergence)

    2 y
  -------
   2   2
  x + y
```

Spherical, Cylindrical and Rectangular Coordinates

MATLAB allows you to easily convert cylindrical and spherical coordinates to rectangular, cylindrical to spherical and their inverse transformations. As the cylindrical and spherical coordinates, we have the following:

In a *cylindrical coordinate* system, a point P in the space is represented by a triplet (r, θ, z), where:

      r is the distance from the origin (O) to the projection P' of P in the XY plane

      θ is the angle between the X axis and the segment OP'

      z is the distance PP'

In a *spherical coordinate* system, a point P in the space is represented by a triplet (ρ, θ, ϕ), where:

r is the distance from P to the origin

θ is the same angle as the one used in cylindrical coordinates

φ is the angle between the positive Z axis and the segment OP

The following conversion equations are easily found:
Cylindrical to rectangular:

$$x = r\cos\theta$$
$$y = r\sin\theta$$
$$z = z$$

Rectangular to cylindrical:

$$r = \sqrt{x^2 + y^2}$$

$$\theta = \tan^{-1}\frac{y}{x}$$

$$z = z$$

Spherical to rectangular:

$$x = \rho\sin\phi\cos\theta$$
$$y = \rho\sin\phi\sin\theta$$
$$z = \rho\cos\phi$$

Rectangular to spherical:

$$\rho = \sqrt{x^2 + y^2 + z^2}$$

$$\theta = \tan^{-1}\frac{y}{x}$$

$$\phi = \cos^{-1}\frac{z}{\sqrt{x^2 + y^2 + z^2}}$$

As a first example we express the surfaces with equations given by $xz = 1$ and $x^2 + y^2 + z^2 = 1$ in spherical coordinates.

```
>> clear all
>> syms x y z r t a
>> f = x * z-1

f =

x * z - 1
```

```
>> equation = simplify (subs (f, {x, y, z}, {r * sin (a) * cos (t), r * sin (a) * sin (t),
r * cos (a)}))

equation =

r ^ 2 * cos (a) * sin (a) * cos (t) - 1

>> pretty (equation)

    2
  r cos (a) sin (a) cos (t) - 1

g =

x ^ 2 + y ^ 2 + z ^ 2 - 1

>> equation1 = simplify (subs (g, {x, y, z}, {r * sin (a) * cos (t), r * sin (a) * sin (t),
r * cos (a)}))

equation1 =

r ^ 2 - 1

>> pretty (equation1)

    2
  r -1
```

EXERCISE 7-1

Study the differentiability of the function:

$$f(x) = x^2 \sin\left(\frac{1}{x}\right) \text{ if } x \neq 0 \text{ and } f(x) = 0 \text{ if } x = 0.$$

We begin by studying the continuity of the function at the point $x = 0$.

```
>> syms x
>> f = x ^ 2 * sin(1/x)

f =

x ^ 2 * sin(1/x)

>> limit(f,x,0, 'right')

ans =

0
```

```
>> limit(f,x,0, 'left')

ans =

0

>>
>> limit(f,x,0)

ans =

0
```

We see that the function is continuous at $x = 0$ because the limit of the function as x tends to zero coincides with the value of the function at zero. It may therefore be differentiable at zero.

We now determine whether the function is differentiable at the point $x = 0$:

```
>> syms h, limit((h^2*sin(1/h) - 0)/h,h,0)

ans =

0
```

Thus, we see that:

$$\lim_{h \to 0} \frac{f(0+h) - f(0)}{h} = f'(0) = 0$$

which indicates that the function f is differentiable at the point $x = 0$.

Let us now see what happens at a non-zero point $x = a$:

```
>> pretty(simple(limit((subs(f,{x},{a+h})-subs(f,{x},{a}))/h,h,a)))

          / 1 \         / 1 \
  4-sin  | --- | -a sin| -- |
          \ 2 a /        \ a /
```

Thus, we conclude that:

$$\lim_{h \to 0} \frac{f(a+h) - f(a)}{h} = f'(a) = 4a\sin\left(\frac{1}{2a}\right) - \sin\left(\frac{1}{a}\right)$$

Thus, we have already found the value of the derivative at any non-zero point $x = a$. We represent the function in the figure below.

```
>> fplot ('x ^ 2 * sin (x)', [-1/10,1/10])
```

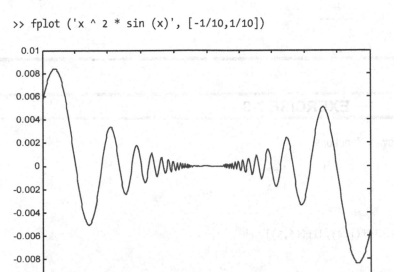

EXERCISE 7-2

Calculate the derivative with respect to x of the following functions:

$$\log(\sin(2x)), \quad x^{\tan(x)}, \quad \frac{4}{3}\sqrt[3]{\frac{x^2-1}{x^2+2}}, \quad \log\left(x+\sqrt{x^2+1}\right).$$

```
>> pretty(simple(diff('log(sin(2*x))','x')))

2 cot(2 x)

>> pretty(simple(diff('x^tanx','x')))

                    tanx
              x         tanx
              ------------
                    x

>> pretty(simple(diff('(4/3)*sqrt((x^2-1)/(x^2+2))','x')))

                        x
           4  ------------------------
                 2      1/2    2      3/2
              (x  - 1)      (x  + 2)
```

```
>> pretty(simple(diff('log(x+(x^2+1)^(1/2))','x')))
```

$$\frac{1}{(x^2 + 1)^{1/2}}$$

EXERCISE 7-3

Calculate the nth derivative of the following functions:

$$\frac{1}{x}, \; e^{x/2}, \frac{1+x}{1+x}$$

```
>> f = '1/x';
>> [diff(f),diff(f,2),diff(f,3),diff(f,4),diff(f,5)]
```

```
ans =
-1/x ^ 2   2/x ^ 3   -6/x ^ 4   24/x ^ 5   -120/x ^ 6
```

We begin to see the pattern emerging, so the nth derivative is given by

$$\frac{(-1)^n n!}{x^{n+1}}.$$

```
>> f = 'exp(x/2)';
>> [diff(f),diff(f,2),diff(f,3),diff(f,4),diff(f,5)]
```

```
ans =

1/2*exp(1/2*x)   1/4*exp(1/2*x)   1/8*exp(1/2*x)   1/16*exp(1/2*x   1/32*exp(1/2*x)
```

Thus the nth derivative is $\frac{e^{x/2}}{2^n}$.

```
>> f = '(1+x)/(1-x)';
>> [simple(diff(f)),simple(diff(f,2)),simple(diff(f,3)),simple(diff(f,4))]
```

```
ans =

2 /(-1+x) ^ 2-4 /(-1+x) ^ 3 12 /(-1+x) ^ 4-48 /(-1+x) ^ 5
```

Thus, the nth derivative is equal to $\frac{2(n!)}{(1-x)^{n+1}}$.

EXERCISE 7-4

Find the equation of the tangent to the curve:

$$f(x) = 2x^3 + 3x^2 - 12x + 7 \text{ at } x = -1.$$

Also find the x for which the tangents to the curve $g(x) = \dfrac{x^2 - x - 4}{x - 1}$ are horizontal and vertical. Find the asymptotes.

```
>> f ='2 * x ^ 3 + 3 * x ^ 2-12 * x + 7';
>> g = diff (f)

g =

6*x^2+6*x-12

>> subs(g,-1)

ans =

-12

>> subs(f,-1)

ans =

20
```

We see that the slope of the tangent line at the point $x = -1$ is -12, and the function has value 20 at $x = -1$. Therefore the equation of the tangent to the curve at the point (–1,20) will be:

$$y - 20 = -12 (x - (-1))$$

We graphically represent the curve and its tangent on the same axes.

```
>> fplot('[2*x^3+3*x^2-12*x+7, 20-12*(x - (-1))]',[-4,4])
```

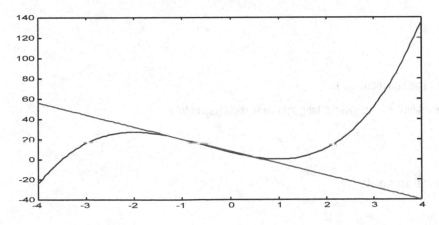

To calculate the horizontal tangent to the curve $y = f(x)$ at $x = x0$, we find the values $x0$ for which the slope of the tangent is zero $(f'(x0) = 0)$. The equation of this tangent will therefore be $y = f(x0)$.

To calculate the vertical tangents to the curve $y = f(x)$ at $x = x0$, we find the values $x0$ which make the slope of the tangent infinite $(f'(x0) = \infty)$. The equation of this tangent will then be $x = x0$:

```
>> g ='(x^2-x+4) /(x-1)'
>> solve(diff(g))

ans =

[ 3]
[-1]

>> subs(g,3)

ans =

5

>> subs(g,-1)

ans =

-3
```

The two horizontal tangents have equations:

$y = g'[-1] (x+1) - 3$, that is, $y = -3$.

$y = g'[3] (x-3) + 5$, that is, $y = 5$.

The horizontal tangents are not asymptotes because the corresponding values of $x0$ are finite (-1 and 3).

We now consider the vertical tangents. To do this, we calculate the values of x that make $g'(x)$ infinite (i.e. values for which the denominator of g' is zero, but does not cancel with the numerator):

```
>> solve('x-1')

ans =

1
```

Therefore, the vertical tangent has equation $x = 1$.

For $x = 1$, the value of $g(x)$ is infinite, so the vertical tangent is a vertical asymptote.

```
subs(g,1)
Error, division by zero
```

Indeed, the line $x = 1$ is a vertical asymptote.

As $\lim\limits_{x \to \infty} g(x) = \infty$, there are no horizontal asymptotes.

Now let us see if there are any oblique asymptotes:

```
>> syms x,limit(((x^2-x+4)/(x-1))/x,x,inf)

ans =

1

>> syms x,limit(((x^2-x+4)/(x-1) - x)/x,x,inf)

ans =

0
```

Thus, there is an oblique asymptote $y = x$.

We now graph the curve with its asymptotes and tangents:

On the same axes (see the figure below) we graph the curve whose equation is $g(x) = (x^2-x + 4)/(x-1)$, the horizontal tangents with equations $a(x) = -3$ and $b(x) = 5$, the oblique asymptote with equation $c(x) = x$ and the horizontal and vertical asymptotes (using the default command *fplot*):

```
>> fplot('[(x^2-x+4)/(x-1),-3,5,x]',[-10,10,-20,20])
```

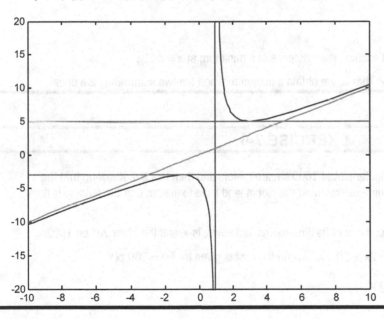

EXERCISE 7-5

Decompose a positive number a as a sum of two summands so that the sum of their cubes is minimal.

Let x be one of the summands. The other will be $a-x$. We need to minimize the sum $x^3 + (a-x)^3$.

```
>> syms x a;
>> f = 'x^3+(a-x)^3'

f =

x^3+(a-x)^3
>> solve(diff(f,'x'))

ans =

1/2 * a
```

The possible maximum or minimum is at $x = a/2$. We use the second derivative to see that it is indeed a minimum:

```
>> subs(diff(f,'x',2),'a/2')

ans =

3 * a
```

As $a > 0$ (by hypothesis), $4a > 0$, which ensures the existence of a minimum at $x = a/2$.

Therefore $x = a/2$ and $a-x = a-a/2 = a/2$. That is, we obtain a minimum when the two summands are equal.

EXERCISE 7-6

Suppose you want to purchase a rectangular plot of 1600 square meters and then fence it. Knowing that the fence costs 200 cents per meter, what dimensions must the plot of land have to ensure that the fencing is most economical?

If the surface area is 1600 square feet and one of its dimensions, unknown, is x, and the other will be $1600/x$.

The perimeter of the rectangle is $p(x) = 2x + 2(1600/x)$, and the cost is given by $f(x) = 200 \, p(x)$:

```
>> f ='200 * (2 * x + 2 *(1600/x))'

f =

200 * (2 * x + 2 *(1600/x))
```

This is the function to minimize:

```
>> solve (diff (f))

ans =

[40]
[-40]
```

The possible maximum and minimum are presented for $x = 40$ and $x = -40$. We use the second derivative to determine their nature:

```
>> [subs (diff(f,2), 40), subs (diff(f,2), - 40)]

ans =

20 - 20
```

$x = 40$ is a minimum, and $x = -40$ is a maximum. Thus, one of the sides of the rectangular field is 40 meters, and the other will measure 1,600/40 = 40 meters. Therefore the optimal rectangle is a square with sides of 40 meters.

EXERCISE 7-7

Given the function of two real variables defined by:

$$f(x,y) = \frac{xy}{x^2+y^2} \text{ if } x^2+y^2 \neq 0 \text{ and } f(x,y) = 0 \text{ if } x^2+y^2 = 0$$

calculate the partial derivatives of f at the origin. Study the differentiability of the function.

To find $\partial f / \partial x$ and $\partial f / \partial y$ at the point (0,0), we directly apply the definition of the partial derivative at a point:

```
>> syms x y h k
>> limit((subs(f,{x,y},{h,0})-0)/h,h,0)

ans =

0

>> limit((subs(f,{x,y},{0,k})-0)/k,k,0)

ans =

0
```

We see that the limits of the two previous expressions when $h \to 0$ and $k \to 0$, respectively, are both zero. That is to say:

$$\lim_{h \to 0} \frac{f(h,0) - f(0,0)}{h} = \frac{\partial f}{\partial x}(0,0) = 0$$

$$\lim_{k \to 0} \frac{f(0,k) - f(0,0)}{k} = \frac{\partial f}{\partial y}(0,0) = 0$$

Thus the two partial derivatives have the same value, namely zero, at the origin.

But the function is not differentiable at the origin, because it is not continuous at (0,0), since it has no limit as $(x,y) \to (0,0)$:

```
>> syms m
>> limit((m*x)^2/(x^2+(m*x)^2),x,0)

ans =

m^2 /(m^2 + 1)
```

The limit does not exist at (0,0), because if we consider the directional limits with respect to the family of straight lines $y = mx$, the result depends on the parameter m.

EXERCISE 7-8

Given the function:

$$f(x,y) = e^{-\frac{x^2+y^2}{8}} \left(\cos^2(x) + \sin^2(y) \right)$$

calculate:

$$\frac{\partial f}{\partial x}, \frac{\partial f}{\partial y}, \frac{\partial^2 f}{\partial x \partial y}, \frac{\partial^2 f}{\partial x^2}, \frac{\partial^2 f}{\partial y^2}, \frac{\partial^3 f}{\partial x \partial y^2}, \frac{\partial^4 f}{\partial x^2 \partial y^2} \text{ and } \frac{\partial^5 f}{\partial x^3 \partial y^2}$$

and find their values at the point $(\pi/3, \pi/6)$.

```
>> f = exp (-(x^2+y^2)/8) * (cos (x) ^ 2 + sin (y) ^ 2)

f =

>> (cos (x) ^ 2 + sin (y) ^ 2) /exp(x^2/8 + y^2/8)

>> pretty(simple(diff(f,x)))
```

$$- \frac{x \cos^2(x) + x \sin^2(y) + 4 \sin(2x)}{4 \exp\left(\frac{x^2}{8} + \frac{y^2}{8}\right)}$$

```
>> pretty (simple (diff(f,y)))
```

$$- \frac{y \cos^2(x) + y \sin^2(y) - 4 - \sin(2y)}{4 \exp\left(\frac{x^2}{8} + \frac{y^2}{8}\right)}$$

```
>> pretty(simple(diff(diff(f,x),y)))
```

$$\frac{x\,y \cos^2(x) + x\,y^{(y)} - 4x \sin(2y) + 4y \sin(2x)}{16 \exp\left(\frac{x^2}{8} + \frac{y^2}{8}\right)}$$

```
>> pretty(simple(diff(diff(f,x),x)))
```

$$\frac{2 \cos(2y) - 34(2x) \cos + 8x \sin(2x) + \dfrac{x^2 \cos(2x)}{2} - \dfrac{x^2 \cos(2y)}{2} + x2 - 4}{16 \exp\left(\frac{x^2}{8} + \frac{y^2}{8}\right)}$$

```
>> pretty (simple (diff (diff(f,y), y)))
```

$$- \frac{2 \cos(2x) - 34 \cos(2y) + 8y \sin(2y) - \dfrac{y^2 \cos(2x)}{2} + \dfrac{y^2 \cos(2y)}{2} - y^2 + 4}{16 \exp\left(\frac{x^2}{8} + \frac{y^2}{8}\right)}$$

```
>> pretty(simple(diff(diff(diff(f,x),y),y)))
```

$$
(8 x + 32 \sin (2 x) + 4 x (2 x) \cos - 68 x \cos(2 y) - 8 y \sin(2 x) - 2 x y +)
$$

$$
16 x y \sin(2 y) - x y \cos^2 (2 x) + x y \cos(2 y)) / \left(128 \exp\left(\frac{x^2}{8} + \frac{y^2}{8} \right) \right)
$$

```
>> pretty(simple(diff(diff(diff(diff(f,x),x),y),y)))
```

$$
(272 \cos^2 (2 x) - 272 \cos(2 y) + 2 x y - 64 x \sin (2 x) + 64 y \sin(2 y) - 4 x \cos(2 x) +)
$$

$$
68 x^2 \cos(2 y) - 68 y^2 \cos (2 x) + 4 y^2 \cos(2 y) - 8 x^2 - 8 y^2 + x^2 y^2 \cos (2 x) -
$$

$$
X^2 y^2 (\cos(2 y) + 16 x y \sin(2 x) - 16 x \sin(2 y) + 32) / \left(512 \exp\left(\frac{x^2}{8} + \frac{y^2}{8} \right) \right)
$$

```
>> pretty(simple(diff(diff(diff(diff(diff(f,x),x),x),y),y)))
```

$$
-(96 x + 2432 \sin (2 x) + 2 x^3 y^2 + 816 x \cos^2 (2 x) - 816 x \cos(2 y) - 4 x^3 \cos(2 x) +)
$$

$$
68 x^3 \cos(2 y) - 96 x \sin^2 (2 x) - 608 y^2 \sin(2 x) - 24 x^3 y^2 - 8 x^3 + x^3 y^2 \cos^2 (2 x) -
$$

$$
x^3 y^2 \cos(2 y) + 24 x^2 y \sin(2 x) + 192 x y^2 \sin(2 y) - 204 x y^2 \cos^2 (2 x) +
$$

$$
12 x y^2 \cos(2 y) - 16 x y^3 \sin(2 y)) / \left(2048 \exp\left(\frac{x^2}{8} + \frac{y^2}{8} \right) \right)
$$

The values of the previous partial derivatives at the point $(\pi/3, \pi/6)$ are calculated as follows (from last to first):

```
>> subs(diff(diff(diff(diff(diff(f,x),x),x),y),y),{x,y},{π/3,π/6})
```

```
ans =

-0.5193
```

```
>> subs(diff(diff(diff(diff(f,x),x),y),y),{x,y},{π/3,π/6})

ans =

-0.3856

>> subs(diff(diff(diff(f,x),y),y),{x,y},{π/3,π/6})

ans =

0.0250

>> subs(diff(diff(f,y),y),{x,y},{π/3,π/6})

ans =

0.5534

>> subs(diff(diff(f,x),x),{x,y},{π/3,π/6})

ans =

1.1481

>> subs(diff(diff(f,x),y),{x,y},{π/3,π/6})

ans =

-0.0811

>> subs(diff(f,y),{x,y},{π/3,π/6})

ans =

0.6745

>> subs(diff(f,x),{x,y},{π/3,π/6})

ans =

-0.8399
```

EXERCISE 7-9

Find and classify the extreme points of the function

$$f(x,y) = 120x^3 - 30x^4 + 18x^5 + 5x^6 + 30xy^2.$$

We begin by finding the possible extreme points. To do so, we equate each of the partial derivatives of the function with respect to each of its variables to zero (i.e. the components of the gradient vector of f) and solve the resulting system in three variables:

```
>> syms x y
>> f = -120 * x ^ 3-30 * x ^ 4 + 18 * x ^ 5 + 5 * x ^ 6 + 30 * x * y ^ 2

f =

5 * x ^ 6 + 18 * x ^ 5-30 * x ^ 4-120 * x ^ 3 + 30 * x * y ^ 2

>> [x y] = solve (diff(f,x), diff(f,y), x, y)

x =

 0
 2
-2
-3

y =

0
0
0
0
```

So the possible extreme points are: (− 2,0), (2,0), (0,0) and (− 3,0).

We will analyze what kind of extreme points these are. To do this, we calculate the Hessian matrix and express it as a function of x and y.

```
>> clear all
>> syms x y
>> f = -120*x^3-30*x^4+18*x^5+5*x^6+30*x*y^2

f =

5*x^6 + 18*x^5 - 30*x^4 - 120*x^3 + 30*x*y^2
```

```
>> H = simplify([diff(f,x,2),diff(diff(f,x),y);diff(diff(f,y),x),diff(f,y,2)])

H =

[- 30 * x *(-5*x^3-12*x^2 + 12*x + 24), 60 * y]
[                               60*y, 60*x]
```

Now we calculate the value of the determinant of the Hessian matrix at the possible extreme points.

```
>> det(subs(H,{x,y},{0,0}))

ans =

        0
```

The origin turns out to be a degenerate point, as the determinant of the Hessian matrix is zero at (0,0).

We will now look at the point (- 2,0).

```
>> det(subs(H,{x,y},{-2,0}))

ans =

        57600
```

```
>> eig(subs(H,{x,y},{-2,0}))

ans =

        -480
        -120
```

The Hessian matrix at the point (- 2,0) has non-zero determinant, and is also negative definite, because all its eigenvalues are negative. Therefore, the point (- 2,0) is a maximum of the function.

We will now analyze the point (2,0).

```
>> det(subs(H,{x,y},{2,0}))

ans =

        288000
```

```
>> eig(subs(H,{x,y},{2,0}))

ans =

        120
        2400
```

The Hessian matrix at the point (2,0) has non-zero determinant, and is furthermore positive definite, because all its eigenvalues are positive. Therefore, the point (2,0) is a minimum of the function.

We will now analyze the point (- 3,0).

```
>> det(subs(H,{x,y},{-3,0}))

ans =

      -243000

>> eig(subs(H,{x,y},{-3,0}))

ans =

      -180
      1350
```

The Hessian matrix at the point (− 3,0) has non-zero determinant, and, in addition, is neither positive definite nor negative, because it has both positive and negative eigenvalues. Therefore, the point (− 3,0) is a saddle point of the function.

EXERCISE 7-10

Find and classify the extreme points of the function:

$$f(x,y,z) = \sqrt{x^2 + y^2} - z$$

subject to the restrictions: $x^2 + y^2 = 16$ and $x + y + z = 10$.

We first find the Lagrangian L, which is a linear combination of the objective function and the constraints:

```
>> clear all
>> syms x y z L p q
>> f = (x^2+y^2) ^(1/2)-z

f =

(x ^ 2 + y ^ 2) ^ (1/2) - z

>> g1 = x ^ 2 + y ^ 2-16, g2 = x + y + z-10

G1 =

x ^ 2 + y ^ 2-16

G2 =

x + y + z - 10
```

```
>> L = f + p * g1 + q * g2

L =

(x ^ 2 + y ^ 2) ^ (1/2) - z + q *(x + y + z-10) + p *(x^2 + y^2-16)
```

Then, the possible extreme points are found by solving the system obtained by setting the components of the gradient vector of L to zero, that is, $\nabla L(x_1, x_2, \ldots, x_n, \lambda) = (0, 0, \ldots, 0)$. Which translates into:

```
>> [x, y z, p, q] = solve (diff(L,x), diff(L,y), diff(L,z), diff(L,p), diff(L,q), x, y z, p, q)

x =

-2 ^(1/2)/8 - 1/8

y =

1

z =

2 * 2 ^(1/2)

p =

2 * 2 ^(1/2)

q =

10 - 4 * 2 ^(1/2)
```

Matching all the partial derivatives to zero and solving the resulting system, we find the values of $x_1, x_2, \ldots, x_n, \lambda_1, \lambda_2, \ldots, \lambda_k$ corresponding to possible maxima and minima.

We already have one possible extreme point:

$(-(1+\sqrt{2})/8, 1, 2\sqrt{2})$

We need to determine what kind of extreme point this is. To this end, we substitute it into the objective function.

```
>> syms x y z
>> vpa (subs (f, {x, y, z}, {-2 ^(1/2)/8-1/8,1,2*2^(1/2)}))

ans =

-1.7838845579619739822874180390S
```

Thus, at the point $(-(1+\sqrt{2})/8, 1/2\sqrt{2})$ the function has a maximum.

EXERCISE 7-11

Given the role $f(x,y) = 10^{-(x+y)}$ and the transformation u = u(x,y) = 2 x + y, v = v(x,y) = x – y, find f(u,v).

We calculate the inverse transformation and its Jacobian in order to apply the change of variables theorem:

```
>> [x, y] = solve('u=2*x+y,v=x-y','x','y')

x =

u + v/3

y =

u - (2 * v) / 3

>> jacobian([u/3 + v/3,u/3-(2*v)/3], [u, v])

ans =

[1/3, 1/3]
[1/3, 2/3]

>> f = 10 ^(x-y);
>> pretty (simple (subs(f,{x,y},{u/3 + v/3,u/3-(2*v)/3}) *))
   abs (det (jacobian([u/3 + v/3,u/3-(2*v)/3], [u, v])))

     v
   10
   ---
    3
```

Thus the requested function is f(u,v) = 10 v/3.

```
EXERCISE 7-12
```

Find the Taylor series at the origin, up to order 2, of the function:

$$f(x,y) = e^{x+y^2}$$

```
>> f = exp(x+y^2)

f =

>> pretty (simplify (subs(f,{x,y},{0,0}) + subs (diff(f,x), {x, y}, {0.0}) * (x) + subs
(diff(f,y), {x, y}, {0.0}) * (y) + 1/2 * (subs (diff(f,x,2), {x, y}, {0.0}) * (x) ^ 2 + subs
(diff(f,x,y), {x, y}, {0.0}) * (x) * (y) + subs (diff(f,y,2), {x, y}, {0,0}) * (y) ^ 2)))


    2
    x         2
    -- + x + y  + 1
    2
```

```
EXERCISE 7-13
```

Express in Cartesian coordinates the surface which is given in cylindrical coordinates by $z = r^2 (1 + \sin(t))$.

```
>> syms x y z r t a
>> f = r ^ 2 * (1 + sin (t))

f =

r ^ 2 * (sin (t) + 1)

>> Cartesian = simplify (subs (f, {r, t}, {sqrt(x^2+y^2), bind (y/x)}))

Cartesian =

(x ^ 2 + y ^ 2) * (y / (x *(y^2/x^2 + 1) ^(1/2)) + 1)

>> pretty (Cartesian)

    2    2 /        y           \
  (x  + y ) | ------------- + 1 |
            |   / 2     \1/2    |
            |  | y      |       |
            | x | -- + 1 |      |
            |  | 2      |       |
            \  \ x      /       /
```

EXERCISE 7-14

Find the unit tangent, the unit normal, and the unit binormal vectors of the twisted cubic: $x = t$, $y = t^2$, $z = t^3$.
We begin by restricting the variable t to the real field:

```
>> x = sym('x','real);
```

We define the symbolic vector V as follows:

```
>> syms t, V = [t,t^2,t^3]
```

V =

[t, t ^ 2, t ^ 3]

The tangent vector is calculated by:

```
>> tang = diff(V)
```

tang =

[1, 2 *, 3 * t ^ 2]

The unit tangent vector will be:

```
>> ut = simple (tang/ sqrt (dot(tang,tang)))
```

tu =

[1/(1+4*t^2+9*t^4)^(1/2),2*t/(1+4*t^2+9*t^4)^(1/2),3*t^2/(1+4*t^2+9*t^4)^(1/2)]

To find the unit normal vector we calculuate $((v' \wedge v'') \wedge v') / (|v' \wedge v''| \, |v'|)$:

```
>> v1 = cross(diff(V),diff(V,2));
>> nu = simple(cross(v1,tang)/(sqrt(dot(v1,v1))*sqrt(dot(tang,tang))))
```

nu =

[(-2*t-9*t^3)/(9*t^4+9*t^2+1)^(1/2)/(1+4*t^2+9*t^4)^(1/2),
   (1-9*t^4)/(9*t^4+9*t^2+1)^(1/2)/(1+4*t^2+9*t^4)^(1/2),
 (6*t^3+3*t)/(9*t^4+9*t^2+1)^(1/2)/(1+4*t^2+9*t^4)^(1/2)]

The unit binormal vector is the vector product of the tangent vector and the unit normal vector.

```
>> bu = simple(cross(tu,nu))
```

bu =

```
[3*t^2/(9*t^4+9*t^2+1)^(1/2),-3*t/(9*t^4+9*t^2+1)^(1/2),1/(9*t^4+9*t^2+1)^(1/2)]
```

The unit binormal vector can also be calculated via (v'^v ") / |v'^v" | as follows:

```
>> bu = simple(v1/sqrt(dot(v1,v1)))
```

bu =

```
[3*t^2/(9*t^4+9*t^2+1)^(1/2),-3*t/(9*t^4+9*t^2+1)^(1/2),1/(9*t^4+9*t^2+1)^(1/2)]
```

We have calculated the Frenet frame for a twisted cubic.

CHAPTER 8

■■■

Optimization of Functions of Complex Variables

8.1 Complex Numbers

MATLAB implements a simple way to work with complex numbers in binary form $a+bi$ or $a+bj$, representing the imaginary unit by means of the symbol i or j. Note that it is not necessary to include the product symbol (asterisk) before the imaginary unit, but if it is included, everything still works correctly. It is important, however, that spaces are not introduced between the imaginary unit i and its coefficient.

Complex numbers can have symbolic or numeric real or imaginary parts. Operations are carried out with a precision that is set by the command *format*. Thus, it is possible to work with complex numbers in exact rational format via the command *format rat*.

The common arithmetical operations with complex numbers (sum, difference, product, division and exponentiation) are carried out in the usual way. Examples are shown in Figure 8-1.

```
>> (3+21)+(5-6i)

ans =

  29.0000 - 6.0000i

>> (3+21)-(5-6i)

ans =

  19.0000 + 6.0000i

>> (3+21)*(5-6i)

ans =

  1.2000e+002 -1.4400e+002i

>> (3+21)/(5-6i)

ans =

  1.9672 + 2.3607i

>> (3+21)^(5-6i)

ans =

  7.7728e+006 -1.7281e+006i
```

Figure 8-1.

Obviously, as the real numbers are a subset of the complex numbers, any function of complex variables will also be valid for real variables.

8.2 General Functions of a Complex Variable

MATLAB has a range of preset general functions of a complex variable, which of course will also be valid for real, rational and integer variables. The following sections present the most important examples.

8.2.1 Trigonometric Functions of a Complex Variable

Below is a table summarizing the trigonometric functions of a complex variable and their inverses that are incorporated in MATLAB, illustrated with examples.

Function	Inverse
sin (z) *sine*	**asin (z)** *arc sine*
>> sin(5-6i)	>> asin(1-i)
ans =	ans =
-1 9343e + 002-5 7218e + 001i	0.6662 - 1.0613i
cos (z) *cosine*	**acos (z)** *arc cosine*
>> cos (3 + 4i)	>> acos (-i)
ans =	ans =
-27.0349 - 3.8512i	1.5708 + 0.8814i
tan (z) *tangent*	**atan(z)** and **atan2(imag(z), real(z))** *arc tangent*
>> tan(pi/4i)	>> atan(-pi*i)
ans =	ans =
0 - 0.6558i	1.5708 - 0.3298i
csc (z) *cosecant*	**acsc (z)** *arc cosecant*
>> csc(1-i)	>> acsc(2i)
ans =	ans =
0.6215 + 0.3039i	0 - 0.4812i
sec (z) *secant*	**asec (z)** *arc secant*
>> sec(-i)	>> asec(0.6481+0i)
ans =	ans =
0.6481	0 + 0.9999i
cot (z) *cotangent*	**acot (z)** *arc cotangent*
>> cot(-j)	>> acot(1-6j)
ans =	ans =
0 + 1.3130i	0.0277 + 0.1635i

8.2.2 Hyperbolic Functions of a Complex Variable

Below is a table of hyperbolic functions of a complex variable and their inverses that are incorporated in MATLAB, illustrated with examples.

Function	Inverse
sinh(z) *hyperbolic sine*	**asinh(z)** *arc hyperbolic sine*
>> sinh(1+i)	>> asinh(0.6350 + 1.2985i)
ans =	ans =
0.6350 i 1.2985i	1.0000 + 1.0000i
cosh(z) *hyperbolic cosine*	**acosh(z)** *arc hyperbolic cosine*
>> cosh(1-i)	>> acosh(0.8337 - 0.9889i)
ans =	ans =
0.8337 0.9889i	1.0000 1.0000i

(continued)

Function	Inverse
tanh(z) *hyperbolic tangent*	**atanh(z)** *arc hyperbolic tangent*
>> tanh(3-5i)	>> atanh(3-41)
ans =	ans =
1.0042 + 0.0027i	-0.0263 - 1.5708i
csch(z) *hyperbolic cosecant*	**acsch (z)** *arc hyperbolic cosecant*
>> csch(i)	>> acsch(- 1.1884i)
ans =	ans =
0 - 1.1884i	0 + 1.0000i
sech(z) *hyperbolic secant*	**asech(z)** *arc hyperbolic secant*
>> sech(i^i)	>> asech(5-0i)
ans =	ans =
0.9788	0 + 1.3694i
coth(z) *hyperbolic cotangent*	**acoth(z)** *arc hyperbolic cotangent*
>> coth(9+i)	>> acoth(1-i)
ans =	ans =
1.0000 0.0000i	0.4024 + 0.5536i

8.2.3 Exponential and Logarithmic Functions of a Complex Variable

Below is a table summarizing the exponential and logarithmic functions that are incorporated in MATLAB, illustrated with examples.

Function	Meaning
exp (z)	*Exponential function to base e (e ^ x)*
	>> exp(1-i)
	ans =
	1.4687 - 2.2874i
log (x)	*Base e logarithm of x*
	>> log(1.4687-2.2874i)
	ans =
	1.0000 1.0000i
log10 (x)	*Base 10 logarithm of x*
	>> log10 (100 + 100i)
	ans =
	2.1505 + 0.3411i

(continued)

Function	Meaning
log2 (x)	*Base 2 logarithm of x*
	`>> log2(4-6i)`
	`ans =`
	`2.8502 1.4179i`
pow2 (x)	*Base 2 power function (2^x)*
	`>> pow2(2.8502-1.4179i)`
	`ans =`
	`3.9998. 6.0000i`
sqrt (x)	*Square root of x*
	`>> sqrt(1+i)`
	`ans =`
	`1.0987 + 0.4551i`

8.3 Specific Functions of a Complex Variable

MATLAB incorporates a specific group of functions of a complex variable which allow you to work with moduli, arguments, and real and imaginary parts. Among these features are the following:

Function	Meaning
abs (z)	*The modulus (absolute value) of z*
	`>> abs(12.425-8.263i)`
	`ans =`
	`14.9217`
angle (z)	*The argument of z*
	`>> angle(12.425-8.263i)`
	`ans =`
	`-0.5869`
conj (z)	*The complex conjugate of z*
	`>> conj(12.425-8.263i)`
	`ans =`
	`12.4250 + 8.2630i`
real (z)	*The real part of z*
	`>> real(12.425-8.263i)`
	`ans =`
	`12.4250`

(*continued*)

Function	Meaning

imag (z)	*The imaginary part of z*
	`>> imag(12.425-8.263i)`
	`ans =`
	`-8.2630`

floor (z)	*Applies the floor function to real(z) and imag(z)*
	`>> floor(12.425-8.263i)`
	`ans =`
	`12.0000 9.0000i`

ceil (z)	*Applies the ceiling function to real(z) and imag(z)*
	`>> ceil(12.425-8.263i)`
	`ans =`
	`13.0000 8.0000i`

round (z)	*Applies the round function to real(z) and imag(z)*
	`>> round(12.425-8.263i)`
	`ans =`
	`12.0000 8.0000i`

fix (z)	*Applies the fix function to real(z) and imag(z)*
	`>> fix(12.425-8.263i)`
	`ans =`
	`12.0000 - 8.0000i`

8.4 Basic Functions with Complex Vector Arguments

MATLAB enables you to work with functions of a complex matrix or vector. Of course, these functions are also valid for real variables since the real numbers are included in the complex numbers. Below is a table summarizing the functions of complex vector variables that are incorporated in MATLAB. Later, when the functions of complex matrix variables are tabulated, we will observe that all of them are also valid for vector variables, a vector being a particular case of a matrix.

max (V)	*The maximum component of V. (max is calculated for complex vectors as the complex number with the largest complex modulus (magnitude), computed with max(abs(V)). Then it computes the largest phase angle with max(angle(V)), if necessary.)*

```
>> max([1-i 1+i 3-5i 6i])
ans =
0 + 6.0000i
>> max([1, 0, -23, 12, 16])
ans =
16
```

min (V)	*The minimum component of V. (min is calculated for complex vectors as the complex number with the smallest complex modulus (magnitude), computed with min(abs(V)). Then it computes the smallest phase angle with min(angle(V)), if necessary.)*

```
>> min([1-i 1+i 3-5i 6i])
ans =
1.0 - 1.0000i
>> min([1, 0, -23, 12, 16])
ans =
-23
```

mean (V)	*Average of the components of V.*

```
>> mean([1-i 1+i 3-5i 6i])
ans =
1.2500 + 0.2500i
>> mean([1, 0, -23, 12, 16])
ans =
1.2000
```

median (V)	*Median of the components of V.*

```
>> median([1-i 1+i 3-5i 6i])
ans =
2.0000 2.0000i
>> median([1, 0, -23, 12, 16])
ans =
1
```

(continued)

std (V) *Standard deviation of the components of V.*
```
>> std([1-i 1+i 3-5i 6i])
ans =
4.7434
>> std([1, 0, -23, 12, 16])
ans =
15.1888
```

sort (V) *Sorts the components of V in ascending order. For complex entries the order is by absolute value and argument.*
```
>> sort([1-i 1+i 3-5i 6i])
ans =
Columns 1 through 2
1.0000 - 1.0000i    1.0000 + 1.0000i
Columns 3 through 4
3.0000 - 5.0000i    0 + 6.0000i
>> sort([1, 0, -23, 12, 16])
ans =
-23 0 1 12 16
```

sum (V) *Returns the sum of the components of V.*
```
>> sum([1-i 1+i 3-5i 6i])
ans =
5.0000 + 1.0000i
>> sum([1, 0, -23, 12, 16])
ans =
6
```

prod (V) *Returns the product of the components of V, so, for example, n! = prod(1:n).*
```
>> prod([1-i 1+i 3-5i 6i])
ans =
60.0000 + 36 0000i
>> prod([1, 0, -23, 12, 16])
ans =
0
```

(continued)

cumsum (V)	*Gives the cumulative sums of the components of V.*

```
>> cumsum([1-i 1+i 3-5i 6i])
ans =
Columns 1 through 2
1.0000 - 1.0000i   2.0000
Columns 3 through 4
5.0000 5.0000i 5.0000 + 1.0000i
>> cumsum([1, 0, -23, 12, 16])
ans =
1 1-22 - 10-6
```

cumprod (V)	*Gives the cumulative products of the components of V.*

```
>> cumprod([1-i 1+i 3-5i 6i])
ans =
Columns 1 through 2
1.0000 - 1.0000i   2.0000
Columns 3 through 4
6.0000 - 10.0000i 60.0000 + 36.0000i
>> cumprod([1, 0, -23, 12, 16])
ans =
1    0    0    0    0
```

diff (V)	*Gives the vector of first differences of V ($V_t - V_{t-1}$).*

```
>> diff([1-i 1+i 3-5i 6i])
ans =
0 + 2.0000i   2.0000 - 6.0000i   -3.0000 + 11.0000i
>> diff([1, 0, -23, 12, 16])
ans =
-1-23 35 4
```

gradient (V)	*Gives the gradient of V.*

```
>> gradient([1-i 1+i 3-5i 6i])
ans =
Columns 1 through 3
0 + 2.0000i   1.0000 - 2.0000i   -0.5000 + 2.5000i
Column 4
-3.0000 + 11.0000i
>> gradient([1, 0, -23, 12, 16])
ans =
-1.0000 - 12.0000 6.0000 19.5000 4.0000
```

(*continued*)

del2 (V)	*Gives the Laplacian of V (5-point discrete).*

```
>> del2([1-i 1+i 3-5i 6i])
ans =
Columns 1 through 3
2.2500 - 8.2500i   0.5000 - 2.0000i  -1.2500 + 4.2500i
Column 4
-3.0000 + 10 5000i
>> del2([1, 0, -23, 12, 16])
ans =
-25.5000 - 5.5000 14.5000 - 7.7500 - 30.0000
```

fft (V)	*Gives the discrete Fourier transform of V.*

```
>> fft([1-i 1+i 3-5i 6i])
ans =
Columns 1 through 3
5.0000 + 1.0000i  -7.0000 + 3.0000i   3.0000 -13.0000i
Column 4
3.0000 + 5.0000i
>> fft([1, 0, -23, 12, 16])
ans =
Columns 1 through 3
6.0000 14.8435 +35.7894i -15.3435 -23.8824i
Columns 4 through 5
-15.3435 +23.8824i   14.8435 -35.7894i
```

fft2 (V)	*Gives the two-dimensional discrete Fourier transform of V.*

```
>> fft2([1-i 1+i 3-5i 6i])
ans =
Columns 1 through 3
5.0000 + 1.0000i  -7.0000 + 3.0000i   3.0000 -13.0000i
Column 4
3.0000 + 5.0000i
>> fft2([1, 0, -23, 12, 16])
ans =
Columns 1 through 3
6.0000 14.8435 +35.7894i -15.3435 -23.8824i
Columns 4 through 5
-15.3435 +23.8824i   14.8435 -35.7894i
```

(*continued*)

ifft (V)	*Gives the inverse discrete Fourier transform of V.*

```
>> ifft([1-i 1+i 3-5i 6i])
ans =
Columns 1 through 3
1.2500 + 0.2500i    0.7500 + 1.2500i    0.7500 - 3.2500i
Column 4
-1.7500 + 0.7500i
>> ifft([1, 0, -23, 12, 16])
ans =
Columns 1 through 3
1.2000 2.9687 - 7.1579i  -3.0687 + 4.7765i
Columns 4 through 5
-3.0687 - 4.7765i    2.9687 + 7.1579i
```

ifft2 (V)	*Gives the inverse two-dimensional discrete Fourier transform of V.*

```
>> ifft2([1-i 1+i 3-5i 6i])
ans =
Columns 1 through 3
1.2500 + 0.2500i    0.7500 + 1.2500i    0.7500 - 3.2500i
Column 4
-1.7500 + 0.7500i
>> ifft2([1, 0, -23, 12, 16])
ans =
Columns 1 through 3
1.2000 2.9687 - 7.1579i  -3.0687 + 4.7765i
Columns 4 through 5
-3.0687 - 4.7765i    2.9687 + 7.1579i
```

8.5 Basic Functions with Complex Matrix Arguments

The functions given in the above table also support complex matrices as arguments, in which case the result is a row vector whose components are the results of applying the function to each column of the matrix. Let us not forget that these functions are also valid for real variables, since the set of real numbers is a subset of the set of complex numbers.

max (Z) *Returns a row vector indicating the maximum component of each column of the matrix Z. (max is calculated for complex vectors V as the complex number with the largest complex modulus (magnitude), computed with max(abs(V)). Then it computes the largest phase angle with max(angle(V)), if necessary.)*

```
>> Z = [1-i 3i 5;-1+i 0 2i;6-5i 8i -7]
Z =
  1.0000 - 1.0000i        0 + 3.0000i    5.0000
 -1.0000 + 1.0000i        0                   0 + 2.0000i
  6.0000 - 5.0000i        0 + 8.0000i   -7.0000
>> Z = [1-i 3i 5-12i;-1+i 0 2i;6-5i 8i -7+6i]
Z =
  1.0000 - 1.0000i        0 + 3.0000i    5.0000 - 12.0000i
 -1.0000 + 1.0000i        0                   0 +  2.0000i
  6.0000 - 5.0000i        0 + 8.0000i   -7.0000 +  6.0000i
>> max(Z)
ans =
  6.0000 - 5.0000i        0 + 8.0000i    5.0000 - 12.0000i
>> Z1 = [1 3 5;-1 0 2;6 8 -7]
Z1 =
   1    3    5
  -1    0    2
   6    8   -7
>> max(Z1)
ans =
   6    8    5
```

min (Z) *Returns a row vector indicating the minimum component of each column of the matrix Z. (min is calculated for complex vectors V as the complex number with the smallest complex modulus (magnitude), computed with min(abs(V)). Then it computes the smallest phase angle with min(angle(V)), if necessary.)*

```
>> min(Z)
ans =
  1.0000 - 1.0000i        0                   0 + 2.0000i
>> min(Z1)
ans =
  -1    0   -7
```

(*continued*)

mean (Z)	*Returns a row vector indicating the mean of the components of each column of Z.*

```
>> mean(Z)
ans =
2.0000 - 1.6667i        0 + 3.6667i  -0.6667 - 1.3333i
>> mean(Z1)
ans =
2.0000    3.6667         0
```

median (Z)	*Returns a row vector indicating the median of the components of each column of Z.*

```
>> median(Z)
ans =
-1.0000 + 1.0000i        0 + 3.0000i  -7.0000 + 6.0000i
>> median(Z1)
ans =
1     3     2
```

std (Z)	*Returns a row vector indicating the standard deviation of the components of each column of Z.*

```
>> std(Z)
ans =
4.7258    4.0415    11.2101
>> std(Z1)
ans =
3.6056    4.0415    6.2450
```

sort (Z)	*Sorts the components of the columns of Z in ascending order. For complex entries the order is by absolute value and argument.*

```
>> sort(Z)
ans =
 1.0000 - 1.0000i        0                 0 +  2.0000i
-1.0000 + 1.0000i        0 + 3.0000i  -7.0000 +  6.0000i
 6.0000 - 5.0000i        0 + 8.0000i   5.0000 - 12.0000i
>> sort(Z1)
ans =
-1     0    -7
 1     3     2
 6     8     5
```

(continued)

sum (Z)   *Returns a row vector indicating the sum of the components of each column of Z.*

```
>> sum(Z)
ans =
6.0000 - 5.0000i       0 + 11.0000i  -2.0000 - 4.0000i
>> sum(Z1)
ans =
6    11    0
```

prod (Z)   *Returns a row vector indicating the product of the components of each column of Z.*

```
> prod(Z)
ans =
1.0e+002 *
0.1000 + 0.1200i          0            -2.2800 + 0.7400i
>> prod(Z1)
ans =
-6     0    -70
```

cumsum (Z)   *Returns a matrix indicating the cumulative sums of the elements in the columns of Z.*

```
>> cumsum(Z)
ans =
1.0000 - 1.0000i       0 +  3.0000i    5.0000 - 12.0000i
     0                 0 +  3.0000i    5.0000 - 10.0000i
6.0000 - 5.0000i       0 + 11.0000i   -2.0000 -  4.0000i
>> cumsum(Z1)
ans =
1     3     5
0     3     7
6    11     0
```

cumprod(Z)   *Returns a matrix indicating the cumulative products of the elements in the columns of Z.*

```
>> cumprod(Z)
ans =
1.0e+002 *
0.0100 - 0.0100i       0 + 0.0300i    0.0500 - 0.1200i
     0 + 0.0200i       0              0.2400 + 0.1000i
0.1000 + 0.1200i       0             -2.2800 + 0.7400i
>> cumprod(Z1)
ans =
1     3     5
-1     0    10
-6     0   -70
```

(*continued*)

diff (Z)   *Returns the matrix of first differences of the components of the columns of Z.*

```
>> diff(Z)
ans =
-2.0000 + 2.0000i       0 - 3.0000i  -5.0000 + 14.0000i
 7.0000 - 6.0000i       0 + 8.0000i  -7.0000 +  4.0000i
>> diff(Z1)
ans =
-2    -3    -3
 7     8    -9
```

gradient (Z)   *Returns the matrix of gradients for the columns of Z.*

```
>> gradient(Z)
ans =
-1.0000 +  4.0000i   2.0000 - 5.5000i   5.0000 - 15.0000i
 1.0000 -  1.0000i   0.5000 + 0.5000i        0 +  2.0000i
-6.0000 + 13.0000i  -6.5000 + 5.5000i  -7.0000 -  2.0000i
>> gradient(Z1)
ans =
2.0000  2.0000   2.0000
1.0000  1.5000   2.0000
2.0000 -6.5000 -15.0000
```

del2 (Z)   *Returns the matrix indicating the Laplacian of the columns of Z (5-point discrete).*

```
>> del2(Z)
ans =
3.7500 - 6.7500i   1.5000 - 2.0000i   1.0000 - 7.2500i
2.0000 - 1.2500i  -0.2500 + 3.5000i  -0.7500 - 1.7500i
2.0000 - 5.7500i  -0.2500 - 1.0000i  -0.7500 + 6.2500i
>> del2(Z1)
ans =
 2.2500    2.7500   -1.5000
 2.5000    3.0000   -1.2500
-2.0000   -1.5000   -5.7500
```

(continued)

fft (Z)	*Returns the matrix with discrete Fourier transforms of the columns of Z.*

```
>> fft(Z)
ans =
  6.0000 - 5.0000i        0 + 11.0000i  -2.0000 -   4.0000i
  3.6962 + 7.0622i  -6.9282 -  1.0000i   5.0359 - 22.0622i
 -6.6962 - 5.0622i   6.9282 -  1.0000i  11.9641 -  9.9378i
>> fft(Z1)
ans =
  6.0000            11.0000                   0
 -1.5000 + 6.0622i  -1.0000 + 6.9282i   7.5000 - 7.7942i
 -1.5000 - 6.0622i  -1.0000 - 6.9282i   7.5000 + 7.7942i
```

fft2 (Z)	*Returns the matrix with the two-dimensional discrete Fourier transforms of the columns of the matrix Z.*

```
>> fft2(Z)
ans =
  4.0000 +  2.0000i  19.9904 - 10.2321i  -5.9904 - 6.7679i
  1.8038 - 16.0000i  22.8827 + 28.9545i -13.5981 + 8.2321i
 12.1962 - 16.0000i  -8.4019 +  4.7679i -23.8827 - 3.9545i
>> fft2(Z1)
ans =
 17.0000             0.5000 -  9.5263i   0.5000 +  9.5263i
  5.0000 + 5.1962i   8.0000 + 13.8564i -17.5000 -  0.8660i
  5.0000 - 5.1962i -17.5000 +  0.8660i   8.0000 - 13.8564i
```

ifft (Z)	*Returns the matrix with the inverse inverse discrete Fourier transform of the columns of the matrix Z.*

```
>> ifft(Z)
ans =
  2.0000 - 1.6667i        0 + 3.6667i  -0.6667 - 1.3333i
 -2.2321 - 1.6874i   2.3094 - 0.3333i   3.9880 - 3.3126i
  1.2321 + 2.3541i  -2.3094 - 0.3333i   1.6786 - 7.3541i
>> ifft(Z1)
ans =
  2.0000             3.6667                   0
 -0.5000 - 2.0207i  -0.3333 - 2.3094i   2.5000 + 2.5981i
 -0.5000 + 2.0207i  -0.3333 + 2.3094i   2.5000 - 2.5981i
```

(continued)

ifft2 (Z)	*Returns the matrix with the inverse two-dimensional discrete Fourier transform of the columns of Z.*

```
>> ifft2(Z)
ans =
0.4444 + 0.2222i   -0.6656 - 0.7520i    2.2212 - 1.1369i
1.3551 - 1.7778i   -2.6536 - 0.4394i   -0.9335 + 0.5298i
0.2004 - 1.7778i   -1.5109 + 0.9147i    2.5425 + 3.2172i
>> ifft2(Z1)
ans =
1.8889               0.0556 + 1.0585i    0.0556 - 1.0585i
0.5556 - 0.5774i     0.8889 - 1.5396i   -1.9444 + 0.0962i
0.5556 + 0.5774i    -1.9444 - 0.0962i    0.8889 + 1.5396i
```

8.6 General Functions with Complex Matrix Arguments

MATLAB incorporates a broad group of hyperbolic, trigonometric, exponential and logarithmic functions that support a complex matrix as an argument. Obviously, all these functions also accept a complex vector as the argument, since a vector is a particular case of matrix. All functions are applied elementwise in the matrix.

8.6.1 Trigonometric Functions of a Complex Matrix Variable

Below is a table summarizing the trigonometric functions of a complex variable and their inverses which are incorporated in MATLAB, illustrated with examples. All the examples use as arguments the matrices Z and Z1 introduced at the beginning of the table in the description of the sine function.

Direct Trigonometric Functions

sin(Z) *sine function*

```
>> Z = [1-i, 1+i, 2i;3-6i, 2+4i, -i;i,2i,3i]
Z =
1.0000 - 1.0000i    1.0000 + 1.0000i        0 + 2.0000i
3.0000 - 6.0000i    2.0000 + 4.0000i        0 - 1.0000i
     0 + 1.0000i         0 + 2.0000i         0 + 3.0000i
>> Z1 = [1,1,2;3,2,-1;1,2,3]
Z1 =
1     1     2
3     2    -1
1     2     3
>> sin(Z)
ans =
1.0e+002 *
0.0130 - 0.0063i    0.0130 + 0.0063i        0 + 0.0363i
0.2847 + 1.9969i    0.2483 - 0.1136i        0 - 0.0118i
     0 + 0.0118i         0 + 0.0363i         0 + 0.1002i
>> sin(Z1)
ans =
0.8415 0.8415  0.9093
0.1411 0.9093 -0.8415
0.8415 0.9093  0.1411
```

cos (Z) *cosine function*

```
>> cos(Z)
ans =
1.0e+002 *
 0.0083 + 0.0099i   0.0083 - 0.0099i   0.0376
-1.9970 + 0.2847i  -0.1136 - 0.2481i   0.0154
 0.0154            0.0376              0.1007
>> cos(Z1)
ans =
 0.5403   0.5403 -0.4161
-0.9900 -0.4161   0.5403
 0.5403 -0.4161 -0.9900
```

(continued)

Direct Trigonometric Functions

tan (Z) *tangent function*

```
>> tan(Z)
ans =
 0.2718 - 1.0839i   0.2718 + 1.0839i        0 + 0.9640i
-0.0000 - 1.0000i  -0.0005 + 1.0004i        0 - 0.7616i
      0 + 0.7616i        0 + 0.9640i        0 + 0.9951i
>> tan(Z1)
ans =
 1.5574   1.5574  -2.1850
-0.1425  -2.1850  -1.5574
 1.5574  -2.1850  -0.1425
```

csc (Z) *cosecant function*

```
>> csc(Z)
ans =
0.6215 + 0.3039i   0.6215 - 0.3039i        0 - 0.2757i
0.0007 - 0.0049i   0.0333 + 0.0152i        0 + 0.8509i
      0 - 0.8509i        0 - 0.2757i        0 - 0.0998i
>> csc(Z1)
ans =
1.1884     1.1884     1.0998
7.0862     1.0998    -1.1884
1.1884     1.0998     7.0862
```

sec (Z) *secant function*

```
>> sec(Z)
ans =
 0.4983 - 0.5911i   0.4983 + 0.5911i   0.2658
-0.0049 - 0.0007i  -0.0153 + 0.0333i   0.6481
 0.6481                0.2658          0.0993
>> sec(Z1)
ans =
 1.8508     1.8508    -2.4030
-1.0101    -2.4030     1.8508
 1.8508    -2.4030    -1.0101
```

(continued)

Direct Trigonometric Functions

cot (Z) *cotangent function*

```
>> cot(Z)
ans =
 0.2176 + 0.8680i    0.2176 - 0.8680i        0 - 1.0373i
-0.0000 + 1.0000i   -0.0005 - 0.9996i        0 + 1.3130i
      0 - 1.3130i          0 - 1.0373i        0 - 1.0050i
>> cot(Z1)
ans =
 0.6421     0.6421    -0.4577
-7.0153    -0.4577    -0.6421
 0.6421    -0.4577    -7.0153
```

Inverse Trigonometric Functions

asin (Z) *arc sine function*

```
>> asin(Z)
ans =
0.6662 - 1.0613i    0.6662 + 1.0613i        0 + 1.4436i
0.4592 - 2.5998i    0.4539 + 2.1986i        0 - 0.8814i
     0 + 0.8814i         0 + 1.4436i         0 + 1.8184i
>> asin(Z1)
ans =
1.5708              1.5708              1.5708 - 1.3170i
1.5708 - 1.7627i    1.5708 - 1.3170i   -1.5708
1.5708              1.5708 - 1.3170i    1.5708 - 1.7627i
```

acos (Z) *arc cosine function*

```
>> acos(Z)
ans =
0.9046 + 1.0613i    0.9046 - 1.0613i    1.5708 - 1.4436i
1.1115 + 2.5998i    1.1169 - 2.1986i    1.5708 + 0.8814i
1.5708 - 0.8814i    1.5708 - 1.4436i    1.5708 - 1.8184i
>> acos(Z1)
ans =
0              0              0 + 1.3170i
0 + 1.7627i    0 + 1.3170i    3.1416
0              0 + 1.3170i    0 + 1.7627i
```

(continued)

184

Inverse Trigonometric Functions

atan(Z) and **atan2 (real(Z), imag(Z))** *arc tangent function*

```
>> atan(Z)
ans =
1.0172 - 0.4024i    1.0172 + 0.4024i   -1.5708 + 0.5493i
1.5030 - 0.1335i    1.4670 + 0.2006i         0 -    Infi
     0 +    Infi   -1.5708 + 0.5493i   -1.5708 + 0.3466i
>> atan(Z1)
ans =
0.7854     0.7854     1.1071
1.2490     1.1071    -0.7854
0.7854     1.1071     1.2490
```

acsc (Z) *arc cosecant function*

```
>> acsc(Z)
ans =
0.4523 + 0.5306i    0.4523 - 0.5306i        0 - 0.4812i
0.0661 + 0.1332i    0.0982 - 0.1996i        0 + 0.8814i
     0 - 0.8814i         0 - 0.4812i        0 - 0.3275i
>> acsc(Z1)
ans =
1.5708     1.5708     0.5236
0.3398     0.5236    -1.5708
1.5708     0.5236     0.3398
```

asec (Z) *arc secant function*

```
>> asec(Z)
ans =
1.1185 - 0.5306i    1.1185 + 0.5306i    1.5708 + 0.4812i
1.5047 - 0.1332i    1.4726 + 0.1996i    1.5708 - 0.8814i
1.5708 + 0.8814i    1.5708 + 0.4812i    1.5708 + 0.3275i
>> asec(Z1)
ans =
     0          0     1.0472
1.2310     1.0472     3.1416
     0     1.0472     1.2310
```

(continued)

Inverse Trigonometric Functions

acot (Z) *arc cotangent function*

```
>> acot(Z)
ans =
0.5536 + 0.4024i   0.5536 - 0.4024i      0 - 0.5493i
0.0678 + 0.1335i   0.1037 - 0.2006i      0 +    Infi
     0 -    Infi        0 - 0.5493i      0 - 0.3466i
>> acot(Z1)
ans =
0.7854    0.7854    0.4636
0.3218    0.4636   -0.7854
0.7854    0.4636    0.3218
```

8.6.2 Hyperbolic Functions of a Complex Matrix Variable

Below is a table summarizing the hyperbolic functions of complex matrix variables and their inverses which are incorporated in MATLAB, illustrated with examples.

Direct Hyperbolic Functions

sinh (Z) *hyperbolic sine function*

```
>> sinh(Z)
ans =
0.6350 - 1.2985i   0.6350 + 1.2985i      0 + 0.9093i
9.6189 + 2.8131i  -2.3707 - 2.8472i      0 - 0.8415i
     0 + 0.8415i        0 + 0.9093i      0 + 0.1411i
>> sinh(Z1)
ans =
 1.1752    1.1752    3.6269
10.0179    3.6269   -1.1752
 1.1752    3.6269   10.0179
```

cosh (Z) *hyperbolic cosine function*

```
>> cosh(Z)
ans =
0.8337 - 0.9889i   0.8337 + 0.9889i   -0.4161
9.6667 + 2.7991i  -2.4591 - 2.7448i    0.5403
0.5403                      -0.4161   -0.9900
>> cosh(Z1)
ans =
 1.5431    1.5431    3.7622
10.0677    3.7622    1.5431
 1.5431    3.7622   10.0677
```

(continued)

Direct Hyperbolic Functions

tanh (Z) *hyperbolic tangent function*

```
>> tanh(Z)
ans =
1.0839 - 0.2718i    1.0839 + 0.2718i       0 - 2.1850i
0.9958 + 0.0026i    1.0047 + 0.0364i       0 - 1.5574i
     0 + 1.5574i         0 - 2.1850i       0 - 0.1425i
>> tanh(Z1)
ans =
0.7616    0.7616    0.9640
0.9951    0.9640    -0.7616
0.7616    0.9640    0.9951
```

csch (z) *hyperbolic cosecant function*

```
>> csch(Z)
ans =
0.3039 + 0.6215i    0.3039 - 0.6215i       0 - 1.0998i
0.0958 - 0.0280i    -0.1727 + 0.2074i      0 + 1.1884i
     0 - 1.1884i         0 - 1.0998i       0 - 7.0862i
>> csch(Z1)
ans =
0.8509    0.8509    0.2757
0.0998    0.2757    -0.8509
0.8509    0.2757    0.0998
```

sech (Z) *hyperbolic secant function*

```
>> sech(Z)
ans =
0.4983 + 0.5911i    0.4983 - 0.5911i   -2.4030
0.0954 - 0.0276i    -0.1811 + 0.2021i   1.8508
1.8508              -2.4030            -1.0101
>> sech(Z1)
ans =
0.6481    0.6481    0.2658
0.0993    0.2658    0.6481
0.6481    0.2658    0.0993
```

(continued)

Direct Hyperbolic Functions

coth (Z) *hyperbolic cotangent function*

```
>> coth(Z)
ans =
0.8680 + 0.2176i   0.8680 - 0.2176i        0 + 0.4577i
1.0042 - 0.0027i   0.9940 - 0.0360i        0 + 0.6421i
     0 - 0.6421i        0 + 0.4577i        0 + 7.0153i
>> coth(Z1)
ans =
1.3130     1.3130     1.0373
1.0050     1.0373    -1.3130
1.3130     1.0373     1.0050
```

Inverse Hyperbolic Functions

asinh (Z) *hyperbolic arc sine function*

```
>> asinh(Z)
ans =
1.0613 - 0.6662i   1.0613 + 0.6662i   1.3170 + 1.5708i
2.5932 - 1.1027i   2.1836 + 1.0969i        0 - 1.5708i
     0 + 1.5708i   1.3170 + 1.5708i   1.7627 + 1.5708i
>> asinh(Z1)
ans =
0.8814     0.8814     1.4436
1.8184     1.4436    -0.8814
0.8814     1.4436     1.8184
```

acosh (Z) *hyperbolic arc cosine function*

```
>> acosh(Z)
ans =
1.0613 - 0.9046i   1.0613 + 0.9046i   1.4436 + 1.5708i
2.5998 - 1.1115i   2.1986 + 1.1169i   0.8814 - 1.5708i
0.8814 + 1.5708i   1.4436 + 1.5708i   1.8184 + 1.5708i
>> acosh(Z1)
ans =
   0                0              1.3170
1.7627            1.3170               0 + 3.1416i
   0              1.3170          1.7627
```

(continued)

Inverse Hyperbolic Functions

atanh (Z) *hyperbolic arc tangent function*

```
>> atanh(Z)
ans =
0.4024 - 1.0172i    0.4024 + 1.0172i        0 + 1.1071i
0.0656 - 1.4377i    0.0964 + 1.3715i        0 - 0.7854i
     0 + 0.7854i         0 + 1.1071i        0 + 1.2490i
>> atanh(Z1)
ans =
   inf                 inf            0.5493 + 1.5708i
0.3466 + 1.5708i    0.5493 + 1.5708i   -inf
   inf              0.5493 + 1.5708i   0.3466 + 1.5708i
```

acsch (Z) *hyperbolic arc cosecant function*

```
>> acsch(Z)
ans =
0.5306 + 0.4523i    0.5306 - 0.4523i        0 - 0.5236i
0.0672 + 0.1334i    0.1019 - 0.2003i        0 + 1.5708i
     0 - 1.5708i         0 - 0.5236i        0 - 0.3398i
>> acsch(Z1)
ans =
0.8814    0.8814     0.4812
0.3275    0.4812    -0.8814
0.8814    0.4812     0.3275
```

asech (Z) *hyperbolic arc secant function*

```
>> asech(Z)
ans =
0.5306 + 1.1185i    0.5306 - 1.1185i    0.4812 - 1.5708i
0.1332 + 1.5047i    0.1996 - 1.4726i    0.8814 + 1.5708i
0.8814 - 1.5708i    0.4812 - 1.5708i    0.3275 - 1.5708i
>> asech(Z1)
ans =
0                   0                   0 + 1.0472i
0 + 1.2310i         0 + 1.0472i         0 + 3.1416i
0                   0 + 1.0472i         0 + 1.2310i
```

(*continued*)

Inverse Hyperbolic Functions

acoth (Z) *hyperbolic arc cotangent function*

```
>> acoth(Z)
ans =
0.4024 + 0.5536i   0.4024 - 0.5536i      0 - 0.4636i
0.0656 + 0.1331i   0.0964 - 0.1993i      0 + 0.7854i
     0 - 0.7854i        0 - 0.4636i      0 - 0.3218i
>> acoth(Z1)
ans =
  Inf       Inf    0.5493
0.3466    0.5493     -Inf
  Inf    0.5493    0.3466
```

8.6.3 Exponential and Logarithmic Functions of a Complex Matrix Variable

Below is a table summarizing the exponential and logarithmic functions which are incorporated in MATLAB, illustrated with examples. The matrices Z1 and Z are the same as those in the previous examples.

Function	Meaning

exp (Z)	*Base e exponential function (e ^ x)*
	
	 ```>> exp(Z)```
	 ```ans =```
	 ``` 1.4687 - 2.2874i 1.4687 + 2.2874i -0.4161 + 0.9093i```
	 ```19.2855 + 5.6122i -4.8298 - 5.5921i 0.5403 - 0.8415i```
	 ``` 0.5403 + 0.8415i -0.4161 + 0.9093i -0.9900 + 0.1411i```
	 ```>> exp(Z1)```
	 ```ans =```
	 ``` 2.7183 2.7183 7.3891```
	 ```20.0855 7.3891 0.3679```
	 ``` 2.7183 7.3891 20.0855```

log (Z)	*Base e logarithm of Z.*
	
	 ```>> log(Z)```
	 ```ans =```
	 ```0.3466 - 0.7854i 0.3466 + 0.7854i 0.6931 + 1.5708i```
	 ```1.9033 - 1.1071i 1.4979 + 1.1071i 0 - 1.5708i```
	 ``` 0 + 1.5708i 0.6931 + 1.5708i 1.0986 + 1.5708i```
	 ```>> log(Z1)```
	 ```ans =```
	 ``` 0 0 0.6931```
	 ```1.0986 0.6931 0 + 3.1416i```
	 ``` 0 0.6931 1.0986```

(*continued*)

Function	Meaning
log10 (Z)	*Base 10 logarithm of Z.*
	`>> log10(Z)`
	`ans =`
	`0.1505 - 0.3411i   0.1505 + 0.3411i   0.3010 + 0.6822i`
	`0.8266 - 0.4808i   0.6505 + 0.4808i        0 - 0.6822i`
	`     0 + 0.6822i   0.3010 + 0.6822i   0.4771 + 0.6822i`
	`>> log10(Z1)`
	`ans =`
	`     0        0    0.3010`
	`0.4771   0.3010        0 + 1.3644i`
	`     0   0.3010   0.4771`
log2 (Z)	*Base 2 logarithm of Z.*
	`>> log2(Z)`
	`ans =`
	`0.5000 - 1.1331i   0.5000 + 1.1331i   1.0000 + 2.2662i`
	`2.7459 - 1.5973i   2.1610 + 1.5973i        0 - 2.2662i`
	`     0 + 2.2662i   1.0000 + 2.2662i   1.5850 + 2.2662i`
	`>> log2(Z1)`
	`ans =`
	`     0        0    1.0000`
	`1.5850   1.0000        0 + 4.5324i`
	`     0   1.0000   1.5850`
pow2 (Z)	*Base 2 exponential function (2^Z).*
	`>> pow2(Z)`
	`ans =`
	` 1.5385 - 1.2779i    1.5385 + 1.2779i    0.1835 + 0.9830i`
	`-4.2054 + 6.8055i   -3.7307 + 1.4427i    0.7692 - 0.6390i`
	` 0.7692 + 0.6390i    0.1835 + 0.9830i   -0.4870 + 0.8734i`
	`>> pow2(Z1)`
	`ans =`
	`2.0000 2.0000 4.0000`
	`8.0000 4.0000 0.5000`
	`2.0000 4.0000 8.0000`

(continued)

Function	Meaning

sqrt (Z)	*Square root of Z.*
	`>> sqrt(Z)`
	`ans =`
	1.0987 - 0.4551i 1.0987 + 0.4551i 1.0000 + 1.0000i
	2.2032 - 1.3617i 1.7989 + 1.1118i 0.7071 - 0.7071i
	0.7071 + 0.7071i 1.0000 + 1.0000i 1.2247 + 1.2247i
	`>> sqrt(Z1)`
	`ans =`
	1.0000 1.0000 1.4142
	1.7321 1.4142 0 + 1.0000i
	1.0000 1.4142 1.7321

8.6.4 Specific Functions of a Complex Matrix Variable

MATLAB incorporates a specific group of functions of a complex variable allowing you to work with moduli, arguments, and real and imaginary parts. Among these functions are the following:

Function	Meaning

abs (Z)	*The complex modulus (absolute value).*
	`>> abs(Z)`
	`ans =`
	1.4142 1.4142 2.0000
	6.7082 4.4721 1.0000
	1.0000 2.0000 3.0000
	`>> abs(Z1)`
	`ans =`
	1 1 2
	3-2-1
	1 2 3

angle (Z)	*Argument function.*
	`>> angle(Z)`
	`ans =`
	-0.7854 0.7854 1.5708
	-1.1071 1.1071 -1.5708
	 1.5708 1.5708 1.5708
	`>> angle(Z1)`
	`ans =`
	0 0 0
	0 0 3.1416
	0 0 0

(continued)

Function	Meaning
conj (Z)	*Complex conjugate.*
	```>> conj(Z)```
	```ans =```
	```1.0000 + 1.0000i 1.0000 - 1.0000i 0 - 2.0000i```
	```3.0000 + 6.0000i 2.0000 - 4.0000i 0 + 1.0000i```
	``` 0 - 1.0000i 0 - 2.0000i 0 - 3.0000i```
	```>> conj(Z1)```
	```ans =```
	```1 1 2```
	```2 -3 -1```
	```1 2 3```
real (Z)	*Real part.*
	```>> real(Z)```
	```ans =```
	```1 1 0```
	```3 2 0```
	```0 0 0```
	```>> real(Z1)```
	```ans =```
	```1 1 2```
	```2 -3 -1```
	```1 2 3```
imag (Z)	*Imaginary part.*
	```>> imag(Z)```
	```ans =```
	```-1 1 2```
	```-4 6 -1```
	``` 1 2 3```
	```>> imag(Z1)```
	```ans =```
	```0 0 0```
	```0 0 0```
	```0 0 0```

(continued)

Function	Meaning
floor (Z)	*Floor function applied to real and imaginary parts.*

```
>> floor(12.357*Z)
ans =
12.0000 -13.0000i  12.0000 +12.0000i       0 +24.0000i
37.0000 -75.0000i  24.0000 +49.0000i       0 -13.0000i
      0 +12.0000i        0 +24.0000i        0 +37.0000i
>> floor(12.357*Z1)
ans =
12   12   24
37   24  -13
12  -24  -37
```

ceil (Z)	*Ceiling function applied to real and imaginary parts.*

```
>> ceil(12.357*Z)
ans =
13.0000 -12.0000i  13.0000 +13.0000i       0 +25.0000i
38.0000 -74.0000i  25.0000 +50.0000i       0 -12.0000i
      0 +13.0000i        0 +25.0000i        0 +38.0000i
>> ceil(12.357*Z1)
ans =
13  13   25
38  25  -12
13  25   38
```

round (Z)	*Round function applied to real and imaginary parts.*

```
>> round(12.357*Z)
ans =
12.0000 -12.0000i  12.0000 +12.0000i       0 +25.0000i
37.0000 -74.0000i  25.0000 +49.0000i       0 -12.0000i
      0 +12.0000i        0 +25.0000i        0 +37.0000i
>> round(12.357*Z1)
ans =
12 -12 -25
37  25 -12
12  25  37
```

(continued)

Function	Meaning
fix (Z)	*Fix applied to real and imaginary parts.*

```
>> fix(12.357*Z)
ans =
12.0000 -12.0000i   12.0000 +12.0000i        0 +24.0000i
37.0000 -74.0000i   24.0000 +49.0000i        0 -12.0000i
      0 +12.0000i          0 +24.0000i        0 +37.0000i
>> fix(12.357*Z1)
ans =
12  12  24
24 -37  12
12 -24 -37
```

8.7 Matrix Operations with Real and Complex Variables

MATLAB includes the usual matrix operations of sum, difference, product, exponentiation and inversion. Obviously all these operations will also be valid for real matrices. The following table summarizes those operations that are valid both for numerical and algebraic real and complex matrices.

A + B	*Sum of matrices.*

```
>> A = [1+i, 1-i, 2i; -i,-3i,6-5i; 2+3i, 2-3i, i]
A =
1.0000 + 1.0000i   1.0000 - 1.0000i        0 + 2.0000i
     0 - 1.0000i        0 - 3.0000i   6.0000 - 5.0000i
2.0000 + 3.0000i   2.0000 - 3.0000i        0 + 1.0000i
>> B = [i, -i, 2i; 1-i,7-3i,2-5i;8-6i, 5-i, 1+i]
B =
     0 + 1.0000i        0 - 1.0000i        0 + 2.0000i
1.0000 - 1.0000i   7.0000 - 3.0000i   2.0000 - 5.0000i
8.0000 - 6.0000i   5.0000 - 1.0000i   1.0000 + 1.0000i
>> A1 = [1 6 2;3 5 0; 2 4 -1]
A1 =
1      6      2
3      5      0
2      4     -1
>> B1 = [-3 -6 1;-3 -5 2; 12 14 -10]
B1 =
-3     -6      1
-3     -5      2
12     14    -10
>> A+B
ans =
 1.0000 + 2.0000i   1.0000 - 2.0000i        0 +  4.0000i
 1.0000 - 2.0000i   7.0000 - 6.0000i   8.0000 - 10.0000i
10.0000 - 3.0000i   7.0000 - 4.0000i   1.0000 +  2.0000i
>> A1+B1
ans =
-2      0      3
 0      0      2
14     18    -11
```

(continued)

A-B	*Difference of matrices.*

```
>> A-B
ans =
  1.0000                1.0000                        0
 -1.0000               -7.0000               4.0000
 -6.0000 + 9.0000i  -3.0000 - 2.0000i  -1.0000
>> A1-B1
ans =
   4     12     1
   6     10    -2
 -10    -10     9
```

A * B	*Product of matrices.*

```
>> A * B
ans =
 11.0000 + 15.0000i    7.0000 -  1.0000i  -  7.0000 -  3.0000i
 16.0000 - 79.0000i   15.0000 - 52.0000i  -  2.0000 -  5.0000i
  2.0000 +  5.0000i    9.0000 - 24.0000i  - 18.0000 - 11.0000i
>> A1*B1
ans =
   3    -8    -7
 -24   -43    13
 -30   -46    20
```

A^n	*nth power of the matrix A.*

```
>> A^3
ans =
1.0e+002 *
0.1000 - 0.3400i  -0.3200 - 0.1200i   0.3400 - 0.3600i
0.0900 - 0.0300i  -1.0700 + 0.2100i  -2.2500 - 0.6700i
0.3700 - 0.7900i  -1.0300 - 0.0300i  -0.0700 - 0.3700i
>> A1^3
ans =
155    358    46
159    347    30
106    232    19
ans =
Columns 1 through 2
1.0000 - 1.0000i    2.0000
Columns 3 through 4
6.0000 - 10.0000i 60.0000 + 36.0000i
>> cumprod([1, 0, -23, 12, 16])
ans =
1    0    0    0    0
```

(continued)

P^^   *Scalar p raised to the power of the matrix A.*

```
>> 3^A
ans =
   0.0159 - 1.2801i   -0.5297 +  2.8779i   -1.9855 +  3.0796i
 -10.3372 + 0.4829i   17.0229 + 12.9445i   14.7327 + 20.1633i
  -5.0438 + 0.2388i    7.0696 +  6.9611i    5.7189 +  9.5696i
>> 3^A1
ans =
1.0e+003 *
2.2230    4.9342    0.4889
2.1519    4.7769    0.4728
1.4346    3.1844    0.3156
```

A'   *Transpose of the matrix A.*

```
>> A'
ans =
1.0000 - 1.0000i        0 + 1.0000i   2.0000 - 3.0000i
1.0000 + 1.0000i        0 + 3.0000i   2.0000 + 3.0000i
       0 - 2.0000i   6.0000 + 5.0000i        0 - 1.0000i
>> A1'
ans =
1    3    2
6    5    4
2    0   -1
```

(continued)

A^-1

Inverse of A.

```
>> A^-1
ans =
-2.5000 + 2.0000i  -0.0500 + 0.6500i   0.8500 - 1.0500i
 0.5000 + 3.0000i   0.5500 + 0.3500i  -0.3500 - 0.9500i
-1.0000 - 1.0000i  -0.2000 + 0.1000i   0.4000 + 0.3000i
>> A1^-1
ans =
-0.2941    0.8235   -0.5882
 0.1765   -0.2941    0.3529
 0.1176    0.4706   -0.7647
>> A*A^-1
ans =
 1.0000                0.0000 - 0.0000i  -0.0000 + 0.0000i
-0.0000 - 0.0000i   1.0000 + 0.0000i   0.0000
 0.0000 + 0.0000i   0.0000                1.0000 + 0.0000i
>> A1*A1^-1
ans =
 1.0000   -0.0000         0
-0.0000    1.0000         0
-0.0000   -0.0000    1.0000
```

A\B

*If A is square A\B= (A^{-1}) * B and if A is not square A\B is the solution in the sense of least-squares of the system AX = B.*

```
>> A\B
ans =
 -0.9000 -15.3000i   6.8000 + 1.1000i   1.0500 - 3.6500i
-10.6000  -5.2000i   5.2000 - 4.1000i  -2.5500 - 2.3500i
  5.9000   0.7000i   0.2000 + 3.4000i   2.2000 - 0.1000i
>> A1\B1
ans =
 -8.6471 -10.5882   7.2353
  4.5882   5.3529  -3.9412
-10.9412 -13.7647   8.7059
```

(*continued*)

B/A
Equivalent to A'\B'

```
>> B/A
ans =
  3.0000 -  5.0000i  -0.5000 -  1.0000i  -0.5000 +  2.0000i
  5.0000 + 27.0000i   5.6000 +  2.7000i  -3.2000 -  8.9000i
 -2.5000 + 43.5000i   6.3000 +  6.6000i  -2.1000 - 17.2000i
>> A'\B'
ans =
  3.0000 +  5.0000i   5.0000 - 27.0000i  -2.5000 - 43.5000i
 -0.5000 +  1.0000i   5.6000 -  2.7000i   6.3000 -  6.6000i
 -0.5000 -  2.0000i  -3.2000 +  8.9000i  -2.1000 + 17.2000i
>> B1/A1
ans =
 -0.0588   -0.2353   -1.1176
  0.2353   -0.0588   -1.5294
 -2.2353    1.0588    5.5294
>> A1'\B1'
ans =
 -0.0588    0.2353   -2.2353
 -0.2353   -0.0588    1.0588
 -1.1176   -1.5294    5.5294
```

EXERCISE 8-1

Given the complex numbers $z_1 = 1-i$, and $z_2 = 5i$, calculate: z_1^3 z_1^2/z_2^4, $z_1^{1/2}$, $z_2^{3/2}$, $\ln(z_1+z_2)$, $\sin(z_1-z_2)$, and $\tanh(z_1/z_2)$.

```
>> Z1 = 1-i

Z1 =

1.0000 - 1.0000i

>> Z2 = 5i

Z2 =

0 + 5.0000i

>> Z1^3

ans =

-2.0000 - 2.0000i
```

```
>> Z1^2/Z2^4

ans =

0 - 0.0032i

>> sqrt(Z1)

ans =

1.0987 - 0.4551i

>> sqrt(Z2^3)

ans =

7.9057 - 7.9057i

>> log(Z1+Z2)

ans =

1.4166 + 1.3258i

>> sin(Z1-Z2)

ans =

1.6974e+002 -1.0899e+002i

>> tanh(Z1/Z2)

ans =

-0.2052 - 0.1945i
```

EXERCISE 8-2

Perform the following operations with complex numbers:

$$\frac{i^8 - i^{-8}}{3 - 4i} + 1, \; i^{\sin(1+i)}, \; (2 + \ln(i))^{1/i}, \; (1+i)^i, \; i^{\ln(1+i)}, \; (1+\sqrt{3i})^{1-i}$$

```
>> (i^8-i^(-8))/(3-4*i) + 1

ans =

1
```

```
>> i^(sin(1+i))

ans =

-0.16665202215166 + 0.329041394503071

>> (2+log(i))^(1/i)

ans =

1.15809185259777 - 1.56388053989023i

>> (1+i)^i

ans =

0.42882900629437 + 0.15487175246425i

>> i^(log(1+i))

ans =

0.24911518828716 + 0.15081974884717i

>> (1+sqrt(3)*i)^(1-i)

ans =

5.34581479196611 + 1.97594883452873i
```

EXERCISE 8-3

Find the real part, imaginary part, modulus and argument of the following expressions:

$$i^{3+i}, \ (1+\sqrt{3i})^{1-i}, \ i^{i^i}, \ i^i$$

```
>> Z1=i^3*i; Z2=(1+sqrt(3)*i)^(1-i); Z3=(i^i)^i;Z4=i^i;

>> format short

>> real([Z1 Z2 Z3 Z4])

ans =

1.0000    5.3458    0.0000    0.2079
```

```
>> imag([Z1 Z2 Z3 Z4])

ans =

    0    1.9759    -1.0000         0

>> abs([Z1 Z2 Z3 Z4])

ans =

1.0000    5.6993    1.0000    0.2079

>> angle([Z1 Z2 Z3 Z4])

ans =

    0    0.3541    -1.5708         0
```

EXERCISE 8-4

Consider the 3×3 matrix M whose elements are the squares of the first nine positive integers, multiplied by the imaginary unit (reading from left to right and top to bottom).

Find the square, the square root and the exponential to base 2 and − 2 of M.

Find the elementwise Naperian logarithm and base e exponential of M.

Find e^M and log(M).

```
>> M = i*[1 2 3;4 5 6;7 8 9]

M =
0 + 1.0000i       0 + 2.0000i       0 + 3.0000i
0 + 4.0000i       0 + 5.0000i       0 + 6.0000i
0 + 7.0000i       0 + 8.0000i       0 + 9.0000i

>> C = M^2

C =

  -30    -36    -42
  -66    -81    -96
 -102   -126   -150

>> D = M^(1/2)

D =

0.8570 - 0.2210i   0.5370 + 0.2445i   0.2169 + 0.7101i
0.7797 + 0.6607i   0.9011 + 0.8688i   1.0224 + 1.0769i
0.7024 + 1.5424i   1.2651 + 1.4930i   1.8279 + 1.4437i
```

```
>> 2^M

ans =

 0.7020 - 0.6146i  -0.1693 - 0.2723i  -0.0407 + 0.0699i
-0.2320 - 0.3055i   0.7366 - 0.3220i  -0.2947 - 0.3386i
-0.1661 + 0.0036i  -0.3574 - 0.3717i   0.4513 - 0.7471i

>> (-2)^M

ans =

 17.3946 - 16.8443i   4.3404 - 4.5696i  -7.7139 + 7.7050i
  1.5685 -  1.8595i   1.1826 - 0.5045i  -1.2033 + 0.8506i
-13.2575 + 13.1252i  -3.9751 + 3.5607i   6.3073 - 6.0038i

>> log(M)

ans =

     0 + 1.5708i   0.6931 + 1.5708i   1.0986 + 1.5708i
1.3863 + 1.5708i   1.6094 + 1.5708i   1.7918 + 1.5708i
1.9459 + 1.5708i   2.0794 + 1.5708i   2.1972 + 1.5708i

>> exp(M)

ans =

 0.5403 + 0.8415i  -0.4161 + 0.9093i  -0.9900 + 0.1411i
-0.6536 - 0.7568i   0.2837 - 0.9589i   0.9602 - 0.2794i
 0.7539 + 0.6570i  -0.1455 + 0.9894i  -0.9111 + 0.4121i

>> logm(M)

ans =

-5.4033 - 0.8472i  11.9931 - 0.3109i  -5.3770 + 0.8846i
12.3029 + 0.0537i -22.3087 + 0.8953i  12.6127 + 0.4183i
-4.7574 + 1.6138i  12.9225 + 0.7828i  -4.1641 + 0.6112i

>> expm(M)

ans =

 0.3802 - 0.6928i  -0.3738 - 0.2306i  -0.1278 + 0.2316i
-0.5312 - 0.1724i   0.3901 - 0.1434i  -0.6886 - 0.1143i
-0.4426 + 0.3479i  -0.8460 - 0.0561i  -0.2493 - 0.4602i
```

EXERCISE 8-5.

Consider the vector sum Z of the complex vector V = (i,-i, i) and the real vector R = (0,1,1). Find the mean, median, standard deviation, variance, sum, product, maximum and minimum of the elements of V, as well as its gradient, the discrete Fourier transform and its inverse.

```
>> Z = [i,-i,i]

Z =

0 + 1.0000i       0 - 1.0000i       0 + 1.0000i

>> R = [0,1,1]

R =

0    1    1

>> V = Z+R

V =

0 + 1.0000i    1.0000 - 1.0000i    1.0000 + 1.0000i

>> [mean(V),median(V),std(V),var(V),sum(V),prod(V),max(V),min(V)]'

ans =

0.6667 - 0.3333i
1.0000 + 1.0000i
1.2910
1.6667
2.0000 - 1.0000i
     0 - 2.0000i
1.0000 + 1.0000i
     0 - 1.0000i

>> gradient(V)

ans =

1.0000 - 2.0000i    0.5000                0 + 2.0000i

>> fft(V)

ans =

2.0000 + 1.0000i  -2.7321 + 1.0000i    0.7321 + 1.0000i

>> ifft(V)

ans =

0.6667 + 0.3333i    0.2440 + 0.3333i   -0.9107 + 0.3333i
```

EXERCISE 8-6.

Given the following matrices:

$$A1 = \begin{bmatrix} 1 & 0 & 0 \\ 0 & 1 & 0 \\ 0 & 0 & 1 \end{bmatrix} \quad A2 = \begin{bmatrix} 0 & 1 & 0 \\ 0 & 0 & 1 \\ 0 & 0 & 0 \end{bmatrix} \quad B1 = \begin{bmatrix} 0 & 1 & 2 \\ 0 & -1 & 3 \\ 0 & 0 & 0 \end{bmatrix} \quad B2 = \begin{bmatrix} -i & i & -i \\ 0 & 0 & i \\ 0 & 0 & i \end{bmatrix}$$

$$C1 = \begin{bmatrix} 1 & -1 & 0 \\ -1 & sqrt(2)i & -sqrt(2)i \\ 0 & 0 & -1 \end{bmatrix} \quad C2 = \begin{bmatrix} 0 & 2 & 1 \\ 1 & 0 & 0 \\ 1 & -1 & 0 \end{bmatrix}$$

First calculate A = A1 + A2, B = B1 - B2 and C = C1 + C2.

Then calculate AB - BA, $A^2 + B^2 + C^2$, ABC, sqrt (A) + sqrt (B) - sqrt(C), $(e^B + e^C)$, their transposes and their inverses.

Finally check that any matrix multiplied by its inverse yields the identity matrix.

```
>> A1 = eye(3)

A1 =

1    0    0
0    1    0
0    0    1

>> A2 = [0 1 0; 0 0 1;0 0 0]

A2 =

0    1    0
0    0    1
0    0    0

>> A = A1+A2

A =

1    1    0
0    1    1
0    0    1

>> B1 = [0 1 2;0 -1 3;0 0 0]

B1 =

0    1    2
0    -1   3
0    0    0
```

```
>> B2 = [-i i -i;0 0 i;0 0 i]

B2 =

0 - 1.0000i        0 + 1.0000i        0 - 1.0000i
0                  0                  0 + 1.0000i
0                  0                  0 + 1.0000i

>> B = B1-B2

B =

0 + 1.0000i   1.0000 - 1.0000i   2.0000 + 1.0000i
0             -1.0000            3.0000 - 1.0000i
0             0                  0 - 1.0000i

>> C1 = [1, -1, 0;-1,sqrt(2)*i,-sqrt(2)*i;0,0,-1]

C1 =

 1.0000           -1.0000              0
-1.0000            0 + 1.4142i        0 - 1.4142i
      0            0                  -1.0000

>> C2 = [0 2 1;1 0 0;1 -1 0]

C2 =

0    2    1
1    0    0
1   -1    0

>> C = C1+C2

C =

1.0000          1.0000             1.0000
     0              0 + 1.4142i        0 - 1.4142i
1.0000         -1.0000            -1.0000

>> M1 = A*B-B*A

M1 =

0          -1.0000 - 1.0000i   2.0000
0           0                  1.0000 - 1.0000i
0           0                  0
```

```
>> M2 = A^2+B^2+C^2

M2 =

 2.0000              2.0000 + 3.4142i   3.0000 - 5.4142i
      0 - 1.4142i   -0.0000 + 1.4142i   0.0000 - 0.5858i
      0              2.0000 - 1.4142i   2.0000 + 1.4142i

>> M3=A*B*C

M3 =

 5.0000 + 1.0000i  -3.5858 + 1.0000i  -6.4142 + 1.0000i
 3.0000 - 2.0000i  -3.0000 + 0.5858i  -3.0000 + 3.4142i
      0 - 1.0000i       0 + 1.0000i        0 + 1.0000i

>> M4 = sqrtm(A)+sqrtm(B)-sqrtm(C)

M4 =

  0.6356 + 0.8361i  -0.3250 - 0.8204i   3.0734 + 1.2896i
  0.1582 - 0.1521i   0.0896 + 0.5702i   3.3029 - 1.8025i
 -0.3740 - 0.2654i   0.7472 + 0.3370i   1.2255 + 0.1048i


>> M5 = expm(A)*(expm(B)+expm(C))

M5 =

 14.1906 - 0.0822i   5.4400 + 4.2724i  17.9169 - 9.5842i
  4.5854 - 1.4972i   0.6830 + 2.1575i   8.5597 - 7.6573i
  3.5528 + 0.3560i   0.1008 - 0.7488i   3.2433 - 1.8406i

>> inv(A)

ans =

 1    -1     1
 0     1    -1
 0     0     1

>> inv(B)

ans =

 0 - 1.0000i  -1.0000 - 1.0000i  -4.0000 + 3.0000i
 0            -1.0000             1.0000 + 3.0000i
 0             0                      0 + 1.0000i
```

```
>> inv(C)

ans =

0.5000                 0              0.5000
0.2500          0 - 0.3536i         -0.2500
0.2500          0 + 0.3536i         -0.2500

>> [A*inv(A) B*inv(B) C*inv(C)]

ans =

1    0    0    1    0    0    1    0    0
0    1    0    0    1    0    0    1    0
0    0    1    0    0    1    0    0    1

>> A'

ans =

1    0    0
1    1    0
0    1    1

>> B'

ans =

     0 - 1.0000i        0                   0
1.0000 + 1.0000i    -1.0000                 0
2.0000 - 1.0000i    3.0000 + 1.0000i    0 + 1.0000i

>> C'

ans =

1.0000                 0              1.0000
1.0000          0 - 1.4142i         -1.0000
1.0000          0 + 1.4142i         -1.0000
```

EXERCISE 8-7

Apply the sine, base e exponential, logarithm, square root, modulus, argument and rounding functions to each of the following matrices:

$$A = \begin{bmatrix} 1 & 2 & 3 \\ 4 & 5 & 6 \\ 7 & 8 & 9 \end{bmatrix}, \quad B = \begin{bmatrix} 1+i & 2+i \\ 3+i & 4+i \end{bmatrix}.$$

Calculate e^B and $\ln(A)$.

```
>> A = [1 2 3; 4 5 6; 7 8 9]

A =

1    2    3
4    5    6
7    8    9

>> sin(A)

ans =

 0.8415    0.9093    0.1411
-0.7568   -0.9589   -0.2794
 0.6570    0.9894    0.4121

>> B   =[1+i 2+i;3+i,4+i]

B =

1.0000 + 1.0000i    2.0000 + 1.0000i
3.0000 + 1.0000i    4.0000 + 1.0000i

>> sin(B)

ans =

1.2985 + 0.6350i    1.4031 - 0.4891i
0.2178 - 1.1634i   -1.1678 - 0.7682i

>> exp(A)

ans =

1.0e+003 *

0.0027    0.0074    0.0201
0.0546    0.1484    0.4034
1.0966    2.9810    8.1031
```

```
>> exp(B)

ans =

  1.4687 +  2.2874i   3.9923 +  6.2177i
 10.8523 + 16.9014i  29.4995 + 45.9428i

>> log(B)

ans =

 0.3466 + 0.7854i   0.8047 + 0.4636i
 1.1513 + 0.3218i   1.4166 + 0.2450i

>> sqrt(B)

ans =

 1.0987 + 0.4551i   1.4553 + 0.3436i
 1.7553 + 0.2848i   2.0153 + 0.2481i

>> abs(B)

ans =

 1.4142    2.2361
 3.1623    4.1231

>> imag(B)

ans =

 1    1
 1    1

>> fix(sin(B))

ans =

 1.0000        1.0000
 0 - 1.0000i  - 1.0000

>> ceil(log(A))

ans =

 0    1    2
 2    2    2
 2    3    3
```

```
>> sign(B)

ans =

0.7071 + 0.7071i    0.8944 + 0.4472i
0.9487 + 0.3162i    0.9701 + 0.2425i
```

The exponential functions, square root and logarithm used above apply element wise to the array, and have nothing to do with the matrix exponential and logarithmic functions that are used below.

```
>> expm(B)

ans =

1.0e+002 *

-0.3071 + 0.4625i   -0.3583 + 0.6939i
-0.3629 + 1.0431i   -0.3207 + 1.5102i

>> logm(A)

ans =

-5.6588 + 2.7896i   12.5041 - 0.4325i   -5.6325 - 0.5129i
12.8139 - 0.7970i  -23.3307 + 2.1623i   13.1237 - 1.1616i
-5.0129 - 1.2421i   13.4334 - 1.5262i   -4.4196 + 1.3313i
```

EXERCISE 8-8

Solve the following equation in the complex field:

$\sin(z) = 2$.

```
>> vpa(solve ('sin (z) = 2'))

ans =

1.3169578969248167086250463473308 * i + 1.5707963267948966192313216916398
1.5707963267948966192313216916398        1.3169578969248167086250463473308 * i
```

EXERCISE 8-9

Solve the following equations:

    a. $1 + x + x^2 + x^3 + x^4 + x^5 = 0$

    b. $x^2 + (6-i)x + 8-4i = 0$

    c. $\tan(Z) = 3i/5$

```
>> solve('1+x+x^2+x^3+x^4+x^5 = 0')

ans =

                   -1
 -1/2 - (3-^(1/2) * i) / 2
  1/2 - (3-^(1/2) * i) / 2
 -1/2 + (3 ^(1/2) * i) / 2
  1/2 + (3 ^(1/2) * i) / 2

>> solve('x ^ 2 +(6-i) * x + 8-4 * i = 0')

ans =

    -4
 i 2

>> vpa(solve('tan(Z) = 3 * i/5 '))

ans =

0.69314718055994530941723212145818 * i
```

EXERCISE 8-10

Find the results of the following operations:

    a.   the fourth root of - 1 and 1;

    b.   the fifth roots of $2 + 2i$ and $- 1 + i\sqrt{3}$;

    c.   the real part of tan (iLn ((a+ib) / (a-ib)));

    d.   the imaginary part of $(2 + i)^{\cos(4+i)}$.

```
>> solve('x^4+1=0')

ans =

2 ^(1/2) *(-i/2-1/2)
2 ^(1/2) *(i/2-1/2)
2 ^(1/2) *(1/2-i/2)
2 ^(1/2) *(i/2 + 1/2)

>> pretty (solve('x^4+1=0'))

    +-                 -+
    |   1/2 / i 1 \ |
    |  2   | - - - | |
    |       \  2  2 / |
    |                 |
    |   1/2 / i 1 \ |
    |  2   | - - - | |
    |       \ 2  2 / |
    |                 |
    |   1/2 / 1 i \ |
    |  2   | - - - | |
    |       \ 2  2 / |
    |                 |
    |   1/2 / i 1 \ |
    |  2   | - + - | |
    |       \ 2  2 / |
    +-                 -+

>> solve('x^4-1=0')

ans =

-1
 1
-i
 i

>> vpa(solve('x^5-2-2*i=0'))

ans =

 0.19259341768888084906125263406469 * i + 1.2159869826496146992458377919696
-0.87055056329612413913627001747975 * i - 0.87055056329612413913627001747975
 0.55892786746600970394985946846702 * i - 1.0969577045083811131206798770216
 0.55892786746600970394985946846702 1.0969577045083811131206798770216 * i
 1.2159869826496146992458377919696 * i + 0.19259341768888084906125263406469
```

```
>> vpa(solve('x^5+1-sqrt(3)*i=0'))

ans =

 0.46721771281818786757419290603946 * i + 1.0493881644090691705137652947201
 1.1424056652180689506550734259384 * i - 0.12007167380592154112409047542855
 0.76862922680258900220179378744147 0.85364923855044142809268986292246 * i
-0.99480195671282768870147766609475 * i - 0.57434917749851750339931347338896
 0.23882781722701229856490119703938 * i - 1.1235965399072191281921551333441

>> simplify(vpa(real(tan(i * log((a+i*b) /(a-i*b))))))

ans =

-0.5 * tanh (conj (log ((a^2 + 2.0*a*b*i-1.0*b^2) /(a^2 + b^2))) *
i + (0.5 * ((a^2 + 2.0*a*b*i-1.0*b^2) ^ 2 /(a^2 + b^2) ^ 2 - 1) * i) /
((a^2 + 2.0*a*b*i-1.0*b^2) ^ 2 /(a^2 + b^2) ^ 2 + 1))

>> simplify(vpa(imag((2+i)^cos(4-i))))

ans =

-0.62107490808037524310236676683417
```

CHAPTER 9

■■■

Algebraic Expressions, Polynomials, Equations and Systems. Tools for Optimization

9.1 Expanding, Simplifying and Factoring Algebraic Expressions

MATLAB incorporates a wide range of commands, including simplification, expansion and factorization, that allow you to work with algebraic expressions. The following table shows the most common commands used when working with algebraic expressions.

expand (expr)	*Expands an algebraic expression, presenting the result as a sum of products and powers, applying multiple angle rules for trigonometric expressions and the formal properties of exponential and logarithmic functions. It also decomposes quotients of polynomials into sums of simpler polynomial quotients.*

```
>> syms x y z t a b
>> pretty(expand((x+2)*(x+3)))
       2
   x  + 5 x + 6
>> pretty(expand((x+2)/(x+3)))
   x         2
  ----- + -----
  x + 3   x + 3
>> pretty(expand(cos(x+y)))
cos(x) cos(y) - sin(x) sin(y)
```

(continued)

factor (expr)	*The reverse operation of expand. Writes an algebraic expression as a product of factors.*

```
>> syms x y
>> pretty(factor(6*x^2+18*x-24))
6 (x + 4) (x - 1)
>> pretty(factor((x^3-y^3) /(x^4-y^4)))
    2       2
x + x y + y
----------------

        2   2
(x + y) (x  + y )
>> pretty(factor(x^3+y^3))
        2           2
(x + y) (x  - x y + y )
```

simplify (expr)	*Simplifies an algebraic expression as much as possible.*

```
>> syms x y b c
>> simplify(sin(x) ^ 2 + cos(x) ^ 2) * 2
ans =

2
>> simplify(log(exp(a+log exp (c)))))
ans =

log (exp(a + c))
```

simple (expr)	*Searches for the simplest form of an algebraic expression.*

```
>> syms a positive;
f = (1/a^3 + 6/a^2 + 12/a + 8)^(1/3);
>> simplify(f)
ans =
(8*a^3 + 12*a^2 + 6*a + 1)^(1/3)/a
>> simple(f)
simplify:
(2*a + 1)/a
radsimp:
(12/a + 6/a^2 + 1/a^3 + 8)^(1/3)
simplify(100):
1/a + 2
combine(sincos):
(12/a + 6/a^2 + 1/a^3 + 8)^(1/3)
combine(sinhcosh):
(12/a + 6/a^2 + 1/a^3 + 8)^(1/3)
```

(continued)

```
combine(ln):
(12/a + 6/a^2 + 1/a^3 + 8)^(1/3)
factor:
(12/a + 6/a^2 + 1/a^3 + 8)^(1/3)
expand:
(12/a + 6/a^2 + 1/a^3 + 8)^(1/3)
combine:
(12/a + 6/a^2 + 1/a^3 + 8)^(1/3)
rewrite(exp):
(12/a + 6/a^2 + 1/a^3 + 8)^(1/3)
rewrite(sincos):
(12/a + 6/a^2 + 1/a^3 + 8)^(1/3)
rewrite(sinhcosh):
(12/a + 6/a^2 + 1/a^3 + 8)^(1/3)
rewrite(tan):
(12/a + 6/a ^ 2 + 1/a ^ 3 + 8) ^(1/3)
mwcos2sin:
(12/a + 6/a ^ 2 + 1/a ^ 3 + 8) ^(1/3)
collect(a):
(12/a + 6/a^2 + 1/a^3 + 8)^(1/3)
ans =
1/a + 2
>> g=simple(f)
g =
1/a + 2
```

collect (expr)   *Groups terms of the expression together into powers of its variables.*

```
>> syms x;
f = x*(x*(x - 6) + 11) - 6;
>> collect(f)
ans =
x^3 - 6*x^2 + 11*x - 6
>> f = (1+x)*t + x*t;
>> collect(f)
ans =
(2*t)*x + t
```

Horner (expr)   *Factors the expression in Horner form.*

```
>> syms x;
f = x^3 - 6*x^2 + 11*x   6;
>> horner(f)
ans =
x*(x*(x - 6) + 11) - 6
```

9.2 Polynomials

MATLAB implements specific commands for working with polynomials, such as finding their roots, differentiation and interpolation. The following table shows the syntax and examples of the most important of these commands.

poly2sym(vector)	*Converts a vector of coefficients into the corresponding symbolic polynomial (from highest to lowest power).*
	
	`>> poly2sym([3 5 0 8 9])`
	
	`ans =`
	
	`3*x^4 + 5*x^3 + 8*x + 9`

poly2sym(vector, 'v')	*Converts a vector of coefficients into the corresponding symbolic polynomial in v (from highest to lowest power).*
	
	`>> poly2sym([3 5 0 8 9],'z')`
	
	`ans =`
	
	`3*z^4 + 5*z^3 + 8*z + 9`

sym2poli(polynomial)	*Converts a symbolic polynomial into a vector of coefficients (the coefficient are given in decreasing order of power).*
	
	`>> syms x`
	
	`>> sym2poly(x^5-3*x^4+2*x^2-7*x+12)`
	
	`ans =`
	
	`1    -3    0    2    -7    12`

q=conv(u,v)	*Gives the coefficients of the polynomial product of two polynomials whose coefficients are given by the vectors u and v.*
	
	`>> u=[3 -1 4 2];v=[2 1 4 6 8 3];`
	
	`>> p=conv(u,v)`
	
	`p =`
	
	`6    1    19    22    36    33    41    28    6`
	
	`>> poly2sym(p)`
	
	`ans =`
	
	`6*x^8 + x^7 + 19*x^6 + 22*x^5 + 36*x^4 + 33*x^3 + 41*x^2 + 28*x + 6`

(continued)

[q, r] = deconv(v,u)	*Gives the polynomial quotient and remainder of the division between polynomials u and v, so that v = conv (u, q) + r.*
| | ```
>> [q,r] = deconv(v,u)
q =
0.6667    0.5556    0.6296
r =
0         0         0    3.0741    4.3704    1.7407
>> poly2sym(q)
ans =
(2*x^2)/3 + (5*x)/9 + 17/27
>> poly2sym(r)
ans =
(83*x^2)/27 + (118*x)/27 + 47/27
``` |
| **p = poly (r)** | *Gives the coefficients of the polynomial p whose roots are specified by the vector r.* |
| | ```
>> p=poly(u)
p =
1    -8    17    2    -24
>> poly2sym(p)
ans =
x^4 - 8*x^3 + 17*x^2 + 2*x - 24
``` |
k = polyder(p)	*Gives the coefficients k of the derivative of the polynomial p.*
k = polyder(a,b)	*Gives the coefficients k of the derivative of the product of polynomials a and b.*
[q,d] = polyder(a,b)	*Gives the numerator q and denominator d of the derivative of a/b*
| | ```
>> polyder([1 -8 17 2 -24])
ans =
4    -24    34    2
>> poly2sym([1 -8 17 2 -24])
ans =
x^4 - 8*x^3 + 17*x^2 + 2*x - 24
>> poly2sym(polyder([1 -8 17 2 -24]))
ans =
4*x^3 - 24*x^2 + 34*x + 2
>> u = [3 - 1 4 2]; v = [2 1 4 6 8 3];
>> k = polyder(u,v)
k =
48    7    114    110    144    99    82    28
>> poly2sym(k)
ans =
48*x^7 + 7*x^6 + 114*x^5 + 110*x^4 + 144*x^3 + 99*x^2 + 82*x + 28
``` |

(continued)
```

```
>> [q, d] = polyder(u,v)
q =
-12    3   -30   -10    8   -29   -30   -4
d =
4     4    17    32    60    76   106   120   100    48    9
```

p = polyfit(x, y, n)

Finds the polynomial of degree n which is the best fit of the set of points (x, y).

[p,S] = polyfit(x,y,n)

Finds the polynomial of degree n which is the best fit of the set of points (x, y) and also returns structure data S of the fit.

[p, S, u] = polyfit (x, y, n)

Finds the coefficients of the polynomial in $\hat{x}=(x-m)/s$ which best fits the data, and also returns the structure data S and the row vector u=[m, s], where m is the mean and s is the standard deviation of the data x.

```
>> u = [3 -1 4 2];v=[2 1 4 6];
>> p = poly2sym(polyfit(u,v,3))
p =
(53*x^3)/60 - (99*x^2)/20 + (119*x)/30 + 54/5
>> [p,S,u] = polyfit(u,v,3)
p =
8.9050    1.6333   -11.3053    6.0000
S =
R: [4x4 double]
df: 0
normr: 1.2686e-014
u =
2.0000
2.1602
```

y = polyval(p,x)

Evaluates the polynomial p at x.

y = polyval(p,x,[],u)

If u=[m,s], evaluates the polynomial p at $\hat{x}=(x-m)/s$.

[y, delta] = polyval (p, x, S)

Uses the optional output structure S generated by polyfit to generate error estimates delta.

[y, delta] = polyval(p,x,S,u)

Does the above with $\hat{x}=(x-m)/s$ in place of x, where u[m,s].

```
>> p = [2 0 -1 7 9]
p =
2    0   -1    7    9
>> poly2sym(p)
ans =
2*x^4 - x^2 + 7*x + 9
>> polyval(p,10)
ans =
19979
```

(continued)

Y = polyvalm (p, X)

For a polynomial p and a matrix X, evaluates p(X) in the matrix sense.

```
>> X = [1 2 3; 4 5 6; 7 8 9]
X =
   1    2    3
   4    5    6
   7    8    9
>> p = [2 0 -1 7 9]
p =
   2    0   -1    7    9
>> A = polyval(p,X)
A =
    17          51         183
   533        1269        2607
  4811        8193       13113
```

[r,p,k] = residue(b,a)

Finds the residues, poles and direct term of the rational expansion of b/a.

$$\frac{b(s)}{a(s)} = \frac{r_1}{s-p_1} + \frac{r_2}{s-p_2} + \cdots + \frac{r_n}{s-p_n} + k(s).$$

[b,a] = residue(r,p,k)

Converts the partial fraction expansion back into a quotient of polynomials.

```
>> u = [3 -1 4 2]; v = [2 1 4 6 8 3];
>> [r,p,k] = residue(v,u)
r =
  0.4751 - 0.6032i
  0.4751 + 0.6032i
  0.0745
p =
  0.3705 + 1.2240i
  0.3705 - 1.2240i
 -0.4076
k =
  0.6667   0.5556   0.6296
>> [v,u] = residue(r,p,k)
v =
  0.6667   0.3333   1.3333   2.0000   2.6667   1.0000
u =
  1.0000  -0.3333   1.3333   0.6667
```

(continued)

r = roots(c)	Gives the column vector r of the roots of the polynomial with coefficients c.
	`>> v = [0.6667    0.3333    1.3333    2.0000    2.6667    1.0000];`
	`>> r = roots(v)`
	`r =`
	`0.6662 + 1.4813i`
	`0.6662 - 1.4813i`
	`-0.6662 + 0.8326i`
	`-0.6662 - 0.8326i`
	`-0.5000`

9.3 Polynomial Interpolation

MATLAB implements both algebraic and graphical commands for polynomial interpolation, the most important of which are summarized in the following table.

Yi = interp1(X, Y, Xi)	Returns a vector Yi such that (Xi, Yi) is the total set of points found by one-dimensional linear interpolation of the given set of points (X, Y).
Yi = interp1(Y,Xi)	Equivalent to interp1(X,Y,Xi) with X = 1: n, where n is the length of Y.
Yi = interp1(X,Y,Xi,method)	Performs the interpolation using the given method, which can be nearest (nearest neighbor), linear, cubic (cubic Hermite), v5cubic (MATLAB 5 cubic), spline or pchip (cubic Hermite).
Yi= interp1(X,Y,Xi, method,ext)	Additionally specifies a strategy for evaluating points that lie outside the domain of X.
	In the following example, 21 points (x,y) are interpolated depending on the function $y = sin (x)$ for x values equally spaced between 0 and 10.
	`>> x = 0:10; y = sin (x); Xi = 0:.5:10; yi = interp1 (x, y, xi);` `points = [xi', yi']`
	`points =`
	`0          0`
	`0.5000     0.4207`
	`1.0000     0.8415`
	`1.5000     0.8754`
	`2.0000     0.9093`
	`2.5000     0.5252`
	`3.0000     0.1411`
	`3.5000    -0.3078`
	`4.0000    -0.7568`
	`4.5000    -0.8579`
	`5.0000    -0.9589`

(continued)

5.5000	-0.6192
6.0000	-0.2794
6.5000	0.1888
7.0000	0.6570
7.5000	0.8232
8.0000	0.9894
8.5000	0.7007
9.0000	0.4121
9.5000	-0.0660
10.0000	-0.5440

We can represent the points in the following form:

```
plot(x,y,'o',xi,yi)
```

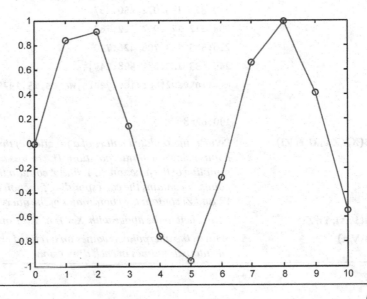

(*continued*)

Zi = interp2(X,Y,Z,Xi,Yi)	*Returns a vector Zi such that (Xi, Yi, Zi) is the set of points found by two-dimensional linear interpolation of the set of given points (X, Y, Z).*
Zi = interp2(Z,Xi,Yi)	*Equivalent to the above with X = 1: n and Y = 1:m where (n, m) = size(Z).*
Zi = interp2(Z,n)	*Returns the interpolated values on a refined grid formed by repeatedly dividing the intervals n times in each dimension.*
Zi = interp2(X,Y,Z,Xi,Yi,*method*)	*In addition specifies the method of interpolation. Possible methods are nearest (nearest neighbor), linear, cubic (cubic Hermite) and spline interpolation.*

In the following example we consider a set of years, years of service and wages and try to find by interpolation the salary earned in 1975 by an employee with 15 years of service.

```
>> years = 10:1950:1990;
service = 10:10:30;
wages = [150.697 199.592 187.625
179.323 195.072 250.287
203.212 179.092 322.767
226.505 153.706 426.730
249.633 120.281 598.243];
w = interp2(service,years,wages,15,1975)
w =
190.6288
```

vi = interp3(X,Y,Z,V,Xi,Yi,Zi)	*Returns interpolated values of a function of three variables at specific query points using linear interpolation. The results always pass through the original sampling of the function. X, Y, and Z contain the coordinates of the sample points. V contains the corresponding function values at each sample point. Xi, Yi, and Zi contain the coordinates of the query points.*
vi = interp3(V, Xi, Yi, Zi)	*Equivalent to the above with X = 1: n, Y = 1:m, Z = 1:p where (n, m, p) = size(V).*
vi = interp3(V,n)	*Returns the interpolated values on a refined grid formed by repeatedly dividing the intervals n times in each dimension.*

(continued)

vi = interp3(...,method)

Performs the interpolation using the specified method.

The following example calculates and represents interpolated values of the MATLAB function *flow* by taking several slices through the data and displaying the interpolated data on each slice. The three axes are sampled in equal intervals of 0.5, for x between 0.1 and 10 and y and z between -3 and 3.

```
>> [x, y, z, v] = flow(10);
[xi, yi, zi] = meshgrid(.1:.5:10,-3:.5:3,-3:.5:3);
vi = interp3(x,y,z,v,xi,yi,zi);
slice(xi,yi,zi,vi,[6 9.5],2,[-2 .2]), shading flat
```

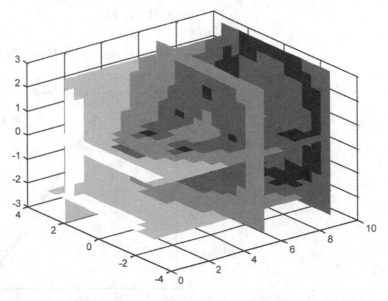

Y = interpft(X,n)

One-dimensional interpolation using the FFT method. Gives the vector containing the values of the periodic function X sampled at n equally spaced points. The original vector X is transformed to the Fourier domain via the fast Fourier transform (FFT).

(continued)

y = interpft (x, n, dim)	*Operates along the specified dimension.*

Below is an example where the original points and the interpolated points using the FFT method are compared.

```
>> y = [0:. 5:2 1.5:-. 5: - 2 - 1.5:. 5:0]; % Equally spaced
points
factor = 5; A factor of 5% Tween
m = length(y) * factor;
x = 1:factor: m;
XI = 1;
Yi = interpft (y, m);
plot(x,y,'o',xi,yi,'*')
Legend ('original data', 'interpolated data')
```

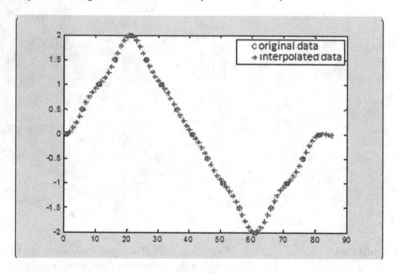

Vi = interpn(X,Y,Z,...V, Xi, Yi, Zi...)	*Returns interpolated values of a function of n variables at specific query points using linear interpolation. The results always pass through the original sampling of the function. X,Y,Z,... contain the coordinates of the sample points. V contains the corresponding function values at each sample point. Xi,Yi,Zi,... contain the coordinates of the query points.*
Vi = interpn (V, Xi, Yi, Zi)	*Equivalent to the above with X = 1: n, Y = 1:m, Z = 1:p,... where (n, m, p,...) = size(V).*
Vi = interpn (V, n)	*Returns the interpolated values on a refined grid formed by repeatedly dividing the intervals n times in each dimension.*
Vi = interpn(...,method)	*Interpolation using the specified method.*
Yi = pchip (X, Y, Xi)	*Returns a vector Yi containing elements corresponding to the elements of Xi and determined by piecewise cubic interpolation within vectors X and Y.*
pp = pchip(X,Y)	*Returns a piecewise polynomial structure for use by ppval.*

(*continued*)

Yi = spline (X, Y, Xi)

Uses a cubic spline interpolation to find Yi, the values of the underlying function Y at the values of the interpolant Xi. The simple points are determined by X.

pp = spline(X,Y)

Returns the piecewise polynomial form of the cubic spline interpolant for later use with ppval and the spline utility unmkpp.

In the following example the original points are compared with the interpolated points obtained using the the *pchip* and *spline* methods.

```
>> x = - 3:3;
y = [- 1 - 1 - 1 0 1 1 1];
t = - 3:. 01:3;
plot(x, y, 'o', t, [pchip(x, y, t); spline(x,y,t)])
legend('data','pchip','spline',4)
```

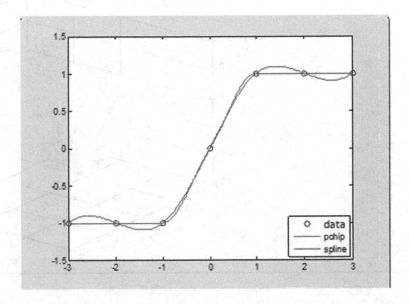

Zi = griddata(X,Y,Z,Xi,Yi)

Fits a surface of the form Z = f(X,Y) to the scattered data in the vectors (X,Y,Z). The function interpolates the surface at the query points specified by (Xi,Yi) and returns the interpolated values, Zi. The surface always passes through the data points defined by X and Y. The method of interpolation is linear by default.

[Xi, Yi, Zi] = griddata(X,Y,Z,Xi,Yi)

Returns in addition to Zi the vectors Xi and Yi.

(continued)

[...] = griddata(...,method)

Interpolation using the specified method.

The example below interpolates scattered data over a grid.

```
x = rand (100.1) * 4-2; y = rand (100.1) * 4-2;
z = x.*exp(-x.^2-y.^2);
ti = -2:.25:2;
[xi,yi] = meshgrid(ti,ti);
Zi = griddata(x,y,z,xi,yi);
mesh(xi,yi,zi), hold on, plot3(x,y,z,'o'),
hold off
```

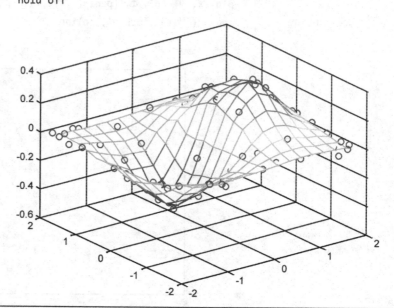

(continued)

W = griddata3(X,Y,Z,V,Xi,Yi,Zi)   *Fits a hypersurface of the form V = f(X,Y,Z) to the scattered data in the vectors (X,Y,Z,V). The function interpolates the hypersurface at the query points specified by (Xi,Yi,Zi) and returns the interpolated values, W. The surface always passes through the data points defined by X, Y and Z. The method of interpolation is linear by default.*

W = griddata3(...,'method')   *Interpolation using the specified method.*

Below is an example of fitting a hypersurface to scattered data by interpolation.

```
>> x = 2*rand(5000,1)-1; y = 2*rand(5000,1)-1; z = 2*rand(5000,1)-1;
v = x.^2 + y.^2 + z.^2;
d = -0.8:0.05:0.8;
[xi,yi,zi] = meshgrid(d,d,d);
w = griddata3(x,y,z,v,xi,yi,zi);
p = patch(isosurface(xi,yi,zi,w,0.8));
isonormals(xi,yi,zi,w,p);
set(p,'FaceColor','blue','EdgeColor','none');
view(3), axis equal, axis off, camlight, lighting phong
```

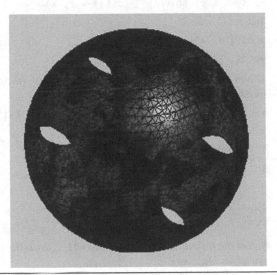

9.4 Solving Equations and Systems of Equations

MATLAB includes multiple commands for solving equations and systems of equations. The following sections present the syntax and main features of these methods.

9.4.1 General Methods

Below are the most common MATLAB commands used to solve equations and systems.

solve('equation', 'x')	*Solve the equation in the variable x.*
	
	The equation $p * sin(x) = r$ is solved as follows:
	
	`>> solve('p*sin(x) = r')`
	
	`ans =`
	
	`asin(r/p)`
	
	`pi - asin(r/p)`

syms x;
solve (equ (x), x)
	Solve the equation equ (x) = 0 in the variable x.
	
	The equation $p * cos(x) = r$ is solved as follows:
	
	`>> syms x r; solve(p * cos(x) - r, x)`
	
	`ans =`
	
	`acos ((8192*r)/1433639)`
	
	`-acos ((8192*r)/1433639)`

solve('eq1,eq2,...,eqn',
'x1, x2,...,xn')
	Solves the n simultaneous equations eq1,..., eqn (the solutions are assigned to the variables x1,..., xn)
	
	`>> [x, y] = solve('x^2 + x*y + y = 3','x^2-4*x + 3 = 0')`
	
	`x =`
	
	`1`
	
	`3`
	
	`y =`
	
	`1`
	
	`-3/2`

syms x1 x2...xn;
solve(eq1,eq2,...,eqn,
x1, x2,...,xn)
	Solves the n simultaneous equations eq1,..., eqn (the solutions are assigned to the variables x1,..., xn)
	
	`>> syms x y; [x, y] = solve(x^2 + x*y + y-3, x^2-4*x + 3)`
	
	`x =`
	
	`1`
	
	`3`
	
	`y =`
	
	`1`
	
	`-3/2`

(*continued*)

X = linsolve (A, B)	*Solves the equation A * X = B where A,B and X are matrices.*

We solve the system:

$$2x + y + z + t = 1$$
$$x + 2y + z + t = 2$$
$$x + y + z + 2t = 3$$
$$x + y + z + 2t = 4.$$

```
>> A = [2,1,1,1;1,2,1,1;1,1,2,1;1,1,1,2];B = [1,2,3,4]';
linsolve(A, B)

ans =

-1

0

1

2
```

x = lscov(A,B)	*Solves the equation A * x = B in the least squares sense, i.e., x is the n×1 vector that minimizes the sum of squared errors (B - A*x)'*(B - A*x).*
x = lscov(A,B,V)	*Solves A * x = B in the least squares sense with covariance matrix proportional to V, i.e. x minimizes (B - A*x)'*inv(V)*(B - A*x).*

```
>> A = [2,1,1,1;1,2,1,1;1,1,2,1;1,1,1,2];B = [1,2,3,4]';
lscov(A, B)

ans =

-1

0

1

2
```

X = A\B	*Solves the system A * X = B.*

```
>> A = [2,1,1,1;1,2,1,1;1,1,2,1;1,1,1,2];B = [1,2,3,4]';
A\B

ans =

-1.0000

-0.0000

1.0000

2.0000
```

X = A/B	*Solves the system X * A = B.*

(*continued*)

roots (A)	*Returns the roots of the polynomial whose coefficients are given by the vector A (from highest to lowest order).*
	
	As example we find the roots of the polynomial $x^4 + 2x^3 + 3x + 4$.
	
	`>> roots([1 2 3 4])`
	
	`ans =`
	
	`-1.6506`
	
	`-0.1747 + 1.5469i`
	
	`-0.1747 - 1.5469i`

poly (V)	*Returns the coefficients of the polynomial whose roots are given by the vector V.*
	
	`>> poly([1 2 3 4])`
	
	`ans =`
	
	`1 1 -10 -10 35 -50 24`

x = fzero x0 (function)	*Returns a zero of the function near x0.*
	
	`>> X = fzero('sin(x) - 1', pi/2)`
	
	`X =`
	
	`1.5708`

[x, fval] = fzero x0 (fun)	*Also returns the objective value of the function at x.*
	
	`>> [F x] = fzero('sin(x) - 1', pi/2)`
	
	`X =`
	
	`1.5708`
	
	`f =`
	
	`0`

9.4.2 The Biconjugate Gradient Method

Below are the MATLAB commands that can be used to solve equations and systems of equations by the biconjugate gradient method.

x = bicg(A,b)	*Tries to solve the system Ax = b by the method of biconjugate gradients.*
	
	`>> A = [2 pi * pi 3 * pi - pi; 1 0 - 1 2; (1) (2) exp exp exp exp (3) (4); i 2i 3i - i];`
	
	`>> B = [1 2 3 4]';`
	
	`>> bicg(A, B)`
	
	`bicg stopped at iteration 4 without converging to the desired tolerance 1e-006`
	
	`because the maximum number of iterations was reached. The iterate returned (number 0) has relative residual 1`
	
	`ans =`
	
	`0`
	
	`0`
	
	`0`
	
	`0`

bicg(A,b,tol)	*Solves Ax = b by specifying tolerance.*

bicg(A,b,tol,maxit)	*Solves Ax = b by specifying the tolerance and the maximum number of iterations.*
	
	`>> bicg(A,B, 1e-009,100)`
	
	`ans =`
	
	`1. 0e + 016 *`
	
	`4.1449 0. 7033i`
	
	`-7.1997 + 1. 2216i`
	
	`3.2729 0. 5553i`
	
	`-0.4360 + 0. 0740i`

bicg(A,b,tol,maxit,M)	*Solves the system inv(M) * A * x = inv (M) * b.*
bicg(A,b,tol,maxit,M1,M2)	*Solves the system inv(M) * A * x = inv (M) * b with M = M1 * M2.*
bicg(A,b,tol,maxit,M1,M2,x0)	*Solves the system inv(M) * A * x = inv (M) * b with M = M1 * M2 and initial value x0.*

[x,f] = bicg(A,b,...)	*Tries to solve the system and also returns a convergence indicator f (0 = convergence, 1 = no-convergence, 2 = ill-conditioned, 3 = stagnation and 4 = very extreme numbers).*
	
	`>> [x, f] = bicg(A,B, 1e-009,100)`
	
	`x =`
	
	`1. 0e + 016 *`
	
	`4.1449 0. 7033i`
	
	`-7.1997 + 1. 2216i`
	
	`3.2729 0. 5553i`
	
	`-0.4360 + 0. 0740i`
	
	`f =`
	
	`3`

(continued)

235

x = bicgstab(A,b)	*Tries to solve the system Ax = b by the method of stabilized biconjugate gradients.*
	`>> bicgstab(A, B)`
	`bicgstab stopped at iteration 4 without converging to the desired tolerance 1e-006`
	`because the maximum number of iterations was reached.`
	`The iterate returned (number 4) has relative residual 0.88`
	`ans =`
	`1. 0e + 011 *`
	`0.6696-0. 4857i`
	`-1.1631 + 0. 8437i`
	`0.5287 0. 3835i`
	`-0.0704 + 0. 0511i`
bicgstab(A,b,tol)	*Solves Ax = b by specifying tolerance.*
bicgstab(A,b,tol,maxit)	*Solves Ax = b by specifying the tolerance and the maximum number of iterations.*
	`>> bicg(A,B, 1e-009,100)`
	`ans =`
	`1.0e   + 016 *`
	`4.1449    0.7033i`
	`-7.1997 + 1.2216i`
	`3.2729    0.5553i`
	`-0.4360 + 0.0740i`
bicgstab(A,b,tol,maxit,M)	*Solves the system inv(M) * A * x = inv (M) * b.*
bicgstab(A,b,tol,maxit,M1,M2)	*Solves the system inv(M) * A * x = inv (M) * b with M = M1 * M2.*
bicgstab(A,b,tol,maxit,M1,M2,x0)	*Solves the system inv(M) * A * x = inv (M) * b with M = M1 * M2 and initial value x0.*
[x,f] = bicgstab(A,b,...)	*Tries to solve the system and returns a convergence indicator f (0 = convergence, 1 = no-convergence, 2 = ill-conditioned, 3 = stagnation and 4 = very extreme numbers).*
[x,f,relres] = bicgstab(A,b,...)	*Also returns the relative residual norm(b-A*x) /norm (b)*

(*continued*)

[x,f,relres,iter] = bicgstab(A,b,...)	*Also returns the number of iterations*

```
>> [x, f, r, i] = bicg(A,B, 1e-006,100)
x =
1. 0e + 016 *
4.1449 0. 7033i
-7.1997 + 1. 2216i
3.2729 0. 5553i
-0.4360 + 0. 0740i
f =
3
r =
26.0415
i =
18
```

9.4.3 The Conjugate Gradients Method

Below are the MATLAB commands that are used to solve equations and systems of equations by the method of conjugate gradients.

x = pcg(A,b)	*Tries to solve the system Ax = b by the pre-conditioned conjugate gradients method.*
pcg(A,b,tol)	*Solves Ax = b by specifying tolerance.*
pcg(A,b,tol,maxit)	*Solves Ax = b by specifying the tolerance and the maximum number of iterations.*
pcg(A,b,tol,maxit,M)	*Solves the system inv(M) * A * x = inv (M) * b.*
pcg(A,b,tol,maxit,M1,M2)	*Solves the system inv(M) * A * x = inv (M) * b with M = M1 * M2.*
pcg(A,b,tol,maxit,M1,M2,x0)	*Solves the system inv(M) * A * x = inv (M) * b with M = M1 * M2 and initial value x0.*
[x,f] = pcg(A,b,...)	*Tries to solve the system and returns a convergence indicator f (0 = convergence, 1 = no-convergence, 2 = ill-conditioned, 3 = stagnation and 4 = very extreme numbers).*
[x,f,relres] = pcg(A,b,...)	*Also returns the relative residual norm (b-A*x) /norm (b).*

(continued)

[x,f,relres,iter] = pcg(A,b,...)	*Also returns the number of iterations.*
	`>> A = [pi 2*pi 3*pi -pi; 1 0 -1 2; exp(1) exp(2) exp(3) exp(4); i 2i 3i -i];`
	`>> B = [1 2 3 4]';`
	`>> [x,f,r,i]=pcg(A,B, 1e-006,1000)`
	`x =`
	`0`
	`0`
	`0`
	`0`
	`f =`
	`4`
	`r =`
	`1`
	`i =`
	`0`
x = lsqr(A,b)	*Tries to solve the system Ax = b by the LSQR method.*
lsqr(A,b,tol)	*Solves Ax = b by specifying tolerance.*
lsqr(A,b,tol,maxit)	*Solves Ax = b by specifying the tolerance and the maximum number of iterations.*
lsqr(A,b,tol,maxit,M)	*Solves the system inv(M) * A * x = inv (M) * b.*
lsqr(A,b,tol,maxit,M1,M2)	*Solves the system inv(M) * A * x = inv (M) * b with M = M1 * M2.*
lsqr(A,b,tol,maxit,M1,M2,x0)	*Solves the system inv(M) * A * x = inv (M) * b with M = M1 * M2 and initial value x0.*
[x,f] = lsqr(A,b,...)	*Tries to solve the system and returns a convergence indicator f (0 = convergence, 1 = no-convergence, 2 = ill-conditioned, 3 = stagnation and 4 = very extreme numbers).*
[x,f,relres] = lsqr(A,b,...)	*Also returns the relative residual norm (b-A*x) /norm (b).*

(continued)

[x,f,relres,iter] = lsqr(A,b,...)	*Also returns the number of iterations.*

```
>> A = [pi 2*pi 3*pi -pi; 1 0 -1 2; exp(1) exp(2) exp(3) exp(4);
i 2i 3i -i];
>> B = [1 2 3 4]';
>> [x, f, r, i] = lsqr(A,B, 1e-006,1000)
x =
 1.1869   0.0910i
 0.4295   0.0705i
-0.5402 - 0.0362i
 0.1364 + 0.0274i
f =
0
r =
0.6981
i =
3
```

9.4.4 The Residual Method

Below are the MATLAB commands that are used to solve equations and systems of equations by the residual method.

x = qmr(A,b)	*Tries to solve the system Ax = b by the quasi-minimal residual method.*
qmr(A,b,tol)	*Solves Ax = b by specifying tolerance.*
qmr(A,b,tol,maxit)	*Solves Ax = b by specifying the tolerance and the maximum number of iterations.*
qmr(A,b,tol,maxit,M)	*Solves the system inv(M) * A * x = inv (M) * b.*
qmr(A,b,tol,maxit,M1,M2)	*Solves the system inv(M) * A * x = inv (M) * b with M = M1 * M2.*
qmr(A,b,tol,maxit,M1,M2,x0)	*Solves the system inv(M) * A * x = inv (M) * b with M = M1 * M2 and initial value x0.*
[x,f] = qmr(A,b,...)	*Tries to solve the system and returns a convergence indicator f (0 = convergence, 1 = no-convergence, 2 = ill-conditioned, 3 = stagnation and 4 = very extreme numbers).*
[x,f,relres] = qmr(A,b,...)	*Also returns the residual waste norm (b-A*x) /norm (b).*

(continued)

[x,f,relres,iter] = qmr(A,b,...)	*Also returns the number of iterations.*
	
	`>> A = [pi 2*pi 3*pi -pi; 1 0 -1 2; exp(1) exp(2) exp(3) exp(4);`
	`i 2i 3i -i];`
	
	`>> B = [1 2 3 4]';`
	
	`>> [x,f,r,i] = qmr(A,B, 1e-006,1000)`
	
	`x =`
	
	`1.0e+016 *`
	
	`0.4810 - 4.0071i`
	
	`-0.8356 + 6.9603i`
	
	`0.3798 - 3.1640i`
	
	`-0.0506 + 0.4215i`
	
	`f =`
	
	`3`
	
	`r =`
	
	`19.5999`
	
	`i =`
	
	`11`

x = gmres(A,b)	*Tries to solve the system Ax = b by the generalized minimum residual method.*
gmres(A,b,tol)	*Solves Ax = b by specifying tolerance.*
gmres(A,b,tol,maxit)	*Solves Ax = b by specifying the tolerance and the maximum number of iterations.*
gmres(A,b,tol,maxit,M)	*Solves the system inv(M) * A * x = inv (M) * b.*
gmres(A,b,tol,maxit,M1,M2)	*Solves the system inv(M) * A * x = inv (M) * b with M = M1 * M2.*
gmres(A,b,tol,maxit,M1,M2,x0)	*Solves the system inv(M) * A * x = inv (M) * b with M = M1 * M2 and initial value x0.*
[x,f] = gmres(A,b,...)	*Tries to solve the system and returns a convergence indicator f (0 = convergence, 1 = no-convergence, 2 = ill-convergence, 3 = stagnation and 4 = very extreme numbers).*
[x,f,relres] = gmres(A,b,...)	*Also returns the relative residual norm(b-A*x) /norm (b).*

(continued)

[x,f,relres,iter] = gmres(A,b,...)	*Also returns the number of iterations.*
| | ```
>> A = [pi 2*pi 3*pi -pi; 1 0 -1 2; exp(1) exp(2) exp(3) exp(4);
i 2i 3i -i];
>> B = [1 2 3 4]';
>> [x,f,r,i] = gmres(A,B)
x =
 1.5504 + 0.0085i
-0.2019 - 0.2433i
-0.2532 + 0.0423i
 0.0982 + 0.0169i
f =
3
r =
0.6981
i =
1    4
``` |
x = minres(A,b)	*Tries to solve the system Ax = b by the minimum residual method.*
minres(A,b,tol)	*Solves Ax = b by specifying tolerance.*
minres(A,b,tol,maxit)	*Solves Ax = b by specifying the tolerance and the maximum number of iterations.*
minres(A,b,tol,maxit,M)	*Solves the system inv(M) * A * x = inv (M) * b.*
minres(A,b,tol,maxit,M1,M2)	*Solves the system inv(M) * A * x = inv (M) * b with M = M1 * M2.*
minres(A,b,tol,maxit,M1,M2,x0)	*Solves the system inv(M) * A * x = inv (M) * b with M = M1 * M2 and initial value x0.*
[x,f] = minres(A,b,...)	*Tries to solve the system and returns a convergence indicator f (0 = convergence, 1 = no-convergence, 2 = ill-conditioned, 3 = stagnation and 4 = very extreme numbers).*
[x,f,relres] = minres(A,b,...)	*Also returns the relative residual norm (b-A*x) /norm (b).*

(*continued*)
```

[x,f,relres,iter] = minres(A,b,...)	*Also returns the number of iterations.*

```
>> A = [pi 2*pi 3*pi -pi; 1 0 -1 2; exp(1) exp(2) exp(3) exp(4);
i 2i 3i -i];
>> B = [1 2 3 4]';
>> [x,f,r,i] = minres(A,B, 1e-006,1000)
x =
 0.0748 - 0.0070i
-0.0761 - 0.0001i
 0.5934 - 0.1085i
-0.1528 + 0.0380i
f =
1
r =
0.0592
i =
1000
```

9.4.5 The Symmetric and Non-Negative Least Squares Method

Below are the MATLAB commands that are used to solve equations and systems of equations by the symmetric and non-negative least squares methods.

x = symmlq(A,b)	*Tries to solve the system Ax = b by the symmetric LQ method.*
symmlq(A,b,tol)	*Solves Ax = b by specifying the tolerance.*
symmlq(A,b,tol,maxit)	*Solves Ax = b by specifying the tolerance and the maximum number of iterations.*
symmlq(A,b,tol,maxit,M)	*Solves the system inv(M) * A * x = inv (M) * b.*
symmlq(A,b,tol,maxit,M1,M2)	*Solves the system inv(M) * A * x = inv (M) * b with M = M1 * M2.*
symmlq(A,b,tol,maxit,M1,M2,x0)	*Solves the system inv(M) * A * x = inv (M) * b with M = M1 * M2 and initial value x0.*
[x,flag] = symmlq(A,b,...)	*Tries to solve the system and returns a convergence indicator (0 = convergence, 1 = no-convergence, 2 = ill-conditioned, 3 = stagnation and 4 = very extreme numbers).*
[x,flag,relres] = symmlq(A,b,...)	*Also returns the relative residual norm (b-A*x) /norm (b).*

(*continued*)

[x,flag,relres,iter] = symmlq(A,b,...)	*Also returns the number of iterations.*
	`>> A = [pi 2*pi 3*pi -pi; 1 0 -1 2; exp(1) exp(2) exp(3) exp(4); i 2i 3i -i];`
	`>> B = [1 2 3 4]';`
	`>> [x,f,r,i] = symmlq(A,B, 1e-006,1000)`
	`x =`
	`0.0121 - 0.0004i`
	`0.0035 - 0.0001i`
	`0.1467 - 0.0061i`
	`0.0001 + 0.0039i`
	`f =`
	`1`
	`r =`
	`0.8325`
	`i =`
	`3`
x = lsqnonneg(C,d)	*Returns the vector x that minimizes norm (C*x-d) subject to x >=0. C and d must be real.*
x = lsqnonneg(C,d,x0)	*Uses x0>=0 as the initial value and a possible option. The options are TolX for termination tolerance on x and Display to show the output ('off' does not display output, 'final' shows just the final output and 'notify' shows the output only if there is no convergence).*
x = lsqnonneg(C,d,x0,opt)	*Returns the value of the squared 2-norm of the residual: norm(C*x-d)^2.*
[x,resnorm] = lsqnonneg(...)	*In addition returns the residual C * x-d.*
[x,resnorm,residual] = lsqnonneg(...)	*In addition gives a convergence indicator f (positive indicates convergence, 0 indicates non-convergence).*
[x,resnorm,residual,f] = lsqnonneg(...)	
[x,resnorm,residual,f, out,lambda] = lsqnonneg(...)	*In addition to the above, returns output data describing the algorithm used, iterations taken and exit message, and also the vector of Lagrange multipliers lambda.*
	`>> A = [1 2 3;5 7 1;2 3 6]; B=[1 3 5]'; lsqnonneg(A,B)`
	`ans =`
	`0.4857`
	`0`
	`0.5714`

9.5 Solving Linear Systems of Equations

In the previous sections we have studied equations and systems in general. We will now focus on linear systems of equations. To solve such systems we could simply use the commands we have seen so far, however MATLAB has a selection of special commands designed especially for linear systems. The following table lists these commands.

X = linsolve (A, B)	*Solves the linear system A * X = B.*
	We solve the system:
	
	$$2x + y + z + t = 1$$
	$$x + 2y + z + t = 2$$
	$$x + y + 2z + t = 3$$
	$$x + y + z + 2t = 4.$$
	
	`>> A = [2,1,1,1;1,2,1,1;1,1,2,1;1,1,1,2];B = [1,2,3,4]';`
	`linsolve(A, B)`
	`ans =`
	`-1`
	`0`
	`1`
	`2`

[X, R] = linsolve (A, B)	*Solves the linear system A * X = B and additionally returns the reciprocal of the condition number of A if A is square, or the rank of A if A is not square.*
	`>> A = [2,1,1,1;1,2,1,1;1,1,2,1;1,1,1,2];B = [1,2,3,4]';`
	`[X, R] = linsolve(A, B)`
	`X =`
	`-1`
	`0`
	`1`
	`2`
	`R =`
	`0.1429`

X = linsolve (A, B, options)	*Solves the linear system A * X = B using various options for the matrix A (UT for upper triangular, LT for lower triangular, SYM for symmetric real or complex hermitian, RECT for general rectangular, POSDEF for positive definite, UHESS for upper Hessenberg and TRANSA for conjugate transpose).*

rank (A)	*Rank of the matrix A.*
	`>> rank(A)`
	`ans =`
	`4`

(continued)

det (A)	*Determinant of the square matrix A.*
	`>> det(A)`
	`ans =`
	`5`
Z = null (A, 'r')	*Rational basis for the null space of A.*

Systems of linear equations can be converted to array form and solved using calculations with matrices. A system can be written in the form $M . X = B$, where X is the vector of variables, B the vector of independent terms and M the matrix of coefficients of the system. If M is a square matrix and the determinant of the matrix M is non-null, M is invertible, and the unique solution of the system can be written in the form: $X = M^{-1}B$. In this case, the commands *solve, linsolve, lscov, bicg, pcg, lsqr, gmr, gmres, minres, symmlq* or $M\backslash B$, already described above, offer the solution.

If the determinant of M is zero, the system has infinitely many solutions, since there are rows or columns in M that are linearly dependent. In this case, the number of redundant equations can be calculated to find out how many variables are needed to describe the solutions. If the matrix M is rectangular (not square), the system may be undetermined (the number of equations is less than the number of variables), overdetermined (the number of equations is greater than the number of variables) or non-singular (the number of equations is equal to number of variables and M has non-zero determinant). An indeterminate system can have infinitely many solutions, or none, and likewise for an overdetermined system. If a system has no solution, it is called inconsistent (incompatible), and if there is at least one solution, it is called consistent (compatible). The system $M . X = B$ is called *homogeneous* when the vector B is the null vector, i.e. the system is of the form $M . X = 0$. If the determinant of M is non-null, the unique solution of the system is the null vector (obtained with the command *linsolve*). If the determinant of M is zero, the system has infinitely many solutions. The solutions can be found using the commands *solve, linsolve, lsqr* or other commands described above for general linear systems.

A fundamental tool in the analysis and solution of systems of equations is the *Rouche-Frobenius theorem*. This theorem says that a system of m equations with n unknowns has a solution if, and only if, the rank of the matrix of coefficients coincides with the rank of the array extended with the vector column of the system-independent terms. If the two ranks are equal, and equal to the number of unknowns, the system has a unique solution. If the two ranks are the same, but less that the number of unknowns, the system has infinitely many solutions. If they are different, the system has no solution.

In summary: Let A be the matrix of coefficients of the system and B the matrix A augmented by the column vector of independent terms.

If $rank(A) \neq rank(B)$, the system is incompatible (without solution).

If $rank(A) = rank(B) < n$, the system is indefinite (has infinitely many solutions).

If $= rank(A) = rank(B) = n$, the system has a unique solution.

This theorem allows us to analyze the solutions of a system of equations before solving it.

We have already encountered *homogeneous systems*. A system $A . X = B$ is said homogeneous if the vector of independent terms B is null, so every homogeneous system is of the form $A . X = 0$. In a homogeneous system, the rank of the matrix of coefficients and the rank of the matrix augmented to include the column vector of independent terms always coincide. If we apply the Rouche-Frobenius theorem, a homogeneous system will have a unique solution when the determinant of the matrix A is non-zero. Since the null vector is always a solution of a homogeneous system, this must be the unique solution. A homogeneous system will have infinitely many solutions when the determinant of the matrix A is zero. In this case, the solutions are calculated as for general systems (using the command *solve*), or by using the function *null (A)*.

As a first example we solve the system:

$$2x + y + z + t = 1$$
$$x + 2y + z + t = 1$$
$$x + y + 2z + t = 1$$
$$x + y + z + 2t = 1$$

We will find the rank of the matrix of the system and the rank of the augmented matrix obtained by extending the matrix by the column vector of independent terms.

```
>> A = [2,1,1,1;1,2,1,1;1,1,2,1;1,1,1,2];
>> B = [2,1,1,1,1;1,2,1,1,1;1,1,2,1,1;1,1,1,2,1];
>> [rank(A), rank(B)]

ans =

4 4
```

We note that the ranks of the two matrices coincide with the number of unknowns. The Rouche-Frobenius theorem then tells us that the system is compatible with a unique solution. We can calculate the solution in the following way:

```
>> B = [1 1 1 1]';
>> linsolve(A, B)

ans =

0.2000
0.2000
0.2000
0.2000
```

The solution could also have been found using the following commands:

```
>> lscov(A, B)

ans =

0.2000
0.2000
0.2000
0.2000

>> bicg(A, B)
bicg converged at iteration 1 to a solution with relative residual 0

ans =

0.2000
0.2000
0.2000
0.2000
```

```
>> pcg(A, B)
PCG converged at iteration 1 to a solution with relative residual 0

ans =

0.2000
0.2000
0.2000
0.2000

>> lsqr(A, B)

lsqr converged at iteration 1 to a solution with relative residual 0

ans =

0.2000
0.2000
0.2000
0.2000

>> qmr(A, B)
QMR converged at iteration 1 to a solution with relative residual 0

ans =

0.2000
0.2000
0.2000
0.2000

>> gmres(A, B)
gmres converged at iteration 1 to a solution with relative residual 1.5e-016

ans =

0.2000
0.2000
0.2000
0.2000

>> symmlq(A, B)
symmlq converged at iteration 1 to a solution with relative residual 0

ans =

0.2000
0.2000
0.2000
0.2000
```

As a second example, we solve the system:

$$x + 2y + 3z = 6$$
$$x + 3y + 8z = 19$$
$$2x + 3y + z = -1$$
$$5x + 6y + 4z = 5$$

We find the rank of the matrix of the system and the rank of the augmented matrix.

```
>> A = [1,2,3;1,3,8;2,3,1;5,6,4];
>> B = [1,2,3,6;1,3,8,19;2,3,1,-1;5,6,4,5];
>> [rank(A), rank(B)]

ans =

3     3
```

We note that the ranks of the two matrices coincide with the number of unknowns. The Rouche-Frobenius theorem then tells us that the system is compatible with a unique solution. We can calculate the solution in the following way:

```
>> A = [1,2,3;1,3,8;2,3,1;5,6,4];
>> B = [19-6 - 5-1]';
>> linsolve(A, B)

ans =

1.0000
-2.0000
3.0000
```

As a third example, we solve the system:

$$x + 2y - z = 0$$
$$2x - y + z = 0$$
$$3x + y = 0$$

As we have a homogeneous system, we will calculate the determinant of the matrix of coefficients of the system.

```
>> A = [1,2, - 1; 2, - 1, 1; 3,1,0];
>> det(A)

ans =

5. 5511e-016
```

This answer is very close to zero, in fact the determinant is actually zero, thus the homogeneous system will have infinitely many solutions, which are calculated with the command *solve* as shown below.

```
>> [x, y, z] = solve('x+2*y-z, 2*x-y+z, 3*x+y', 'x,y,z')

x =

-z1/5


y =

(3 * z1) / 5


z =

z1
```

Thus the infinite set of solutions depend on a parameter z1 and are described as $\{(-z1/5, 3z1/5, z1)\}$, $z1 \in R$.

EXERCISE 9-1

Expand the following algebraic expressions:

$$(x+1)(x+2), \quad \frac{x+1}{x+2},$$

$$\sin(x+y), \quad \cos(2x), \quad e^{a+\ln(b)}, \quad \ln\left(\frac{x}{(1-x)^2}\right), \quad (x+1)(y+z).$$

```
>> syms x y z b t
>> pretty(expand((x + 1) * (x+2)))

  2
 x + 3 x + 2

>> pretty(expand((x + 1) / (x+2)))

   x          1
 ------  +  -------
 x + 2      x + 2

>> pretty(expand(sin(x + y)))

 sin(x) cos(y) + cos(x) sin(y)
```

```
>> pretty(expand(cos(2*x)))
```

```
      2
2 cos (x) - 1
```

```
>> pretty(expand(exp(a+log(b))))
```

```
exp (a) b
```

```
>> pretty(expand(log(x/(1-x)^ 2)))
```

```
log (x) - 2-log(1-x)
```

```
>> pretty(expand((x + 1) * (y+z)))
```

```
x y + x z + y + z
```

EXERCISE 9-2

Factorize the following algebraic expressions:

$$6x^2 + 18x - 24, \quad x^4 - y^4, \quad x^3 + y^3, \quad \frac{x^3 - y^3}{x^4 - y^4}$$

```
>> syms x y
>> pretty(factor(6*x^2+18*x-24))
```

```
6 (x + 4) (x - 1)
```

```
>> pretty(factor(x^4-y^4))
```

```
            2   2
(x y) (x + y) (x + y)
```

```
>> pretty(factor(x^3+y^3))
```

```
          2       2
(x + y) (x - x y + y )
```

```
>> pretty(factor((x^3-y^3) /(x^4-y^4)))
```

```
2        2
x + x y + y
-----------------
        2   2
(x + y) (x + y )
```

EXERCISE 9-3

Simplify the following algebraic expressions:

$$\sin^2(x)+\cos^2(x),\ e^{a+\ln(be^c)},\ \cos(3a\cos(x)),\ \frac{x^2-y^2}{(x-y)^3}.$$

```
>> syms x y b c
>> simplify(sin(x) ^ 2 + cos(x) ^ 2)

ans =

1

>> pretty(simplify(exp (a+log(b * exp(c)))))

b exp(a + c)

>> pretty(sym(simple(cos(3 * acos(x)))))

   3
4 x - 3 x

>> pretty(simple((x^2-y^2) /(x-y) ^ 3))

x + y
--------
     2
(x - y)
```

EXERCISE 9-4

Rewrite the following algebraic expressions in terms of powers of x:

$$f(x) = a^3x - x + a^3x + a,\ p(x)= y/x+2z/x+x^{1/3}-y*x^{1/3},\ q(x)=(x+1)(x+2)$$

Rewrite the following expression in terms of powers of sin(x): $y(\sin(x) + 1) + \sin(x)$

Rewrite the following expression in terms of powers of ln(x): $f = a\ln(x) - x\ln(x) - x$

Rewrite the following expression in terms of powers of x and y: $p = xy + zxy + yx^2 + zyx^2 + x + zx$

```
>> syms x y z
>> pretty(collect(a^3*x-x+a^3+a, x))

   3         3
(a -1) x + a + a
```

```
>> pretty(collect(y / x+2 * z/x + x ^(1/3) - y * ^(1/3) x, x))
```

$$y + 2 z - x^{4/3} y + x^{4/3}$$

$$x$$

```
>> pretty(collect((x+1) * (x+2)))
```

```
 2
x + 3 x + 2
```

```
>> p = x * y + z * x * y + y * x ^ 2-z * y * x ^ 2 + x + z * x;
>> pretty(collect(p, [x,y]))
```

```
      2
(1-z) x y + (z + 1) x y + (z + 1) x
```

```
>> f = a * log(x) - log(x) * x-x;
```

```
>> pretty(collect(f, log(x)))
```

```
(a - x) log (x) - x
```

EXERCISE 9-5

Combine the terms as much as possible in the following expression:

$$a ln(x) + 3 ln(x) - ln(1 - x) + ln(1 + x)/2$$

Simplify it assuming that a is real and x > 0.

```
>> pretty(sym(simple(a * log(x) + 3 * log(x) - log(1-x) + log(1+x)/2)))
```

```
log(x + 1)/2- log(1-x) + 3 log (x) + log(x)
```

```
>> x = sym('x', 'positive')
```

```
x =
```

```
x
```

```
>> a = sym('a', 'real')
```

```
a =
```

```
a
```

```
>> pretty(sym(simple(a * log(x) + 3 * log(x) - log(1-x) + log(1+x)/2)))

       /        x - 1        \
 -log| -  ---------------- |
       |       3  a    1/2 |
       \    x  x  (x + 1)    /
```

EXERCISE 9-6

Expand and simplify the following trigonometric expressions:

$$(a)\ \sin[3x]\cos[5x]$$

$$(b)\ [(\cot[a])^2 + (\sec[a])^2 - (\csc[a])^2$$

$$(c)\ \sin[a] / (1+\cot[a]^2\,) - \sin[a]^3$$

```
>> pretty(simple(expand(sym(sin(3*x) * cos(5*x)))))

sin(8 x)   sin(2 x)
-------- - --------
   2          2
```

```
>> pretty(simple(expand(((cot(a)) ^ 2 + (sec(a)) ^ 2-(csc(a)) ^ 2))))

   1
------- - 1
   2
cos(a)
```

```
>> pretty(simple(expand(sin(a) / (1 + cot(a) ^ 2)- sin(a) ^ 3)))

0
```

EXERCISE 9-7

Simplify the following algebraic expressions as much as possible:

$$\frac{x}{x+y} - \frac{y}{x-y} + \frac{2\,x\,y}{x^2 - y^2} \quad , \quad \frac{1+a^2}{b} + \frac{1-b^2}{a} - \frac{a^3 - b^3}{a\,b}$$

```
>> pretty(simple(expand(x / (x + y) - y /(x-y) + 2 * x * y /(x^2-y^2))))
```

```
1
```

```
>> pretty(simple(expand((1+a^2)/b + (1-b ^ 2) /a - (a ^ 3-b ^ 3) /(a*b))))
```

```
1   1
- + -
a   b
```

EXERCISE 9-8

Simplify the following algebraic fractions as much as possible:

$$\frac{a^3 - a^2 b + ac^2 - bc^2}{a^3 + ac^2 + a^2 b + b c^2} \quad , \quad \frac{(x^2 - 9)\,(x^2 - 2\,x + 1)\,(x - 3)}{(x^2 - 6\,x + 9)\,(x^2 - 1)\,(x - 1)}$$

```
>> pretty(simple(factor(a^3-a^2*b+a*c^2-b*c^2)/(a^3+a*c^2+a^2*b+b*c^2)))
```

```
a - b
-----
a + b
```

```
>> pretty(simple(factor((x^2-9)*(x^2-2*x+1)*(x-3))/((x^2-6*x+9)*(x^2-1) *(x-1))))
```

```
  2
----- + 1
x + 1
```

EXERCISE 9-9

Calculate the roots of the following polynomials:

$$x^3 - 6x^2 - 72x - 27, \ 2x^4 - 3x^3 + 4x^2 - 5x + 11 \ x^{11} - 1$$

Evaluate the first polynomial at the identity matrix of order 3, the second at the unit matrix of order 3 and the third at a uniformly random matrix of order 3.

Find the coefficients of the derivatives of the given polynomials and display the results in polynomial form.

```
>> p1 = [1 - 6 -72 - 27]; r = roots(p)

r =

12.1229
-5.7345
-0.3884

>> p2 = [2 -3 4 -5 11]; r = roots(p)

r =

1.2817 + 1.0040i
1.2817 - 1.0040i
-0.5317 + 1.3387i
-0.5317 - 1.3387i

>> p3 = [1 0 0 0 0 0 0 0 0 0 0 1]; r = roots(p)

r =

-1.0000
-0.8413 + 0.5406i
-0.8413 - 0.5406i
-0.4154 + 0.9096i
-0.4154 - 0.9096i
 0.1423 + 0.9898i
 0.1423   0.9898i
 0.6549 + 0.7557i
 0.6549 - 0.7557i
 0.9595 + 0.2817i
 0.9595   0.2817i

>> Y1 = polyval(p1, eye(3))

Y1 =

-104 - 27 - 27
-27  -104 - 27
-27  - 27 -104
```

```
>> Y2 = polyval(p2, ones(3))

Y2 =

9 -9 -9
9 -9 -9
9 -9 -9

>> Y3 = polyval(p3, rand(3))

Y3 =

1.1050 1.3691 1.0000
1.3368 1.0065 1.0013
1.0000 1.0000 1.6202

>> d1 = polyder(p1)

D1 =

3 -12 -72

>> pretty(poly2sym(d1,'x'))

    2
3 x - 12 x - 72

>> d2 = polyder(p2)

D2 =

8 -9  8 - 5

>> pretty(poly2sym(d2,'x'))

    3     2
8 x - 9 x + 8 x - 5

>> d3 = polyder(p3)

D3 =

11    0    0    0    0    0    0    0    0    0    0

>> pretty(poly2sym(d3,'x'))

     10
11 x
```

EXERCISE 9-10

Consider the equally spaced set of points in the interval [0,5] separated by one tenth. Interpolate the error function at these points and adjust a polynomial of degree 6 thereto. Represent the original data and the interpolated curve on the same graph.

```
>> x = (0: 0.1: 5)';
y = erf (x);
f = polyval(p,x);
>> p = polyfit(x,y,6)

p =

0.0012 - 0.0173 0.0812 - 0.0791 - 0.4495 1.3107 - 0.0128

>> f = polyval(p,x);
plot(x,y,'o',x,f,'-')
axis([0 5 0 2])
```

EXERCISE 9-11

Calculate the second degree interpolating polynomial passing through the points (- 1,4), (0,2), and (1,6) in the least squares sense.

```
>> x = [- 1, 0, 1]; y = [4,2,6]; p = poly2sym(polyfit(x,y,2))

p =

3 * x ^ 2 + x + 2
```

EXERCISE 9-12

Represent 200 points of cubic interpolation between the points (x, y) given by y= e^x for x values in 20 equally spaced intervals between 0 and 2.

First, we define the 20 points *(x, y)*, for *x* equally spaced between 0 and 2:

```
>> x = 0:0.1:2;
>> y = exp(x);
```

Now we find cubic interpolation points *(xi, yi)*, for *x* values in 200 equally spaced between 0 and 2, and represent them on a graph together with the initial points *(x, y)* (indicated by asterisks).

```
>> xi = 0:0. 01:2;
>> yi = interp1(x,y,xi,'cubic');
>> plot(x,y,'*',xi,yi)
```

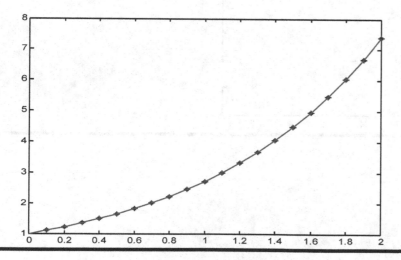

EXERCISE 9-13

Find interpolation points of the parametric function X = cosh (t), Y = sinh (t), Z = tanh (t) for values of t between 0 and π /6 in 25 equally spaced intervals.

First, we define the given points *(x, y, z)*, for equally spaced values of *t* between 0 and π/6.

```
>> t = 0: pi/150: pi/6;
>> x = cosh(t); y = sinh(t); z = tanh(t);
```

Now we find the 26 points of interpolation (x_i, y_i, z_i), for values of the parameter *t* equally spaced between 0 and π /6.

```
>> xi = cosh(t); yi = sinh(t);
>> zi = griddata(x,y,z,xi,yi);
>> points = [xi, yi, zi]

points =

1.0000 0 0
1.0002 0.0209 0.0209
1.0009 0.0419 0.0419
1.0020 0.0629 0.0627
1.0035 0.0839 0.0836
1.0055 0.1049 0.1043
1.0079 0.1260 0.1250
1.0108 0.1471 0.1456
1.0141 0.1683 0.1660
1.0178 0.1896 0.1863
1.0220 0.2110 0.2064
1.0267 0.2324 0.2264
1.0317 0.2540 0.2462
1.0373 0.2756 0.2657
1.0433 0.2974 0.2851
1.0498 0.3194 0.3042
1.0567 0.3414 0.3231
1.0641 0.3636 0.3417
1.0719 0.3860 0.3601
1.0802 0.4085 0.3782
1.0890 0.4312 0.3960
1.0983 0.4541 0.4135
1.1080 0.4772 0.4307
1.1183 0.5006 0.4476
1.1290 0.5241 0.4642
1.1402 0.5479 0.4805
```

EXERCISE 9-14

Using fast Fourier transform (FFT) interpolation, find the 30 points (xi, yi) approximating the function y = sinh (x) for values of x that are in equally spaced intervals between 0 and 2π, interpolating them between values of (x, y) given by y = sinh (x) for x values in 20 evenly spaced intervals in $(0,2\pi)$. Graph the points.

First, we define the *x* values equally spaced in 20 intervals between 0 and 2π.

```
>> x = (0:pi/10:2*pi);
```

Now we find the interpolation points *(x, y)*.

```
>> y = interpft(sinh(x), 30);
>> points = [y ', (asinh(y))']
```

```
points =

 -0.0000 - 0.0000
-28.2506 - 4.0346
 23.3719   3.8451
 -4.9711 - 2.3067
 -7.7918 - 2.7503
 14.0406   3.3364
 -4.8129 - 2.2751
 -0.8717 - 0.7877
 11.5537   3.1420
 -3.3804 - 1.9323
  4.4531   2.1991
 11.8616   3.1682
 -0.2121 - 0.2105
 10.9811   3.0914
 15.1648   3.4132
  6.1408   2.5147
 21.2540   3.7502
 23.3792   3.8455
 18.5918   3.6166
 39.4061   4.3672
 40.6473   4.3982
 42.8049   4.4499
 73.2876   4.9876
 74.8962   5.0093
 89.7159   5.1898
139.0371   5.6279
139.3869   5.6304
180.2289   5.8874
282.4798   6.3368
201.7871   6.0004
```

```
>> plot(points)
```

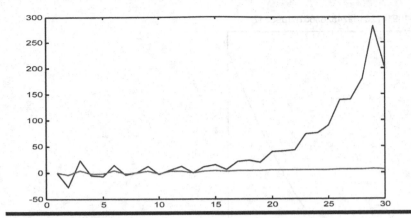

EXERCISE 9-15

Find the polynomial of degree 3 which is the best fit through the points (i, i^2) $1 \le i \le 7$, in the least squares sense. Evaluate this polynomial at $x = 10$ and graphically represent the best fit curve.

```
>> x = (1:7); y = [1,4,9,16,25,36,49]; p = vpa(poly2sym(polyfit(x,y,2))))
```

```
p =
```

```
x ^ 2 - 0.0000000000000009169181662272871686413366801652 * x +
0.0000000000000020761891472015924526365781895317
```

Now we calculate the numerical value of the polynomial p at $x = 10$.

```
>> subs(p,10)
```

```
ans =
```

```
100.0000
```

Next we graph the polynomial:

```
>> ezplot(p,[-5,5])
```

x^2 -...+ 0.0000000000000020761891472015924526365781895317

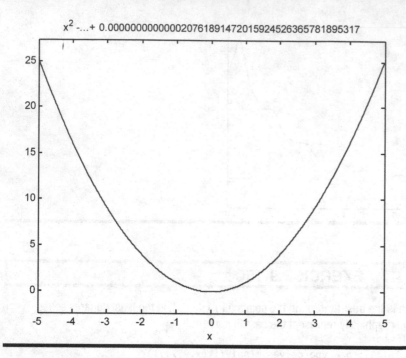

EXERCISE 9-16

Find the solutions to the following equations:

$$\sin(x)\cos(x) = 0, \; \sin(x) = a\cos(x), \; ax^2 + bx + c = 0 \text{ and } \sin(x) + \cos(x) = \text{sqrt}(3) / 2$$

```
>> solve('sin(x) * cos(x) = 0')

ans =

[        0]
[1/2 * pi]
[-1/2 * pi]

>> solve('sin(x) = a * cos(x) ',' x')

ans =

atan(a)
```

```
>> solve('a*x^2+b*x+c=0','x')

ans =

[1/2/a * (-b + (b ^ 2-4 * a * c) ^(1/2))]
[1/2/a * (-b-(b^2-4*a*c) ^(1/2))]

>> solve(' sin(x) + cos(x) = sqrt(3) / 2')

ans =

[1/2 * 3 ^(1/2)]
[1/2 * 3 ^(1/2)]
```

EXERCISE 9-17

Find at least two solutions for each of the following two trigonometric and exponential equations:

$$x \sin(x) = 1/2 \ and \ 2^{2^3} = 4(2^{3x}).$$

First, we use the command *solve*:

```
>> vpa(solve('x * sin(x) = 1/2 ', 'x'))

ans =

matrix([[-226.19688152398440474751335389781]])

>> vpa(solve('2 ^(x^3) = 4 * 2 ^(3*x)', 'x'))

ans =

2.0
-1.0
-1.0
```

For the first equation we get no solutions, but for the second we do. To better analyze the first equation, we graphically represent the function to determine approximate intervals where the possible solutions can be found.

```
>> fplot('[x * sin(x) - 1/2.0]', [0, 4 * pi])
```

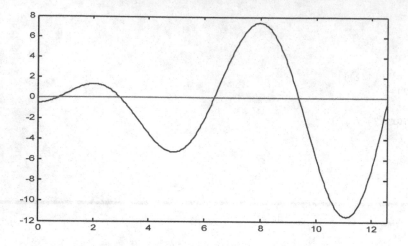

We observe that there is a solution between 0 and 2, another between 2 and 4, another between 4 and 8, and so on. We can calculate three of them with the command *fzero*.

```
>> s1 = fzero('x * sin(x) - 1/2 ', 2)

s1 =

0.7408

>> s2 = fzero('x * sin(x) - 1/2 ', 4)

s2 =

2.9726

>> s3 = fzero('x * sin(x) - 1/2 ', 6)

S3 =

6.3619
```

EXERCISE 9-18

Solve each of the following two logarithmic and surd equations:

$$x^{3/2} \log(x) = x \log(x^{3/2}), \quad \text{sqrt}[1 - x] + \text{sqrt}[1 + x] = a.$$

```
>> vpa(solve('^(3/2) x * log(x) = x * log(x) ^(3/2)'))
```

```
ans =
1.0
0.31813150520476413531265425158766  1.33723570143068940089011621431937 * i
```

We graph the function to determine the intervals in which a solution can be found. The plot indicates that x=1 is the only real solution.

```
>> fplot('[^(3/2) x * log(x), x * log(x) ^(3/2)]', [0.3, - 1, 6])
```

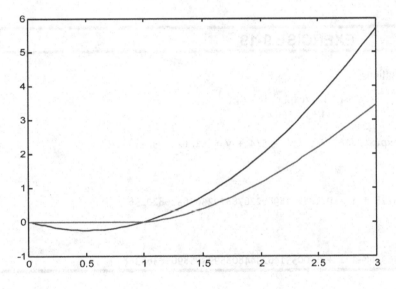

Now, we solve the surd equation:

```
>> pretty(sym(solve('sqrt(1-x) + sqrt(1 + x) = a ', 'x')))
```

```
+-                  -+
|             2 1/2  |
|   a (4 - a )       |
|   -------------    |
|        2           |
|                    |
|             2 1/2  |
|   a (4 - a )       |
| - -------------    |
|        2           |
+-                  -+
```

EXERCISE 9-19

Solve the following system of two equations:

$$\cos(x/12)\,/\exp(x^2/16) = y$$
$$-5/4 + y = \sin(x^{3/2})$$

```
>> [x, y] = solve('cos(x/12) /exp(x^2/16) = y ',' - 5/4 + y = sin(x ^(3/2))')
```

x =

0.34569744170126319331033283636228 * i - 0.18864189802267887925036526820236

y =

0.0086520715192230549621145978569268 * i + 1.0055146234480859930589058368368

EXERCISE 9-20

Find the intersection of the hyperbolas with equations $x^2 - y^2 = r^2$ and $a^2x^2 - b^2y^2 = a^2b^2$ with the parabola $z^2 = 2px$.

```
>> [x, y, z] = solve('a^2*x^2-b^2*y^2=a^2*b^2','x^2-y^2=r^2','z^2=2*p*x','x,y,z')
```

x =

```
((4*a^2*b^2*p^2-4*b^2*p^2*r^2) /(a^2-b^2)) ^(1/2) /(2*p)
((4*a^2*b^2*p^2-4*b^2*p^2*r^2) /(a^2-b^2)) ^(1/2) /(2*p)
((4*a^2*b^2*p^2-4*b^2*p^2*r^2) /(a^2-b^2)) ^(1/2) /(2*p)
```

```
-((4*a^2*b^2*p^2-4*b^2*p^2*r^2) /(a^2-b^2)) ^(1/2) /(2*p)
 ((4*a^2*b^2*p^2-4*b^2*p^2*r^2) /(a^2-b^2)) ^(1/2) /(2*p)
-((4*a^2*b^2*p^2-4*b^2*p^2*r^2) /(a^2-b^2)) ^(1/2) /(2*p)
-((4*a^2*b^2*p^2-4*b^2*p^2*r^2) /(a^2-b^2)) ^(1/2) /(2*p)
-((4*a^2*b^2*p^2-4*b^2*p^2*r^2) /(a^2-b^2)) ^(1/2) /(2*p)
```

```
y =
```

```
 a * ((b^2-r^2) /(a^2-b^2)) ^(1/2)
-a * ((b^2-r^2) /(a^2-b^2)) ^(1/2)
 a * ((b^2-r^2) /(a^2-b^2)) ^(1/2)
 a * ((b^2-r^2) /(a^2-b^2)) ^(1/2)
-a * ((b^2-r^2) /(a^2-b^2)) ^(1/2)
 a * ((b^2-r^2) /(a^2-b^2)) ^(1/2)
-a * ((b^2-r^2) /(a^2-b^2)) ^(1/2)
-a * ((b^2-r^2) /(a^2-b^2)) ^(1/2)
```

```
z =
```

```
 ((4*a^2*b^2*p^2-4*b^2*p^2*r^2) /(a^2-b^2)) ^(1/4)
 ((4*a^2*b^2*p^2-4*b^2*p^2*r^2) /(a^2-b^2)) ^(1/4)
-((4*a^2*b^2*p^2-4*b^2*p^2*r^2) /(a^2-b^2)) ^(1/4)
 ((4*a^2*b^2*p^2-4*b^2*p^2*r^2) /(a^2-b^2)) ^(1/4) * i
-((4*a^2*b^2*p^2-4*b^2*p^2*r^2) /(a^2-b^2)) ^(1/4)
-((4*a^2*b^2*p^2-4*b^2*p^2*r^2) /(a^2-b^2)) ^(1/4) * i
 ((4*a^2*b^2*p^2-4*b^2*p^2*r^2) /(a^2-b^2)) ^(1/4) * i
-((4*a^2*b^2*p^2-4*b^2*p^2*r^2) /(a^2-b^2)) ^(1/4) * i
```

EXERCISE 9-21

Study and solve the system:

$$x_1 - x_2 + x_3 = 1$$
$$4x_1 + 5x_2 - 5x_3 = 4$$
$$2x_1 + x_2 - x_3 = 2$$
$$x_1 + 2x_2 - 2x_3 = 1$$

```
>> A = [1, - 1, 1; 4, 5, - 5; 2, 1, - 1; 1, 2, - 2]

A =

1  -1 -1
5  -4 -5
2  -1 -1
2  -1 -2
```

```
>> B = [1, - 1, 1, 1; 4, 5, - 5, 4; 2, 1, - 1, 2; 1, 2, - 2, 1]

B =

1 -1 -1 -1
5  4 -5  4
1  2 -1  2
2  1 -2  1

>> [rank(A), rank(B)]

ans =

2 2
```

We see that the ranks of A and B coincide and its value is 2, which is less than the number of unknowns in the system (3). Therefore, the system will have infinitely many solutions. We try to solve it with the command *solve*:

```
>> [x 1, x 2, x 3] = solve('x1-x2+x3=1','4*x1+5*x2-5*x3=4','2*x1+x2-x3=2',
'x1+2*x2-2*x3=1','x1','x2','x3')
Warning: 4 equations in three variables.

x 1 =

1

x 2 =

z

x 3 =

z
```

Infinitely many solutions are obtained in terms of the parameter z, namely $\{1, z, z\}$, $z \varepsilon R$. Note that the trivial solution $\{1,0,0\}$ is obtained by setting the parameter equal to zero.

EXERCISE 9-22

Study and solve the system:

$$x + 2y + 3z + t = 6$$
$$x + 3y + 8z + t = 19$$

```
>> A = [1,2,3,1;1,3,8,1]

A =

1 2 3 1
1 3 8 1

>> B = [1,2,3,1,6;1,3,8,1,19]

B =

1 2 3 1  6
1 3 8 1 19

>> [rank(A), rank(B)]

ans =

2 2
```

We see that the ranks of *A* and *B* coincide, and their common value is 2, which is less than the number of unknowns for the system (4). Therefore, the system has infinitely many solutions. We try to solve it:

```
>> [x, y, z, t] = solve('x+2*y+3*z+t=6','x+3*y+8*z+t=19','x','y','z','t')
Warning: 2 equations in 4 variables. New variables might be introduced.

x =

7 * z1 - z2 - 20

y =

z2

z =

13 - 5 * z1

t =

z1
```

This time the solution depends on two parameters $z1$ and $z2$. As these parameters vary over the real numbers (x,y,z,t) varies over all solutions of the system. These solutions form a two-dimensional subspace of the four dimensional real vector space which can be expressed as follows:

{7z1-z2-20, z2, 13-5z1, z1}, z1, z2∈R

EXERCISE 9-23

Study and solve the system:

$$3x_1 + x_2 + x_3 - x_4 = 0$$
$$2x_1 + x_2 - x_3 + x_4 = 0$$
$$x_1 + 2x_2 + 4x_3 + 2x_4 = 0$$
$$2x_1 + x_2 - 2x_3 - x_4 = 0$$

```
>> det([3,1,1,-1;2,1,-1,1;1,2,4,2;2,1,-2,-1])

ans =

-30
```

As the determinant of the coefficient matrix is non-zero, the system has only the trivial solution:

```
>> [(x1,x2,x3,x4]=solve('3*x1+x2+x3-x4=0','2*x1+x2-x3+x4=0','x1+2*x2-4*x3-2*x4=0',
'x1-x2-3*x3-5*x4=0','x1','x2','x3','x4')]

x 1 =

0

x 2 =

0

x 3 =

0

x 4 =

0
```

EXERCISE 9-24

Study and solve the following system, according to the values of m:

$$mx + y + z = 1$$
$$x + my + z = m$$
$$x + y + mz = m^2$$

```
>> syms m
>> A = [m,1,1;1,m,1;1,1,m]

A =

[ m, 1, 1]
[ 1, m, 1]
[ 1, 1, m]

>> det(A)

ans =

m^3 - 3*m + 2

>> solve('m^3 - 3*m + 2=0','m')

ans =

-2
1
1
```

The values of m which determine the rank of the matrix are - 2 and 1.

We now consider the augmented matrix extended to include a fourth column with values 1, m and m^2:

```
>> B = [m,1,1,1;1,m,1,m;1,1,m,m^2]

B =

[ m, 1, 1,   1]
[ 1, m, 1,   m]
[ 1, 1, m, m^2]
```

We will study the case $m = -2$:

```
>> rank(subs(A,{m},{-2}))

ans =

2
```

```
>> rank(subs(B,{m},{-2}))
```

ans =

3

We see that the ranks of the two arrays are different, hence the system is inconsistent (i.e. it has no solution) if $m = -2$.

Now we study the case $m = 1$:

```
>> rank(subs(A,{m},{1}))
```

ans =

1

```
>> rank(subs(B,{m},{1}))
```

ans =

1

Now the rank of both matrices is 1, which is less than the number of unknowns. In this case, the system has infinitely many solutions. We find them by substituting $m = 1$ into the initial system:

```
>> [x,y,z] = solve('x+y+z=1','x','y','z')
Warning: 1 equation in 3 variables. New variables might be introduced.
```

x =

1 - z2 - z1

y =

z2

z =

z1

Thus the solutions are given in terms of two parameters. The two-dimensional subspace of solutions is:

{1-z2-z1, z2, z1}, z1, z2∈R

If we consider the case where m is neither - 2 nor 1, the system has a unique solution, which is given by the command *solve*:

```
>> [x,y,z] = solve('m*x+y+z=1','x+m*y+z=m','x+y+m*z=m^2','x','y','z')

x =

-(m + 1)/(m + 2)

y =

1 /(m + 2)

z =

(m ^ 2 + 2 * m + 1) /(m + 2)
```

EXERCISE 9-25

Study and solve the following system, according to the values of m:

$$my = m$$
$$(1 + m)\,x - z = m$$
$$y + z = m$$

```
>> syms m
>> A = [0, m, 0; m + 1, 0, - 1; 0,1,1]

A =

[    0, m,  0]
[m + 1, 0, - 1]
[    0, 1,  1]

>> det(A)

ans =

-m ^ 2 - m

>> solve('-m^2-m=0','m')

ans -

-1
0
```

We see that the values of m which determine the rank of the matrix of coefficients of the system are $m = 1$ and $m = 0$.

We now consider the augmented matrix:

```
>> B = [0, m, 0, m; m + 1, 0, - 1, m; 0,1,1,m]

B =

[0, m, 0, m]
[m + 1, 0, - 1, m]
[0, 1, 1, m]

>> rank(subs(A,{m},{-1}))

ans =

2

>> rank(subs(B,{m},{-1}))

ans =

3
```

If $m = -1$, we see that the system has no solution because the rank of the matrix of coefficients of the system is 2 and the rank of the augmented matrix is 3.

Now, we analyze the case $m = 0$:

When m is zero the system is homogeneous, since the independent terms are all null. We analyze the determinant of the matrix of coefficients of the system.

```
>> det(subs(A,{m},{0}))

ans =

0
```

Since the determinant is zero, the system has infinitely many solutions:

```
>> [x, y, z] = solve('x-z=0','y+z=0','x','y','z')
Warning: 2 equations in three variables. New variables might be introduced.

x =

z1

y =

-z1
```

z =

z1

Thus the solutions are given in terms of one parameter. The one-dimensional subspace of solutions is:

{z1,-z1, z1},   z1 ∈R

If *m* is neither 0 nor - 1, the system has a unique solution, since the ranks of the matrix of the system and of the augmented matrix coincide. The solution, using the function *solve*, is calculated as follows.

```
>> [x, y, z] = solve('m * y = m', '(1+m) * x-z = m ',' y + z = m', 'x', 'y', 'z')
```

x =

(2 * m - 1) /(m + 1)

y =

1

z =

m - 1

EXERCISE 9-26

Study and solve the system:

$$2x + y + z + t = 1$$
$$x + 2y + z + t = 1$$
$$x + y + 2z + t = 1$$
$$x + y + z + 2t = 1$$

```
>> A = [2,1,1,1;1,2,1,1;1,1,2,1;1,1,1,2];
>> B = [2,1,1,1,1;1,2,1,1,1;1,1,2,1,1;1,1,1,2,1];
>> [rank(A), rank(B)]

ans =

4 4

>> b = [1,1,1,1]';
```

We see that the matrices *A* and *B* (the augmented matrix) both have rank 4, which also coincides with the number of unknowns. Thus the system has a unique solution. To calculate the solution we can use any of the commands shown below.

```
>> x = nnls(A,b)

x =

0.2000
0.2000
0.2000
0.2000

>> x = bicg(A,b)
bicg converged at iteration 1 to a solution with relative residual 0

x =

0.2000
0.2000
0.2000
0.2000

>> x = bicgstab(A,b)
bicgstab converged at iteration 0.5 to a solution with relative residual 0

x =

0.2000
0.2000
0.2000
0.2000

>> x = pcg(A,b)
pcg converged at iteration 1 to a solution with relative residual 0

x =

0.2000
0.2000
0.2000
0.2000
```

```
>> gmres(A,b)
gmres converged at iteration 1 to a solution with relative residual 0

ans =

0.2000
0.2000
0.2000
0.2000

>> x = lsqr(A,b)
lsqr converged at iteration 2 to a solution with relative residual 0

x =

0.2000
0.2000
0.2000
0.2000

>> A\b'

ans =

0.2000
0.2000
0.2000
0.2000
```

Get the eBook for only $10!

Now you can take the weightless companion with you anywhere, anytime. Your purchase of this book entitles you to 3 electronic versions for only $10.

This Apress title will prove so indispensible that you'll want to carry it with you everywhere, which is why we are offering the eBook in 3 formats for only $10 if you have already purchased the print book.

Convenient and fully searchable, the PDF version enables you to easily find and copy code—or perform examples by quickly toggling between instructions and applications. The MOBI format is ideal for your Kindle, while the ePUB can be utilized on a variety of mobile devices.

Go to www.apress.com/promo/tendollars to purchase your companion eBook.